Bank Soundness and Macroeconomic Policy

Bank Soundness and Macroeconomic Policy

Carl-Johan Lindgren,
Gillian Garcia, and Matthew I. Saal

International Monetary Fund

Cataloging-in-Publication Data

Lindgren, Carl-Johan.
  Bank soundness and macroeconomic policy / Carl-Johan Lindgren, Gillian
Garcia, and Matthew I. Saal — [Washington, D.C.] : International Monetary
Fund, [1996]
     p.   cm.
  ISBN 1-55775-599-X

  1. Banks and banking.   2. Financial institutions.   3. Economic policy.
4. Macroeconomics.   I. Garcia, G. G.   II. Saal, Matthew I..
HG1573 L56 1996

Price: $23.50

Address orders to:
International Monetary Fund, Publication Services
700 19th Street, N.W., Washington D.C. 20431, U.S.A.
Telephone: (202) 623-7430
Telefax: (202) 623-7201
Internet: publications@imf.org

Foreword

Globalization of economies creates opportunities and risks, but in this new global environment, it is clear from the vantage point of the International Monetary Fund that the soundness of banking and financial systems must be of worldwide concern. The banking problems experienced by Fund member countries in recent years have not just affected them individually: the global economy and the international financial system have also suffered from costly financial crises. This book is a welcome addition to the literature, because it takes a global view of the causes and consequences of banking sector problems and points to ways in which banking systems can be strengthened nationally and internationally.

In March 1996, the IMF's Executive Board discussed the papers that are the core of this volume. The discussion confirmed that concern over bank soundness is widespread, not only in economies that face banking sector problems, but also in every country that might be affected by spillovers from disturbances that originate elsewhere. It also made clear that there is broad agreement on the principles that must guide policymakers as they seek to strengthen their own banking systems and contribute to the stability of the international financial system: (1) the soundness of a bank is first and foremost the responsibility of its owners and managers; yet the soundness of a banking system is a public policy concern; (2) bank soundness is crucially linked to sound macroeconomic policies; (3) a framework for sound banking must include structures to support internal governance and market discipline, as well as official regulation and supervision; and (4) international cooperation and coordination can play an important role not only in strengthening the global financial system but also in improving the soundness of national banking systems.

The authors of this book have pointed to the need for further efforts by all concerned—national authorities, regional groups, and international bodies at all levels—to upgrade the standards of banking around the world and the structure of international cooperation so as to strengthen financial systems. The Fund, entrusted with particular responsibility for multilateral surveillance of its 181 members, will continue to do its part to assist in these efforts, not only through surveillance over member country policies but also through technical assistance programs, and any appropriate action its members would agree on in order to ensure that banking and financial institutions continue contributing to global prosperity rather than imperiling it.

MICHEL CAMDESSUS
Managing Director
International Monetary Fund

Preface

For some time now, it has been recognized that an appropriate macro-economic policy stance, however necessary to attain balance in an economy, is unlikely to be sufficient to maintain it, unless supported by adequate microeconomic conditions. That a symbiosis exists between macroeconomics and microeconomics has not only been accepted as a general policy proposition, but has also been recognized as having a dual dimension in specific policy areas. In the fiscal area, durable balance will require, besides an appropriate fiscal policy stance (the macroeconomic component), efficient expenditure and tax management (the microeconomic component). The potential role of the exchange rate as a nominal anchor for the economy is very much an aspect of macroeconomic management, it is concerned with absolute price level objectives. Yet, the ability of an exchange rate to anchor an economy durably will depend on whether it also ensures external competitiveness, a key microeconomic concern in that it addresses a relative price issue. A similar duality arises in the context of external debt-management policy: on the one hand, recourse to foreign debt can allow for a higher level of domestic demand (a macro-economic question); but, on the other, efficient use of foreign savings will enhance the economy's productive potential (a question typical of micro-economics).

Monetary policy also exhibits this bidimensional character, yet it is hardly recognized by most of the literature on the subject. For example, analyses of the microeconomic foundations of macroeconomics and of monetary theory have had limited bearing on monetary policy prescriptions. Instead they have emphasized the macroeconomic aspect of monetary policy: on its role to secure stability in the standard of value, either internally, through domestic price discipline, or externally, through exchange rate discipline.

Needless to say, such emphasis on the stability of the standard of value is essential for attaining balance in an economy. But it is by no means sufficient to maintain that balance. Besides an efficient mix of monetary and exchange policy instruments, sustained monetary equilibrium requires a sound and competitive banking sector, and more generally, a sound and competitive financial system. These are microeconomic aspects of monetary management, in that they focus on a specific sector rather than on the economy at large. While the significance of an efficient policy instrument mix is being increasingly recognized, the aims of a sound and competitive banking and financial sector have been rarely, if at all, perceived as integral aspects of monetary and macroeconomic policy. This book attempts to redress that deficiency by examining how the soundness of a banking system and macroeconomic policy are linked.

In recent years, the experiences of a broad range of countries, from industrial to developing and transition economies, have made clear the importance of bank soundness from a macroeconomic perspective. Such experiences illustrate the extent to which unsound, uncompetitive banking systems and inadequate institutional and regulatory frameworks weaken efficient credit allocation, distort the structure of interest rates, disrupt monetary policy signals, and impose significant fiscal costs, with adverse consequences for macroeconomic stabilization and balance.

These issues are of legitimate concern to the IMF given their linkage with macroeconomic management and performance. A clear illustration of this institutional interest is the technical assistance program of the Monetary and Exchange Affairs Department (MAE), which for some time now has been deeply involved in the supervisory and regulatory aspects of central banking. The IMF has also been addressing banking sector problems through its regular policy consultations with all of its members countries, as well as through its policy research. This volume is one product of that research effort, drawing upon the experience MAE has accumulated over several decades. The present work is based on internal policy papers that explore the macroeconomic implications of banking and financial sector issues and that were presented to the Executive Board of the IMF in March 1996. But it takes its place in a broader body of policy research that includes the papers gathered in *Banking Crises: Cases and Issues* (International Monetary Fund, 1991) and studies currently under way regarding payments systems risk management and systemic bank restructuring.

There can hardly be a more opportune time than the present to address the issues surrounding the linkages of bank soundness and macroeconomic policy. Not only is there a significant number of countries with vulnerable banking sectors or confronting banking crises, but there is also a renewed focus on the need for international cooperation in this area. The communiqué of the Group of Seven at their summit meeting in June 1996 in Lyons noted that the globalization of financial markets has created a more complex financial environment, in which improved prudential regulation and supervision in the financial markets are essential to preserve the stability of the international monetary and financial system.

Concern for such stability is at the core of the IMF's mandate to promote international monetary cooperation and exchange stability. It is hoped that the contribution of this book to the policy discussion will be of help to those involved with the interrelationship of the banking sector with macroeconomic policy, and that it will add to the understanding of how structural and macroeconomic policies can be formulated to underpin safe and sound banking.

MANUEL GUITIÁN
Director
Monetary and Exchange Affairs Department
International Monetary Fund

Acknowledgment

The views expressed in this book are those of the authors and should not be interpreted as those of the IMF. The authors are indebted, however, to a great many people within the IMF who encouraged and assisted in the preparation of this text.

A particular debt of gratitude goes to Manuel Guitián, Director of the Monetary and Exchange Affairs Department (MAE), who initiated this project and provided the intellectual inspiration for our focus on the duality between macroeconomic policy and bank soundness. Our work also benefited tremendously from the support and wisdom of V. Sundararajan, Mario Blejer, and Ernesto Feldman, who offered guidance and comments during the preparation of the initial policy papers.

Our colleagues in the Banking Supervision and Regulation Division of MAE, in particular David Hoelscher, made invaluable contributions in their reviews of our drafts and through discussions that helped inform our views about a range of issues. IMF area department country desks provided materials for the survey of banking problems and the case studies.

Secretarial assistance was provided by Norma Anamisis, Noella Eanos, Kim Holloway, and Liliana Vendeuvre, and research assistance by Anil Bhatia. The project also benefited from the editorial expertise of Juanita Roushdy of the External Relations Department, who also coordinated the publication process.

CARL-JOHAN LINDGREN
GILLIAN GARCIA
MATTHEW I. SAAL

Contents

		Page
Foreword	....	v
Preface	....	vii
Acknowledgement	....	xi

Part I   Worldwide Experience with Bank Fragility

1	Introduction	3
2	Banking in the Economy—Why Banks Warrant Special Attention	6
3	Defining, Measuring, and Predicting Soundness	9
	Defining a Sound Banking System	9
	Measuring Unsoundness	10
	Predicting Unsoundness	11
Annex	Survey of Banking Problems Worldwide	20

Part II   Macroeconomic Causes and Consequences of Unsound Banking Systems

4	Macroeconomic Causes of Bank Unsoundness	39
	Economic Conditions and Sound Banking	46
	Monetary Policy Instruments	52
	Fiscal Instruments	53
	Exchange Rate Policy	53
	Overall Policy Stance	54
5	Macroeconomic Consequences of an Unsound Banking System	57
	Behavior of Unsound Banks	57
	Impact on the Real Sector	58
	Monetary Policy Implications	63
	Fiscal Impact	74
	External Sector Effects	75
Annex	Selected Case Studies —Quantitative Analysis	82

Part III   Maintaining a Sound Banking System

  6 Operating Environment 93
      Economic Infrastructure 94
      Economic Conditions and Noneconomic Shocks 99
      Financial Sector Liberalization 100

  7 Internal Governance 105
      Ownership 105
      Management 109
      Internal Oversight 111
      Governance Failures 112

  8 External Governance: Market Discipline 114
      Private Sector 114
      Public Sector 116
      Failures in Market Discipline 117

  9 External Governance: Regulation and Supervision 123
      Banking Regulation 123
      Supervision 129

  10 Challenges Confronting Regulation and Supervision 136
      Regulatory Failure 136
      Supervisory Failure 141
      Macroeconomic Effects of Prudential Regulations 143

  11 International Governance 148
      International Cooperation to Reinforce the
        Operating Environment 148
      International Cooperation to Reinforce Internal
        Governance 151
      International Cooperation to Reinforce Market
        Discipline 152
      International Cooperation to Reinforce Supervision .. 152
      International Coordination Failures 155

Part IV   Conclusions: Policy Design and Flexibility

  12 Macroeconomic Policy Design 161
      Stabilization Policies 161
      Monetary Instruments 164
      Fiscal Balance 166
      Foreign Capital Flows 167

  13 The Banking System and Macroeconomic Policy
      Flexibility 169

Appendices

I The Value of a Bank 173

    Annex: Business Accounting 182

II Supervisory Instruments 185

References **205**

Part I

Worldwide Experience with Bank Fragility

1

Introduction

Since 1980, over 130 countries, comprising almost three fourths of the International Monetary Fund's member countries, have experienced significant banking sector problems (see Figure 1 and the annex to Part I). Developing and industrial market economies alike have been affected—as have all economies in transition. Their experiences demonstrate that chronic weaknesses and crises in banking can have significant costs and highlight the importance of a sound banking sector for macroeconomic stability and the efficient conduct of stabilization programs. They also underscore the influence of macroeconomic and structural policies on the soundness of a country's banking system.

An appropriate macroeconomic policy stance is unlikely to be sufficient to maintain balance in the economy unless it is supported by sound underlying microeconomic conditions. This is true on the fiscal front, where expenditure and tax management must be adequate to sustain the fiscal stance, and in the external sector, where the ability of an exchange rate to anchor an economy on a sustained basis depends on whether it also ensures competitiveness. It is no less true in the monetary policy area, where maintaining a policy stance geared to price level stability requires a sound and competitive banking system to transmit monetary policy signals and ensure the efficient allocation of financial resources.[1]

This volume discusses the linkages between macroeconomic policy and bank soundness and places macroeconomic policy within the framework of policies and structural elements that are required to maintain a sound banking system. Part I outlines why banking is a particularly important activity in most economies and discusses how bank soundness may be defined, measured, and predicted.

---

[1] See Guitián (1993).

3

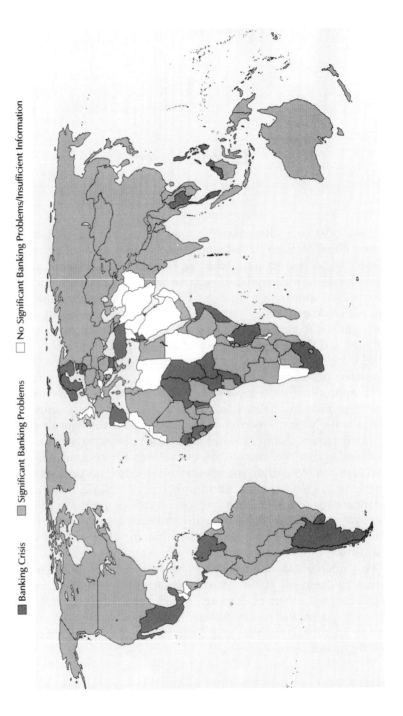

Figure 1. Banking Problems Worldwide, 1980–96

Banking Crisis

Significant Banking Problems

No Significant Banking Problems/Insufficient Information

Part II discusses the macroeconomic causes and consequences of unsound banking systems. Conditions and policies across all aspects of the economy may have an impact on the condition of a banking system. Banks cannot remain sound if the economy in which they operate is unstable, or banks' clients are themselves weak. In addition, some policies or policy instruments may have a particularly adverse effect on banks. The unsoundness of a banking system, in turn, will have important macroeconomic consequences, particularly in the monetary and fiscal areas. The behavior of unsound banks is often very different from that of sound banks: unsound banks tend to be less responsive to market signals, and this may impede the transmission of monetary policy. As most governments are reluctant to permit widespread bank failures, a fragile banking system often has significant fiscal consequences. The analysis presented is supplemented by references to a set of country cases presented in a series of tables throughout these and subsequent chapters.

Part III discusses the contributions of the operating environment, internal governance, market discipline, official oversight, and appropriate macroeconomic policies in supporting banking system soundness. Bank soundness depends crucially on the environment in which banks operate. However, internal governance in individual banks is the most important ingredient for sound banking. Internal governance is both encouraged and reinforced by adequate market discipline and external governance by regulators and supervisors. The balance between market discipline and traditional regulation and supervision may shift over time. As an economy and financial system develop, increasing reliance can be placed on market forces to regulate bank behavior; however, even in advanced market economies, internal governance and market discipline do fail. Thus official governance continues to play a role. In recent years, oversight by domestic regulators has increasingly been supplemented by various forms of international regulation, which are discussed in the concluding chapter of Part III.

Part IV concludes with an examination of the role of macroeconomic management in the two-way linkage between macro policy and banking system soundness. The effects of policy on the banking system may come to the fore in designing stabilization programs, choosing monetary instruments, pursuing fiscal balance, and coping with capital flows. At the same time, the presence of an unsound banking system may constrain policy choices. Thus banking sector soundness itself must be considered a goal of macroeconomic policy.

2

Banking in the Economy—Why Banks Warrant Special Attention

The legal definitions of banking, and the permitted activities of banks, vary across countries. Nevertheless, the essential characteristics of banks are the same. They issue liquid, nominally valued liabilities, many of which are payable on demand at par, and they mainly acquire assets that are illiquid, relatively difficult to value, and of longer maturity than their liabilities.[2]

While the role of banking in the economy is declining in some industrial countries, banks continue to dominate the financial systems of most developing and transition countries. A sound banking system is important because of the key roles it plays in the economy: intermediation, maturity transformation, facilitating payments flows, credit allocation, and maintaining financial discipline among borrowers. Banks provide important positive externalities as gatherers of savings, allocators of resources, and providers of liquidity and payments services. In transition and developing economies with less well-developed financial markets, banks typically are the only institutions producing the information necessary for intermediation, providing the portfolio diversification required for maturity transformation and risk reduction, and helping monitor corporate governance. Even in economies with highly developed financial markets, banks remain at the center of economic and financial activity and stand apart from other institutions as primary providers of payments services and as a fulcrum for monetary policy implementation.

Banks are particularly subject to market failures arising from asymmetries of information. On the asset side, they take on the risk of valuing projects and funding borrowers whose ability to repay is uncertain. On the liability side, the confidence of creditors and depositors who have imper-

---

[2] See Diamond and Dybvig (1983), Fama (1985), and Christopher James (1987).

6

6

fect information on the bank's actual position is essential to a bank's ability to provide deposit and payments services. High leverage and the illiquidity and intransparency of bank assets render banks particularly vulnerable to losses of creditor confidence. Because of sequential servicing (where the first in line is served first), depositors and other creditors have an incentive to run when confidence is lost.[3]

The vulnerability of banks leads to public policy concerns because of the negative externalities related to bank failures. These negative externalities occur when bank failures spill over to harm other banks and economic agents. Contagious runs and attendant domino effects and payments system disruptions are the main negative externalities associated with bank fragility. Runs to quality, that is, from unsound banks to safer havens, may be rational but can disrupt the financial system. When, because of deficient information, depositors cannot distinguish sound banks from unsound banks, they may precipitate unjustified runs against sound banks, which could cause a systemic crisis.[4] The evidence on the actual susceptibility of banks to contagion is mixed, and research has focused on only a few countries. For example, Pozdena (1991) provides evidence of spillovers at U.S. banks, but Kaufman (1994) argues that a wealth of evidence for the United States shows that depositors have been able to distinguish sound banks from unsound ones.

In addition to worries over the potential for contagion, public policy concern is often justified on the grounds that banks provide public goods. Banking services do not fit the definition of a pure public good—one where consumption by one person does not diminish the supply available to another (often referred to as "nonrivalry in consumption," see Sandmo, 1987). Nevertheless some bank services, such as the mobilization of financial resources and the provision of payments services, do have quasi-public good properties.

Both the potential negative externalities in banking due to depositor runs and the public good aspects of banking deriving from savings mobilization and payments services are linked to the traditional banking business of taking demand deposits and making loans. Moreover, it is the juxtaposition of par-valued deposits with opaque and illiquid loans that gives rise to many of the most significant difficulties in maintaining soundness in both universal banks and commercial banks operating with a more limited scope. However, banks in many countries engage in a broad range of activities. For example, they provide a wide variety of financial services

---

[3] Diamond and Dybvig (1983) discuss banks' vulnerability to runs.

[4] Sundararajan and Baliño (1991, p. 3) define a financial crisis as, "a situation in which a significant group of financial institutions have liabilities exceeding the market value of their assets, leading to runs and other portfolio shifts, collapse of some financial firms, and government intervention."

and trade and invest for their own accounts, as well as for clients. Even though these activities add to the risks that banks undertake, draw a new set of clients into contact with the banking system, and provide new avenues through which the core obligations to depositors may be jeopardized, they do little to alter the public policy concerns surrounding the functioning of the banking system.[5]

Regardless of the extent of bank involvement in broader financial services and investment activities, the banking system plays a central role in the economy. Therefore, virtually no government will permit widespread bank failures or forbear from intervening to support depositors in the event of systemic bank insolvencies. Such public involvement has political as well as economic determinants. The difference in treatment of banks compared with other types of enterprises—typically reflected in lender-of-last-resort accommodation of banks and explicit and implicit guarantees of bank liabilities by governments—has implications for the design of macroeconomic and prudential policies. The impact of macroeconomic conditions on the banking system requires special attention for two reasons: first, a well-functioning banking system is important for the effectiveness of macroeconomic policies, and second, weaknesses that emerge in the banking system, if left unattended, could pose a threat to macroeconomic stability.

Public policy concerns with banking soundness should be focused on the banking system as a whole, rather than on individual banks. Only when the deterioration of a particular bank has systemic implications due to possible contagion or domino effects, or when the bank represents a large portion of the banking system, would the consequent damage to the system as a whole warrant public policy attention. Prevention of stress in a banking system requires well-balanced institutional and regulatory structures, as well as a macroeconomic policy mix that is sensitive to banks' financial soundness.

---

[5] Nor does involvement in such activities diminish the importance of the framework for sound banking, which includes both internal and external governance, as is discussed in Chapter 3.

3

Defining, Measuring, and Predicting Soundness

Bank soundness is a concept commonly used to denote, for example, an ability to withstand adverse events. Nevertheless, its usage is typically imprecise and gives rise to questions regarding its definition, measurement, and prediction.

Defining a Sound Banking System

A sound banking system may be defined as one in which most banks (those accounting for most of the system's assets and liabilities) are solvent and are likely to remain so. Solvency is reflected in the positive net worth of a bank, as measured by the difference between the assets and liabilities (excluding capital and reserves) in its balance sheet. In other words, the distance between soundness and insolvency can be gauged in terms of capitalization, since net worth is equivalent to capital plus reserves. The likelihood of remaining solvent will depend, inter alia, on banks' being profitable, well managed, and sufficiently well capitalized to withstand adverse events. In a dynamic and competitive market economy, efficiency and profitability are linked, and their interaction will indicate the prospects for future solvency. Inefficient banks will make losses and eventually will become insolvent and illiquid.[6] Undercapitalized banks, that is, those with low net worth, will be fragile in the sense of being more prone to collapse when faced with a destabilizing shock, such as a major policy change, a sharp asset price adjustment, financial sector liberalization, or a natural disaster.

---

[6] Although problems may first become public through illiquidity, insolvency normally precedes illiquidity. Banks can conceal losses and fund them by attracting new deposits or other liabilities. When problems become severe enough, which is usually well after insolvency, net flows of funds turn negative and illiquidity results.

It is difficult to precisely classify a banking system as "sound" or "unsound," because there is no benchmark measure of systemic insolvency that determines when a banking system is unsound or when a crisis will occur. Banking systems may exhibit different degrees of vulnerability over time. They may be functioning poorly, or may be working relatively well now but exhibit signs (e.g., low earnings or capitalization) of probable future problems or potential crises. Nonetheless, having no precise classification does not detract from the usefulness of the concept of soundness, proxied by solvency, any more than the difficulty of precisely defining concepts like a realistic exchange rate or a sustainable balance of payments has barred the application of those useful notions.

Measuring Unsoundness

Accepting the usefulness of a definition is one thing; practical application from a macroeconomic policy perspective is another. Using current solvency as a proxy for the soundness of a banking system abstracts from important measurement and projection issues.

While solvency is straightforward to define, it is difficult to measure. Bank loans, which represent the bulk of bank assets in most countries, are extremely difficult to value; that is one reason why even in countries with well-developed capital markets bank loans are not readily traded or securitized.[7] From an economic standpoint, insolvency results when the present value of the expected stream of future net cash flows becomes negative and exceeds capital. Obviously, a high reported level of nonperforming loans would indicate fragility. However, there is always an element of judgment in projecting and valuing uncertain future receipts. In addition, owners and managers of unsound banks have incentives to accrue unearned income and show loans as performing in order not to lose their bank. Thus, balance sheet figures on asset value and on nonperforming loans may not represent a bank's actual circumstances. Assessing insolvency is further complicated by off-balance-sheet items and problems of consolidating the balance sheets of bank subsidiaries and other related financial units.

These weaknesses in information explain why banking problems emerge with little apparent warning even in the most advanced countries. Even the combined resources of external auditors, credit rating agencies, stock market analysts, and supervisors may not spot banking problems in time.

To the extent that it can be measured, solvency can be aggregated across banks; clearly a banking system in which a large portion of banks are insolvent at current valuation would be unsound. Aggregation across

---

[7] Valuation is discussed further in Appendix I.

banks, however, may mask problems. For example, a key payments center bank whose net worth is slightly negative might have more significant systemic implications than a savings bank with a highly negative net worth.

Predicting Unsoundness

Apart from the difficulties in measuring current solvency is the additional complexity that the concept of a sound banking system should encompass its dynamic development and its susceptibility to shocks. Solvency is essentially a static concept: it characterizes a bank (or a banking system) at a point in time. A forward-looking measure of banking system health should capture the determinants of bank insolvency, which include poor asset quality and earnings, as well as less quantifiable factors such as management weaknesses, failures of internal and external control, and the potential impact of exogenous events. Thus, if a significant portion of bank profits derives from speculative activities, or if bank governance structures are such that they facilitate high-risk transactions, such as related-party lending, the probability of future insolvency will be higher.

Predicting Unsoundness at Individual Banks

Supervisors in some countries have constructed sets of indicators to provide an early warning that a particular bank is likely to experience difficulties. These indicators consist principally of bank-specific information provided by the reports banks make to the supervisory authority ("call reports"). Early warning indicators are usually used to determine where scarce supervisory resources would best be deployed in on-site examination.

Bank-reported data are often used in conjunction with complementary statistics from other sources and qualitative indicators, many of which are based on supervisory inspections. To the extent that bank data are inaccurate, the quality of such indicators and models is impaired. Even in such circumstances, though, the data may contain significant information: for example, an increase in loans past due provides a warning, even if such loans are systematically underestimated. Thus, specific indicators and trends derived from bank statistics, along with complementary data and judgment, can help to predict bank unsoundness.

Where data are available, some supervisors have constructed more complex econometric models to identify where severe problems are likely to develop. These empirical models identify factors that raise or reduce the probability of bank insolvency in any period. The characteristics of an individual bank can then be fed into the estimated equation to gauge the bank's soundness. The relevant characteristics are mostly bank specific, but may also incorporate sectoral information (such as the concentration of the local banking market) and macroeconomic information (such as the regional unemployment rate). Supervisors then use the results of these models to identify banks that warrant greater supervisory attention, for example, in the form of more frequent on-site inspections.

There has been considerable published academic work in this area as well.[8] Again, models try to predict whether a particular bank is likely to experience difficulties, often defined as insolvency. Published work has focused on the additional question of predicting failure, which is distinct from insolvency. Insolvency is determined by events in the banking market; a bank either is insolvent or is not. Failure in most cases hinges upon a supervisory decision, which may or may not be taken, and may be taken before or after insolvency. Failure usually depends on the same variables that determine insolvency, but as a regulatory decision, failure is subject to misincentives, forbearance, and political interference. Thus, the likelihood of insolvency and the timing of failure may hinge on different factors.

Insolvency should be the dependent variable in empirical exercises, but because banks are difficult to value, market value insolvency may not be observed or measured except after failure. Nevertheless, since regulators and other analysts all define an unsound bank in a similar fashion (focusing principally on insolvency), comparable sets of variables are used in most approaches. One key difference is that models used by regulators have access to a bank's prior supervisory ratings. For example, the U.S. Federal Reserve's Financial Institutions Monitoring System (FIMS) uses prior composite supervisory ratings as one of the predictors of future ratings and risk of failure.[9] Such information is not normally available to outside investigators. While they do have access to some of the data underlying supervisory ratings, such as capital and earnings data, they would not normally have access to information on management and asset quality derived from on-site examinations. Research by supervisors has shown that using data from on-site inspections and from reports submitted by banks results in more accurate forecasts than relying on either alone; FIMS provides one example. In practice, however, supervisors tend to watch a larger number of variables than those identified by researchers.[10] Despite the difficulties, models using publicly available data have been successfully formulated and applied.

Research has generally concluded that a small number of variables can accurately identify at an early stage those individual banks that will ulti-

---

[8] Demirgüc-Kunt (1989) provides a survey. See also Cole and Gunther (1995), Gilbert and Park (1994), Thomson (1992), and Whalen (1991).

[9] See Cole, Cornyn, and Gunther (1995).

[10] For example, see U.S. Office of the Comptroller of the Currency (1989).

mately become insolvent (while avoiding incorrectly flagging banks that will survive). A summary of some of the variables used is provided in Table 1, along with the expected direction of the effect of each variable on the probability of insolvency.

These variables include traditional measures of capital adequacy, asset quality, management, earnings, and liquidity. The impact of macroeconomic conditions on banks is captured in some of the variables used. Recognizing that a bank will not remain well capitalized unless it operates efficiently, some models also include measures of operating efficiency. Assessing efficiency through financial performance indicators, such as earnings relative to assets or relative to employees, requires some control for market structure; a monopolist may be inefficient but still show high earnings. Thus some studies have included market structure variables as well.

Most of the anticipated effects are straightforward, but some are complex. In general, supervisors should be concerned about banks with unusually high or low financial ratios. For example, a high capital-to-asset ratio, which will cause a low rate of return on equity (ROE), may lead to hostile takeover activity that can have positive or negative implications for bank soundness, while a low capital ratio implies a high probability of failure. A low loan-to-asset ratio implies that banks are not carrying out their intermediation role and may be involved in other, possibly speculative, activities, whereas a high ratio indicates high exposure to credit risk.

Much of the published work in this area has focused on the United States, whose large banking sector, extensive recent experience with bank failures, and well-developed statistical reporting systems have provided abundant data. Translating this work to other banking environments will require further research. Since the basic financial operations of banking are the same across countries, the sets of relevant variables would be expected to be similar. It must be recognized, however, that in many countries individual bank data do not exist, or are inaccurate and outdated, presenting such a large errors-in-variables problem as to call into question the validity of any empirical estimates of the probability of insolvency for those economies.

A different approach to gauging insolvency has recently been adopted by a number of researchers. If financial markets can assess a bank's value, and the market price for equity reflects it, then an asset pricing model can be used to infer the risk of insolvency that the market has assigned to each bank. The capital asset pricing model was applied by Hall and Miles (1990) to assess bankruptcy risk for several U.K. banks and for a set of U.S. banks, including a subset that subsequently did fail. Clare (1995) used an arbitrage pricing model based principally on macroeconomic variables to estimate the probabilities of failure among individual U.K.

Table 1. Early Warning Indicators of the Probability of Bank Insolvency

Variables[1]	Expected Effect[2]	Federal Reserve FIMS[3]	Bank Balance Sheet Models[4]	Asset-Pricing Models	Macro Studies
Capital					
Capital adequacy	−	×			
Loan-loss reserves/assets	−	×			
Bank size (ability to raise capital)	−		×		
Asset quality					
Loans past due 30–89 days/assets	+	×			
Loans past due 90 plus days/assets	+	×			
Nonaccrual loans/assets	+	×			
Foreclosed real estate/assets	+	×			
Safe investment securities/assets	−	×			
Rate of asset growth	+	×		×	×
Loans/capital	+		×		
Loans/assets	+/−		×		
Sectoral loans/assets (various sectors)	+/−		×		
Management					
Examiners' on-site rating of management	−	×			
Previous overall on-site rating	−	×			
Corporate structure	+/−		×		
Expenses/total revenue	+		×		
Earnings					
Net income/assets	−	×			
Loan revenue/total revenue	+/−		×		
Revenue from secure assets/total revenue	−		×		
Change in interest and fee income/assets	−		×		
Change in interest expenses/assets	+		×		
Liquidity					
Large certificates of deposit/assets	+	×			
Liquid assets/total assets	−		×		
Interest-sensitive funds/total funds	+		×		
Market structure					
Local banking market concentration	+/−		×		
State of the economy					
Deposit growth rate	+/−		×		
Price of oil	+/−		×	×	
Corporate default risk	+			×	×
Current account imbalance	+			×	

Table 1 *(concluded)*

Variables[1]	Expected Effect[2]	Federal Reserve FIMS[3]	Bank Balance Sheet Models[4]	Asset-Pricing Models	Macro Studies
Inflation/deflation	+			×	×
Market interest rates/bond yields	+/–			×	×
Equity prices/yields	+/–			×	×
Terms of trade	–				×
Real GDP	–				×
International capital flows	+/–				×
Exchange rate changes	+				×
Government deficit, banking sector claims on government	+				×
Policy shocks	+				×

[1] Similar variables have been grouped together; for example, for capital adequacy, studies use various versions of capital/assets. These are not shown separately.

[2] This column indicates the direction of effect that an increase in each explanatory valuable is expected to have on the probability of bank insolvency. Thus, for example, a better on-site rating of management would be expected to correlate with a lower probability of insolvency. The direction of effect of some individual variables will depend also on other factors; these variables are idicated as +/–.

[3] Financial Institutions Monitoring System. See Cole, Cornyn, and Gunther (1995).

[4] As surveyed in Demirgüc-Kunt (1989).

merchant banks. Fischer and Gueyie (1995) applied an option pricing model to estimate the implied variance of bank assets in a number of countries that had liberalized their financial systems. The asset pricing approach has the advantages of using data that are publicly available, principally market prices for bank securities, and of incorporating the information inherent in financial market prices (see Table 1). However, to the extent that financial markets are less than fully informed and efficient, the inferences drawn from these models may be insufficient as an early warning of bank unsoundness (for a critical view, see Simons and Cross (1991)).

Predicting Systemic Unsoundness

Relatively little empirical work has been done on predicting systemic unsoundness. In part this is because supervisors use a bottom-up approach; they are concerned initially with individual banks, and the system is then viewed as the sum of all banks. Most early warning models focus on predicting problems at individual banks and require access to bank-specific data. There is potential, however, to measure or project systemic banking problems from aggregate economic data as well. Three possible approaches to predicting systemic unsoundness are summarized here, followed by a brief review of some recent literature.

Bottom-Up Approach

A bottom-up approach to systemic soundness estimates the probability of insolvency developing for each individual bank in the economy, based, for example, on a balance sheet model. These data then provide the basis for constructing a distribution of bank assets by probability of insolvency. A concern for systemic stability would be warranted when the probability of insolvency becomes significant for a large proportion of the country's banking assets, or when that probability increases substantially in any period of time. The critical range is a matter of judgment and will depend in part on the risk-aversion of the supervisor or policymaker undertaking the evaluation.

While a full distribution provides a more complete picture, a single measure of the condition of the banking system might be constructed as an asset-weighted probability of insolvency based on the probability of insolvency for each bank. The sum of asset-weighted probabilities will range between zero (when all banking assets are housed in banks with no probability of insolvency) and 100 (when all the nation's banking assets are in banks with a probability of insolvency equal to 1).

The principal drawback to applying this methodology is that sufficient bank-specific data to estimate the underlying model are not readily available for most countries. A secondary drawback is that it does not systematically take into account the different functions that banks may play in a market, and the degree of interaction between banks. Banks with certain functions, such as key payments centers, may be more important to the functioning of the system than simple asset weighting shows. The degree of interaction between banks, for example, interbank market exposure or overlapping exposure to certain sectors, will determine the extent of potential domino or contagion effects.

Aggregative Approach

Given the difficulty in obtaining bank-by-bank data, it might be useful to estimate the probability of systemic insolvency using aggregate banking sector data, which are often published by central banks or other official statistical sources. The approach here would be to apply a model based on single bank characteristics similar to those summarized in Table 1 to a synthetic aggregate bank. In this case, the model would have to be developed using cross-sectional data from countries with similar financial systems, since time-series data for a single country might not provide sufficient instances of systemic insolvency to establish the necessary econometric relationships. The model could then be applied to the aggregate bank data to determine the probability of systemic insolvency for that system.

One significant drawback to this approach is that aggregation may hide problems. For example, while the capital-to-asset ratio is used as an indicator of individual bank condition, it is not possible to adequately assess the strength of the banking sector as a whole by looking at an average, even an asset-weighted average of the capital-to-asset ratio. Two banking systems each with ten equally sized banks might have an average capital-to-asset ratio of zero percent. In one system, each bank could have zero capital and so offer the public no sound banking options. The other might consist of half the banks with capital ratios of 10 percent and the other half with minus 10 percent. This system offers sound options to the public. Thus a distribution of bank assets by capital ratio is needed to assess the vulnerability of the banking system to systemic crisis. When a significant proportion of banking assets is held by undercapitalized or insolvent banks, the banking system would be considered unsound. An aggregate measure, however, would not always provide this information.

Another drawback would be the difficulty in estimating the model from cross-country data. First, as noted, defining systemic insolvency presents a number of challenges, although one might alternatively focus on predicting the extent of likely undercapitalization. Second, legal, regulatory, financial infrastructure, political and even cultural factors come into play in determining the degree to which a bank may be subject to losses, runs, and failure. Direct comparability across countries will be difficult to establish, but analysis using countries with similar economic structures or at similar stages of development might yield worthwhile insights.

Macroeconomic Approach

Banks are derivative institutions in that their health reflects the health of their customers, which in turn reflects the health of the economy as a whole. Instead of looking at bank balance sheet data for internal sources of unsoundness, it should be possible to establish systematic relationships between economywide variables and an indicator of bank soundness, such as capitalization. A number of macroeconomic variables would be expected to affect the banking system or reflect its condition. Indeed, some of the models summarized in the first columns of Table 1 employ macroeconomic variables to predict problems at specific banks. One would expect these same variables to be significant for the soundness of the system as a whole.

Broadly speaking, these macroeconomic factors can be grouped as indicators of macroeconomic conditions and indicators of financial fragility. The former group would include GDP and sectoral growth rates, indices of industrial activity, and indicators of macroeconomic balance, such as capital account, current account, and fiscal balances. For example, if an economy or certain important sectors are in a prolonged recession, there is cause for concern about the soundness of the banking system; indicators of macroeconomic conditions would be relevant in these cases.

Indicators of financial fragility would include data on money and credit, interest rates, asset price indices, consumer credit, corporate indebtedness, and bankruptcy rates. For example, excessive credit growth relative to GDP and rapid rises in asset prices have been associated with a weakening of the quality of bank portfolios and an increase in risk exposure. Indicators of systemic distress would include frequent requests by banks for liquidity support and a tiered interbank market. Qualitative variables reflecting the political situation, legal and financial infrastructure, and regulatory environment might also be useful barometers in that the resilience of banking systems will depend to a significant degree on the framework in which they operate, as discussed in Part III.

Data availability for most of these variables should be high. Some researchers have looked at the history of banking crises in a particular country over time; an example is Gorton (1988), who studied the national banking era in the United States (1865–1914), during which there were numerous panics. Under current institutional structures in most countries, estimation of an insolvency probability model at the systemic level would again require cross-country data. Such an approach might provide a means of estimating the impact of particular events, such as a fall in asset prices, on the banking system as a whole. Where bank-specific data are available, macroeconomic factors could be applied to individual banks to derive their sensitivities to particular factors. Even where bank-specific data are not available, some insight into the sensitivity of the banking system as a whole to these factors could be derived from aggregate data, as described (and subject to the caveats noted) above.

Recent Literature

Recent literature has begun to look systematically at banking crises across countries with a view to better understanding the contributing factors. The methodology applied has been a case study approach: examples of countries that have experienced crises are selected, and common macroeconomic trends surrounding the crises are analyzed. The papers in Sundararajan and Baliño (1991) and the studies of Baer and Klingebiel (1995), Caprio and Klingebiel (1996), and Garcia (1994 and 1995) identify a number of the macroeconomic and financial fragility variables listed above as contributors to banking sector crises. The analysis of these studies is largely retrospective, focusing on explanation rather than prediction.

A few recent works have taken a more forward-looking view. Mishkin (1994) attempts to outline signals that a financial crisis is in prospect.

These include declines in stock prices, increases in interest rates and corporate indebtedness, and unanticipated declines in inflation. Hausmann and Gavin (1995) note that loan delinquencies are lagging indicators, and focus instead on macroeconomic shocks to asset quality and bank funding, and the role of credit booms in fostering financial fragility. Kaminsky and Reinhart (1996) focus on the links between balance of payments and banking crises and conclude that financial liberalization helps to predict banking crises across a range of countries, although this may be due to selection bias. As precursors, they identify recessionary conditions, declining economic activity, export sector weakening, sinking asset prices, rapid credit expansion, reversals of capital inflows, increases in the money multiplier, and high real interest rates. Fischer and Gueyie (1995) use a combination of bank balance sheet, macroeconomic, and policy variables to explain changes in bankruptcy probability (as gauged by an option pricing model).

Some of the variables that have been characterized by these studies as contributing to the emergence of a crisis are listed in Table 1. The studies are largely qualitative; no formal model to predict the onset of a crisis or the emergence of an unsound system has been estimated. An appropriate set of early warning signals will vary across countries, depending on the quality and availability of banking and macroeconomic data, and the specific institutional setting. However, as guides to policy these studies are important contributions. The logic underlying the importance of the identified macroeconomic factors is explored further in the next chapters.

Annex
Survey of Banking Problems Worldwide

A review of the experiences since 1980 of the 181 current Fund member countries reveals that 133 have experienced significant banking sector problems at some stage during the past fifteen years.[11] This figure represents 73.5 percent of Fund member countries. A summary of the review is presented in Table 2. Two general classes are identified: "crisis" (41 instances in 36 countries) and "significant" problems (108 instances). There is some degree of judgment in these classifications, but in general, following Sundararajan and Baliño (1991), we refer to cases where there were runs or other substantial portfolio shifts, collapses of financial firms, or massive government intervention, as crises. Extensive unsoundness short of a crisis is termed significant.

As is evident from the table, several countries experienced repeated problems. In others there were problems in some banks that did not have a significant impact on either the functioning of the banking sector as a whole or the macroeconomy; information on 7 such cases was available and is recorded as well but not categorized as crisis or significant.

---

[11] Sources for this review and for the more detailed accounts of a sample of countries presented in Table 2 include IMF desk economists, Sheng (1996), Caprio and Klingebiel (1996), the studies in Sundararajan and Baliño (1991), and various official and news publications.

Table 2. Survey of Banking Problems: 1980–Spring 1996[1]

Country	Type of Problem	Measure of Extent
Albania (1992–present)	Significant	Thirty-one percent of "new" (post-July 1992 cleanup) loans are nonperforming; some banks are facing liquidity problems owing to a logjam of interbank liabilities.
Algeria (1990–92)	Significant	Fifty percent of loans were nonperforming and were taken over by the treasury; operations covered all the 5 commercial banks, and were followed by ongoing structural reforms.
Angola (1991–present)	Significant	The two-tier banking system (established in 1991) is still not consolidated; 2 commercial banks (state-owned) are experiencing solvency problems.
Argentina (1980–82)	Crisis	Nine percent of loans were nonperforming in 1980 and 30% in 1985; 168 institutions were closed.
(1989–90)	Crisis	Nonperforming assets constituted 27% of the aggregate portfolio and 37% of the portfolios of state-owned banks. Failed banks held 40% of financial system assets.
(January to September 1995)	Crisis	Through September 1995, 45 of 205 institutions were closed or merged.
Armenia (1994–present)	Significant	The central bank has closed half of the active banks since August 1994, but the nonperforming asset problem of the large banks remains to be tackled. The Savings Bank has negligible capital.
Australia (1989–92)	Significant	Nonperforming loans rose to 6% of total assets in 1991–92. State-owned banks, especially in Victoria and South Australia, had to be rescued at a cost to the state governments of 1.9% of GDP. A large building society failed.
Azerbaijan (1995–present)	Significant	One large state-owned bank is facing a serious liquidity problem; new management has been appointed; 12 private banks have been closed owing to noncompliance with regulations; 3 large state-owned banks will be insolvent if loan losses are written off.
Bahrain		The system withstood deposit withdrawals from the offshore center during the Persian Gulf war.
Bangladesh (1980s–present)	Significant	In 1987, 20% of the loans of 4 major banks, whose assets accounted for 70% of all lending, were nonperforming.
Belarus (1995–present)	Significant	Many banks are undercapitalized; forced mergers have burdened some banks with poor loan portfolios; the regulatory environment is uncertain.

Table 2 *(continued)*

Country	Type of Problem	Measure of Extent
Benin (1988)	Crisis	All three commercial banks collapsed; 78% of loans were nonperforming at the end of 1988.
Bhutan (Early 1990s–present)	Significant	Nonperforming loans amount to approximately 7% of total loans.
Bolivia (1986–87)	Significant	Nonperforming loans reached 30% of banking assets.
(1994–present)	Significant	Two banks with 11% of assets were closed in November 1994. Four of 15 domestic banks, with 30% of assets, were undercapitalized and had liquidity problems and high levels of nonperforming loans in 1995.
Bosnia-Herzegovina (1992–present)	Significant	There has been no major bank closure. Loans made in the late 1980s and early 1990s are in default owing to the breakup of the former Yugoslavia and the war; this also translates into unrepayable commercial bank debt to international lenders.
Botswana (1994–95)	Significant	One problem bank was merged in 1994, a small bank was liquidated in 1995, and the state-owned National Development Bank was recapitalized at a cost of 0.6% of GDP.
Brazil (1994–present)	Significant	Twenty-nine banks, holding 15.4% of total deposits, were subjected to official intervention, placed under special administration, or received assistance to merge.
Brunei Darussalam (Mid-1980s)	Significant	Several financial firms failed in the mid-1980s. The second largest bank failed in 1986. In 1991, 9% of loans were past due; the level of such loans has subsequently declined.
Bulgaria (1991–present)	Crisis	About 75% of nongovernment loans were nonperforming in 1995, leaving many banks insolvent. Runs on banks have been reflected in pressure on reserve money and a queue of unsettled interbank payments.
Burkina Faso (1988–94)	Significant	Thirty-four percent of loans were nonperforming.
Burundi (1994–present)	Significant	Twenty-five percent of loans were nonperforming in 1995; one bank was liquidated.
Cambodia (Ongoing)	Significant	Commercial banks have rapidly expanded in the past two years. A number of banks do not meet prudential regulations. As supervisory capacity is rudimentary, there is no current information on the quality of the banks' portfolios.

Table 2 *(continued)*

Country	Type of Problem	Measure of Extent
Cameroon (1989–93)	Crisis	In 1989, 60–70% of loans were nonperforming.
(1995–present)	Crisis	About 30% of loans were nonperforming in 1996.
Canada (1983–85)	Significant	Fifteen members of the Canadian Deposit Insurance Corporation, including 2 banks, failed.
Cape Verde (1993–present)	Significant	In September 1993, the central bank was separated from the principal commercial bank. An estimated 30% of loans of the commercial bank were nonperforming at the end of 1995. This is in addition to nonperforming loans of public enterprises amounting to about 7% of GDP that remained with the central bank and were transferred to the government in September 1994.
Central African Republic (1976–92)	Crisis	Four banks were liquidated.
(1995–present)	Significant	Forty percent of loans are nonperforming; one state-owned bank is being taken over by a private group.
Chad (1979–83)	Crisis	Full banking operations were resumed after the 1979 civil war, with a moratorium on some loans and deposits.
(1992)	Significant	Thirty-five percent of loans to the private sector were nonperforming. The central bank consolidated those loans held by the 3 main commercial banks.
Chile (1981–87)	Crisis	The authorities intervened in 4 banks and 4 nonbank financial institutions (with 33% of outstanding loans) in 1981; 9 other banks and 2 more nonbanks (with 45% of outstanding loans) were subject to intervention in 1982–83, and many others were assisted. At the end of 1983, 19% of loans were nonperforming.
China[2] (1980s–present)	Significant	Problems have been recognized, but their size is very unclear; official estimates suggest that between 10% and 20% of bank loans could be nonperforming.
Colombia (1982–85)	Significant	The authorities intervened in 6 major banks and 8 finance companies. 15% of loans were nonperforming in 1984–85 (5.5% in 1980, 6.6% in 1988). Some insolvent banks were nationalized in 1985–86.
Congo, Republic of (1994–present)	Crisis	Seventy-five percent of loans to the private sector are nonperforming; 2 state-owned banks are being liquidated and 2 other state-owned banks are being privatized.

Table 2 *(continued)*

Country	Type of Problem	Measure of Extent
Costa Rica (Mid-1994–present)	Significant	One large state-owned commercial bank was closed in December 1994. The ratio of overdue loans (net of provisions) to net worth in state commercial banks exceeded 100% in June 1995.
Côte d'Ivoire (1988–90)	Significant	Five specialized financial institutions and one commercial bank were restructured. Nonperforming loans reached 12% of bank credit.
Croatia (1995)	Significant	Banks accounting for 47% of bank credit have been found to be unsound and have been, or are scheduled to be, taken over by the Bank Rehabilitation Agency during 1996.
Czech Republic (1991–present)	Significant	In 1994–95, 38% of loans were nonperforming. Several banks have been closed since 1993.
Denmark (1987–92)	Significant	Cumulative loan losses over the period 1990–92 were 9% of loans; 40 of the 60 problem banks were merged.
Djibouti (1991–93)	Significant	Two of 6 commercial banks ceased operations in 1991 and 1992; their bankruptcy is being finalized. Another bank experienced difficulties.
Dominican Republic (1992–present)	Significant	More than 5% of the total loans of the financial system are estimated to be nonperforming. In the past three years, 3 small banks have been liquidated. In April 1996, the Monetary Board intervened in the third largest bank, which represents 7% of the assets of the banking system.
Ecuador (1995–present)	Significant	High levels of nonperforming loans; the authorities intervened in several smaller financial institutions in late 1995 to early 1996 and in the fifth largest commercial bank in March 1996.
Egypt (1991–95)	Significant	Four main public sector banks were given capital assistance.
El Salvador (1989)	Significant	Nine state-owned commercial banks (later privatized between 1991 and 1993) had 37% of loans nonperforming in 1989.
Equatorial Guinea (1983–85)	Crisis	Two of the country's largest banks were liquidated.
(1995)	Significant	The principal bank's main shareholder has been placed in liquidation.
Eritrea (1994)	Significant	State-owned banks were undercapitalized, but information on the quality of bank portfolios is scarce.

Table 2 *(continued)*

Country	Type of Problem	Measure of Extent
Estonia (1992–95)	Crisis	Insolvent banks held 41% of banking system assets. The licenses of 5 banks have been revoked, 2 major banks were merged and nationalized, and 2 large banks were merged and converted to a loan-recovery agency.
Ethiopia (1994–95)	Significant	A government-owned bank was restructured, and its nonperforming loans were taken over by the government.
Fiji (1995–present)	Significant	Ten percent of the loans are nonperforming. The problems are concentrated in one large bank that has 30% nonperforming loans.
Finland (1991–94)	Crisis	Nonperforming loans and credit losses reached 13% of total exposure at their peak in 1992; there was a liquidity crisis in September 1991.
France (1991–95)	Significant	Nonperforming loans were 8.9% of total loans in 1994. Fifteen percent ($27 billion) of Crédit Lyonnais' loans were nonperforming, and some other banks have posted large losses.
Gabon (1995–present)	Significant	Nine percent of loans are nonperforming; one bank was temporarily closed in 1995.
Gambia, The (1985–92)	Significant	Ten percent of bank credit was nonperforming in 1992. A government bank was restructured and privatized in 1992.
Georgia (1991–present)	Significant	About a third of banks' outstanding loans are nonperforming; most large banks would be insolvent if adequate provisions were made for all nonperforming assets.
Germany (1990–93)	Significant	There were major problems at state-owned banks in East Germany following unification. The costs were handled by an extrabudgetary fund.
Ghana (1983–89)	Significant	Forty percent of bank credit to nongovernment borrowers was nonperforming in 1989; one bank was closed and two were merged.
Greece (1991–95)	Significant	There were localized problems that required significant injections of public funds into specialized lending institutions.
Guatemala		Two small state-owned banks had high nonperforming assets; these banks discontinued operations in the early 1990s.

Table 2 *(continued)*

Country	Type of Problem	Measure of Extent
Guinea (1980–85)	Crisis	The state-owned banking system collapsed; 80% of loans were nonperforming.
Guinea-Bissau (Ongoing)	Significant	After transition to a system in which the central bank and private commercial banks operate separately, sizable nonperforming loans (equivalent to 3.5% of GDP) were assumed by the treasury in early 1996.
(1988–present)	Significant	In August 1995, 26% of loans were nonperforming.
Guyana (1993–95)	Significant	One public bank was liquidated and merged with another public bank, holding more than one third of financial sector deposits. The surviving bank is to be restructured because of high levels of nonperforming loans. In 1993–94, US$28 million (approximately 7% of GDP) in nonperforming loans were written off.
Haiti (1991–present)	Significant	The political situation in 1994 resulted in a disruption of normal banking and a run on banks.
Hungary (1987–present)	Significant	Eight banks, accounting for 25% of financial system assets, became insolvent. At the end of 1993, 23% of total loans were problematic.
Iceland (1985–86)	Significant	One of three state-owned banks became insolvent and was eventually privatized in a merger with 3 private banks.
(1993)	Significant	The government was forced to inject capital into one of the largest state-owned commercial banks after it had suffered serious loan losses.
India (1991–present)	Significant	The nonperforming domestic assets of the 27 public sector banks were estimated at 19.5% of total loans and advances of these banks as of the end of March 1995. At that time, 15 banks did not meet Basle capital adequacy standards.
Indonesia (1992–present)	Significant	Nonperforming loans, which were concentrated in state-owned banks, were over 25% of total lending in 1993 but declined to 12% in September 1995. A large private bank was closed in 1992.
Ireland (1985)	Significant	One of the four clearing banks wrote off one fourth of its capital when its insurance subsidiary sustained losses and was placed under administration.
Israel (1983–84)	Significant	The government nationalized major banks accounting for 90% of the market; there had been an undercapitalization problem exacerbated by a crisis in the stock market.

Table 2 *(continued)*

Country	Type of Problem	Measure of Extent
Italy (1990–95)	Significant	Problems were concentrated in the south, affecting particular institutions. Systemwide, nonperforming loans were 10% of total in 1995. During 1990–94, 58 banks (accounting for 11% of total lending) were in difficulties and were merged with other institutions, and 3 of the 10 largest banks received significant injections of public funds; 10 banks were undercapitalized in 1994.
Jamaica (1994–present)	Significant	A merchant banking group was closed in December 1994; a medium-sized bank was supported in 1995.
Japan (1992–present)	Significant	In early 1996, the Ministry of Finance estimated problem loans at around 8% of GDP.
Jordan (1989–90)	Crisis	The third largest bank collapsed in August 1989; six other financial institutions encountered difficulties. The central bank provided overdrafts equivalent to 10% of GDP to meet a run on deposits and allow banks to settle foreign obligations.
Kazakstan (1991–95)	Significant	Forty percent of assets are to be written off; 80% of banks would be insolvent if all loan losses were written off.
Kenya (1993)	Significant	About 66% of loans of one third of the commercial banks were nonperforming. The local subsidiary of Meridien BIAO was closed in 1995 with little spillover.
Korea (Mid-1980s)	Significant	Nonperforming loans of deposit money banks rose significantly in the first half of the 1980s, exceeding 7% of total assets in 1986. The ratio of nonperforming loans to total assets declined subsequently to 0.9% in 1995.
Kuwait (Mid-1980s)	Crisis	There was a banking collapse associated with problems in the informal stock market. An estimated 40% of loans were nonperforming in 1986.
(1990–91)	Significant	A large part of the private sector's loan portfolio became nonperforming due to the loss of property and collateral.
Kyrgyz Republic (Ongoing)	Significant	Eighty to ninety percent of all loans are doubtful; 4 small commercial banks were closed in the past year and 2 large state banks are facing problems.
Lao People's Democratic Republic (Early 1990s)	Significant	Nonperforming loans dominated the portfolios of the state-owned commercial banks. In 1994, these banks were recapitalized with an injection of cash and bonds equivalent to 1.5% of GDP.

Table 2 *(continued)*

Country	Type of Problem	Measure of Extent
Latvia (1995–present)	Crisis	Two thirds of audited banks recorded losses in 1994. Eight bank licenses were revoked in 1994 and 15 more were revoked during the first seven months of 1995. The subsequent closure of the largest bank (with 30% of deposits) and two other major banks triggered a banking crisis in the spring of 1995.
Lebanon (1988–90)	Crisis	Four banks became insolvent; 11 banks had to resort to central bank lending.
Lesotho (1988–present)	Significant	Of 4 commercial banks, 1 that serves mostly the agricultural sector and has only a small share of bank assets has had a large portfolio of nonperforming loans. Banking services were disrupted for two months in 1991 owing to a strike.
Liberia (1991–95)	Crisis	Seven out of 11 banks are not operational; their assets were equivalent to 60% of total bank assets at mid-1995.
Lithuania (1995–present)	Crisis	Of 25 banks, 12 small ones are being liquidated and 4 larger ones do not meet the capital adequacy requirements. The fourth largest bank was closed. The operations of 2 banks, which accounted for 15% of deposits, were supported in 1995.
Macedonia, former Yugoslav Republic of (1993–94)	Crisis	Seventy percent of loans were nonperforming. The government took responsibility for banks' foreign debts and closed the second largest bank.
Madagascar (1988)	Significant	Five major banks had nonperforming loans ranging from 45% to 75% of their portfolios.
(1991–95)	Significant	There were severe management problems in the 2 remaining state-owned banks. Loan losses resulted in reserve deficiencies and the need for substantial provisions in 1994.
Malaysia (1985–88)	Crisis	The largest domestic bank wrote off nonperforming loans equivalent to approximately 1.4% of GDP in 1983. Nonperforming loans were estimated at 32% of total loans in 1988.
Mali (1987–89)	Significant	The largest bank was nearly illiquid, with 75% of its loans nonperforming; it was restructured in 1989 with equity injection and government loan guarantees.
(1995)	Significant	The government made an "equity" loan to strengthen the capital of one bank following the collapse of Meridien Bank.

Table 2 *(continued)*

Country	Type of Problem	Measure of Extent
Mauritania (1991–93)	Significant	The Development Bank ceased operations and was liquidated in 1994; 3 of the 4 commercial banks required substantial recapitalization.
Mauritius		The central bank closed 2 of 12 commercial banks for fraud and other irregularities in 1996.
Mexico (1982)	Crisis	The government took over the troubled banking system.
(1994–present)	Crisis	The ratio of nonperforming to total loans rose from 9% at the end of 1994 to 12% in December 1995. The authorities intervened in 2 banks in September 1994 and 4 of the remaining 35 banks (holding 17.5% of total end-1994 assets) in 1995. An additional 2 were taken under the administration of FOBAPROA (the deposit insurance agency). The overall cost of the several programs to support the banking system is estimated (in present value) at 6.5% of GDP.
Moldova (1994–present)	Significant	A significant stock of nonperforming assets has built up in most banks, largely resulting from earlier directed credits. Audits of the 4 largest banks will help quantify the extent of the problem.
Mongolia (1991–present)	Significant	Twenty-five percent of loans were nonperforming in 1995.
Mozambique (1988–93)	Significant	Most of the loans outstanding at the end of 1988 were written off with central bank assistance.
(1994–95)	Significant	The 2 dominant state-owned banks became increasingly dependent on central bank support, pending privatization.
Myanmar (Ongoing)	Significant	The banking system is dominated by 4 state-owned commercial banks, the largest of which is experiencing heavy losses and has a large portfolio of nonperforming loans. The other state-owned banks are widely recognized to be undercapitalized, but information on the quality of these banks' portfolios is scarce.
Nepal (Late 1980s–present)	Significant	Official estimates indicate that nonperforming loans amount to between 10% and 15% of total loans in the two large public banks, which account for nearly 70% of total bank deposits.
Netherlands		Banks overcame problems with mortgage loans in the late 1970s.

Table 2 *(continued)*

Country	Type of Problem	Measure of Extent
New Zealand (1989–90)	Significant	Of 4 large banks, 1 that was state-owned and accounted for one fourth of banking assets required a capital injection of almost 1% of GDP because of bad loan problems.
Nicaragua (Late 1980s–present)	Significant	Two large state-owned banks have had long-standing financial problems. About 50% of loans are nonperforming.
Niger (1983–present)	Crisis	In the mid-1980s, 50% of loans were nonperforming. Four banks were liquidated and 3 restructured in the late 1980s. Reform was initiated in 1987–90, and the restructuring process is still under way.
Nigeria (1991–95)	Significant	In 1991, 77% of loans were nonperforming. Of 115 banks, 34, accounting for 10% of deposits, were technically insolvent at the end of 1994.
Norway (1987–93)	Crisis	Six percent of commercial bank loans were nonperforming. Heavy losses and insolvencies led to a crisis at the end of 1991. The government became the principal owner of the three largest banks, whose share of total commercial bank assets was approximately 85%.
Pakistan (1980–present)	Significant	Nonperforming loans are estimated to be 10% of bank assets.
Panama (1988–89)	Crisis	A bank holiday that lasted for nine weeks was declared in March 1988. As a result of uncertainty and loss of confidence caused by a political crisis, the public banks were particularly affected by a loss of deposits and a rapid deterioration in their loan portfolios that stemmed from poor lending decisions and the sharp contraction of the economy. The financial position of most commercial banks also weakened, and 15 banks ceased operations.
Papua New Guinea (1989–present)	Significant	A severe economic downturn in 1989 led sharp increases in loan losses at commercial banks. Eighty-five percent of the savings and loan associations ceased operations as a result of the economic problems, mismanagement, or fraud. The public lost confidence in the banking system and withdrew deposits in 1994.
Paraguay (1995–present)	Significant	The authorities invervened in institutions accounting for some 10% of financial system deposits during the summer of 1995. There have been interventions in 6 other financial institutions

Table 2 *(continued)*

Country	Type of Problem	Measure of Extent
		since then. Depositor restitution and operations to facilitate borrowing by distressed institutions cost an estimated 4% of GDP by the end of 1995.
Peru (1983–90)	Significant	Two large banks failed. There were high levels of nonperforming loans and financial disintermediation following nationalization of the banking system in 1987.
Philippines (1981–87)	Crisis	Banks accounting for 1.6% of banking system assets failed in 1981. Through the mid-1980s, a number of institutions failed or were taken over by government financial institutions. Nonperforming assets of two state-owned institutions were transferred to a government agency. These assets accounted for nearly 30% of total banking assets. In 1986, 19% of loans were nonperforming.
Poland (1991–present)	Significant	Sixteen percent loans were classified as losses, 22% as doubtful, and 24% as substandard in 1991.
Romania (1990–present)	Significant	Five major state-owned commercial banks had 35% of their accrued interest receivables overdue as of June 30, 1994.
Russia (1992–present)	Significant	Official estimates of loan arrears were 40% of total credit to the private sector at the end of 1995.
Rwanda (1991–present)	Significant	There is a substantial amount of nonperforming loans. One bank, with a well-established network, has been closed.
São Tomé and Príncipe (1980–present)	Crisis	Over 90% of loans of the monobank were nonperforming in 1992. In 1993, a new central bank began operations. The commercial and development departments of the former monobank were liquidated, as was the only other financial institution. At the same time, 2 new banks were licensed and took over many of the assets of their predecessors. The credit operations of one newly created bank have been suspended since the end of 1994.
Senegal (1983–88)	Crisis	In 1988, 50% of loans were nonperforming. Reform was implemented in 1988–91; 8 banks were liquidated and the remaining 8 were restructured.
Sierra Leone (1990–present)	Significant	In 1995, 40–50% of loans were nonperforming. Recapitalization and restructuring is ongoing. The license of one bank was suspended in 1994.

Table 2 *(continued)*

Country	Type of Problem	Measure of Extent
Singapore		Nonperforming loans at domestic commercial banks reached 0.6% of GDP in 1982.
Slovak Republic (1991–95)	Significant	Loans classified as nonstandard were high at the end of August 1995. There were no runs or major bank closures, but all 5 major banks required government-sponsored restructuring operations.
Slovenia (1992–94)	Significant	Three banks, with two thirds of banking system assets, were restructured during this period. The percentage of bad loans is not known. Bank rehabilitation was completed in 1995.
Somalia (1990)	Crisis	There were nonperforming claims on both private and public sector borrowers during the civil unrest.
South Africa (1985)	Crisis	Banks built up large short-term foreign liabilities owing to high domestic interest rates. When foreign banks began to reduce their exposure, in part owing to political factors, the exchange depreciation and liquidity squeeze on banks resulted in an official moratorium on external capital repayments.
(1989–present)		In 1989–90, one major bank, which held about 15% of banking assets, was recapitalized and reorganized after suffering loan losses and management problems. Since 1991, several small banks have been liquidated or put into curatorship, with no systemic repercussions.
Spain (1977–85)	Crisis	From 1978 through 1982, 110 banks, accounting for 20% of deposits, were rescued. In addition, in 1983 one group that controlled 100 enterprises and 20 banks was nationalized.
Sri Lanka (Early 1990s)	Significant	Thirty-five percent of the portfolios of the two state-owned commercial banks, which accounted for over 60% of banking system assets, were nonperforming. In March 1993, bonds equivalent to 4.8% of GDP were issued to recapitalize these banks.
St. Vincent and the Grenadines (1994–present)	Significant	The only domestic bank is a state-owned commercial bank, which accounts for 30% of deposits. About 10% of its assets are nonperforming.
Sudan		Smaller banks are being encouraged to merge with larger banks to ensure compliance with the Basle capital standards before June 1997.
Swaziland (1995)	Significant	Meridien BIAO Swaziland was taken over by the central bank. The central bank also took over the

Table 2 *(continued)*

Country	Type of Problem	Measure of Extent
		Swaziland Development and Savings Bank (SDSB), which faced severe portfolio problems; the government is now expected to sign an agreement that will allow a foreign bank to take over the management of the SDSB.
Sweden (1990–93)	Crisis	Eighteen percent of total unconsolidated bank loans were reported lost and the two main banks were assisted.
Tajikistan (Ongoing)	Significant	One of the largest banks is insolvent; 1 small bank has been closed and another (out of 17) is in the process of liquidation.
Tanzania (1988–present)	Crisis	State-owned commercial banks, accounting for over 95% of the system, were insolvent. At the end of 1994, 60% to 80% of all loans were nonperforming and the losses of the largest bank were equivalent to 70% of deposits.
Thailand (1983–87)	Crisis	Fifteen percent of bank assets were nonperforming. There were runs during the crisis of 1983–85 and 15 finance companies failed. More than 25% of the financial system's assets were affected.
Togo (1989–91)	Significant	One of 10 commercial banks with 7% of bank credit was insolvent and liquidated and its credits were taken over by the government.
Trinidad and Tobago (Early 1982–93)	Significant	The banking sector expanded rapidly in the mid-1970s in a time of lax supervisory and prudential controls. With the onset of the general downturn in the economy in the early 1980s, some financial institutions experienced solvency problems, resulting in the merging of three government–owned banks in 1993 as an intermediate stage to the planned privatization of the merged bank.
Tunisia (1991–95)	Significant	Introduction of new loan classification and provisioning standards and capital adequacy requirements in 1991, coupled with extensive portfolio audits in 1992, made clear that most commercial banks were undercapitalized. (State-owned banks accounted for over 65% of total lending.) From 1991 to 1994, the banking system raised equity equivalent to 1.5% of GDP and made provisions equivalent to another 1.5%. Thus recapitalization through 1994 required at least 3% of GDP, and some banks remained undercapitalized; recapitalization continued through 1996.

Table 2 *(continued)*

Country	Type of Problem	Measure of Extent
Turkey (1982)	Crisis	Several small banks and most brokerage houses collapsed.
(1991)	Crisis	The start of the Persian Gulf war led to bank runs.
(1994)	Significant	Depositor runs in the spring of 1994 resulted in the closure of 3 medium-sized banks. To stem further runs, the government introduced full deposit insurance in May 1994.
Uganda (1990–present)	Significant	A small bank failed in early 1993. Several other banks are in difficulty or insolvent, including state-owned banks accounting for more than 40% of banking system assets.
Ukraine (1994–present)	Significant	In 1994, many banks did not meet capital and other prudential requirements. Audits indicated that one of the five largest banks was insolvent. Approximately 30% of loans outstanding were in arrears. The authorities intervened at 20 small to medium-sized banks in 1995.
United Kingdom[3]		No systemic problems, but several notable bank failures, including Johnson Matthey (1984), Bank of Credit and Commerce International (1991), and Barings (1995), have occurred.
United States (1980–92)	Significant	During the period, 1,142 savings and loan (S&L) associations and 1,395 banks were closed; 4.1% of commercial bank loans were nonperforming in 1987.
Uruguay (1981–85)	Crisis	Eleven percent of loans were nonperforming in 1982, 59% in 1986.
Uzbekistan (1993–present)	Significant	Almost 10% of loans were reported to be overdue in October 1995.
Venezuela (1994–present)	Crisis	In 1993, before the crisis started, 8.5% of loans were reported as nonperforming. The authorities intervened in 13 of 47 banks, which held 50% of deposits, in 1994, and 5 additional banks in 1995. Support by the government and the central bank to the banking system amounted to almost 17% of GDP in 1994–95.
Vietnam (Ongoing)	Significant	State-owned banks are widely recognized to be undercapitalized, but information on the quality of their portfolios remains scarce.
Yemen Arab Republic (Ongoing)	Significant	Banks have extensive nonperforming loans and heavy foreign currency exposure.

Table 2 *(concluded)*

Country	Type of Problem	Measure of Extent
Zaïre (1991–present)	Significant	Four state-owned banks are insolvent; a fifth bank is to be recapitalized with private participation.
Zambia (1994–present)	Significant	One of the largest commercial banks, the local Meridien BIAO subsidiary, failed in early 1995 and received official support equivalent to approximately 1.5% of GDP. Two small banks failed in late 1995, and several others are fragile.
Zimbabwe (1995–present)	Significant	Two of the 5 commercial banks are unable to meet their statutory reserve requirements owing to a high percentage of nonperforming loans.

[1] Under "Problems," a blank space indicates that there was a problem but that it was neither "significant" nor a "crisis." Years in parentheses denote the period of banking problems.

[2] In 1995, fraud resulted in major losses and depositor runs at two institutions in Taiwan Province of China; one was taken over by a state-owned bank and the other supported by the central bank and a state-owned bank. The large state-owned banks are reported to have an overhang of bad loans to real estate projects.

[3] From 1982–86, 16 Hong Kong banks and other deposit-taking institutions failed, were liquidated, or were taken over. The closure of the BCCI subsidiary in Hong Kong in 1991 led to minor runs on several local banks.

Part II

Macroeconomic Causes
and Consequences of Unsound
Banking Systems

4

Macroeconomic Causes of Bank Unsoundness

The linkage between macroeconomic policy and microeconomic structures and policies runs in both directions: microeconomic structures affect macroeconomic performance, and macroeconomic policies have microeconomic consequences. Structural policies that encourage real sector growth are ultimately reflected in the prosperity of individual enterprises and affect macroeconomic policy objectives and outcomes. A loose fiscal stance will tend to put pressure on government revenue sources and systems, the microeconomic elements of fiscal operations. Macroeconomic shocks, particularly in the monetary domain, will tend to put pressure on bank balance sheets and banking system health. The banking system, however, plays a central role in the economy and is linked to more than just monetary policy and interest rate determination. The following chapters consider four traditional areas of policy analysis (real sector policy, monetary policy, fiscal policy, and external sector policy), and discuss the two-way linkage between the soundness of the banking system and each of these areas.

Economic conditions and policies are key determinants of the soundness of the banking system. Banks fail, and banking systems become unsound, for many reasons, including poor or negligent management, excessive risk taking, a poor operating environment, fraud, or a sharp deterioration in the economic environment that invalidates the assumptions on which loans and investments were initially made. Although bank soundness is first an issue for individual banks, it is more likely to be systemic when unsoundness is due to macroeconomic conditions, because all banks will be exposed to those conditions. In addition, individual banking problems could become systemic owing to the spread of liquidity or solvency problems through contagion and domino effects, and this could compound the effects of macroeconomic shocks on banks. This chapter first outlines how macroeconomic conditions affect the banking system and then turns to the effects that particular monetary, fiscal, and exchange policies and instruments may have on bank soundness. Finally, the impact of the overall policy stance is considered.

Banking system fragility can impair the efficient working of markets and implementation of macroeconomic policy. An unsound banking system not only fails to provide the microeconomic channels necessary for the efficient implementation of monetary policy, but may also impair economic growth prospects, impose significant fiscal costs, and interfere with the smooth functioning of the exchange system. These effects, discussed in Chapter 5, arise from the impact of banks' portfolio weaknesses and constraints on the level and structure of interest rates, on the volume and allocative efficiency of credit, and on the responses of the banks and of other economic agents to monetary conditions.

The following discussion draws on a sample of country experiences to illustrate both aspects of this two-way linkage between banking systems and macroeconomic policy. The sample comprises 34 countries that have recently experienced significant banking sector problems or crises and for which data on a range of aspects of both the causes and consequences of these problems were available. It includes 19 developing countries, 8 countries that are in transition from a command to a market economy, and 7 industrial countries. In terms of geography, it includes 5 countries from Africa and the Middle East, 8 from the Western Hemisphere, 8 from Asia, and 13 from Europe. The European experience is heavily represented to include a number of transition economies. Nine of the banking problems featured here happened principally or entirely in the 1980s, 23 occurred mainly in the 1990s, and 4 are longstanding. At least 17 of the problems were still ongoing at the time of writing (mid-1996). Eight cases for which sufficient data were available are analyzed quantitatively in the annex to this Part; the conclusions drawn from that analysis are incorporated into the discussion throughout the book.

While an effort was made to choose cases that were representative of different regions, types of country, and problems (e.g., developing countries, problems caused by the transition from a planned economy), to a great extent the sample was dictated by the availability of information, and even among the sample countries there was, unfortunately, a great degree of disparity in the type and quality of information. Thus, while the tables that follow summarize these countries' experiences in order to provide illustrative examples of the various issues covered in this study, they should not be construed as providing an exhaustive survey of all cases in which these issues arose.

Table 3 provides summary information on these 34 cases: it lists the types of financial institution in each country that were affected and a brief description of the problems. The experience of these countries is tracked

Table 3. Selected Cases: Institutions Affected and Description of Problems1

Country	Institutions Affected	Description of Problems
Argentina (1980–82)	Businesses, banks, and other financial institutions.	Nine percent of loans were nonperforming in 1980 and 30% in 1985, and 168 institutions were closed.
(1989–90)	State banks and the central bank.	Nonperforming assets constituted 27% of the aggregate portfolio and 37% of the portfolios of state-owned banks. Failed banks held 40% of financial system assets. There were depositor runs, high levels of nonperforming assets, 8 banks holidays, and a forced renewal of time deposits.
(1995)	Banks and finance companies.	The financial system experienced currency outflows and flight to quality. Eighteen percent of depositors were withdrawn between December 1994 and May 1995. Forty-five of 205 institutions were closed or merged through September 1995.
Bangladesh (1980s–present)	All domestic banks, accounting for 95% of banking assets.	In 1987, 20% of the loans of 4 major banks, whose assets accounted for 70% of all lending, were nonperforming.
Bolivia (1994–present)	Private commercial banks.	Two banks with 11% of assets were closed in November 1994. There were depositor runs. Four of 15 domestic banks, with 30% of assets, were undercapitalized and had liquidity problems and high levels of nonperforming loans in 1995.
Brazil (1994–present)	State banks, private commercial banks, and other financial institutions.	Of 246 banks, 17 small private banks have been liquidated, 3 private banks have been subjected to official intervention, and 5 state banks have been placed under special temporary administration. These 25 banks held 8.8% of total deposits in mid-1994. In addition, 2 large and 2 medium-sized banks (representing 6.6% of deposits) have received assistance to merge.
Chile (1981–86)	Banks and other financial institutions.	The authorities intervened in 4 banks and 4 nonbank financial institutions (with 33% of outstanding loans) in 1981; 9 other banks and 2 more nonbanks (with 45% of outstanding loans) were subject to intervention in 1982–83, and many others were assisted. At the end of 1983, 19% of loans were nonperforming. The central bank purchased substandard loans at par to help recapitalize banks; such purchases continued through 1987, although the largest intervened banks were recapitalized and sold by 1986.

Table 3 *(continued)*

Country	Institutions Affected	Description of Problems
Czech Republic (1991–present)	State and private commercial banks and savings banks.	38% of loans were nonperforming in 1994–95. There was a bank run. Three small banks were closed in 1993–94, and 1 failed in 1995 and another early in 1996.
Egypt (1991–95)	Commercial banks.	Four main public sector banks were given capital assistance.
Estonia (1992–95)	Commercial banks.	Insolvent banks held 41% of banking system assets. Two major banks were merged and nationalized, and the licenses of 5 others (1 large) were revoked. Although in early 1994 it appeared that the problems had been resolved, in 1995 the nationalized entity experienced severe difficulties. In addition, during 1994, 2 more large banks were found to be insolvent and were merged and converted to a loan-recovery agency.
Finland (1991–94)	Commercial, savings, and cooperative banks.	Nonperforming loans and credit losses reached 13% of total exposure at their peak in 1992; there was a liquidity crisis in September 1991.
France (1991–95)	Crédit Lyonnais (a large state-owned bank) and some privately owned banks.	Nonperforming loans were 8.9% of total loans in 1994. 15% ($27 billion) of Crédit Lyonnais' loans were nonperforming. Some other banks have posted large losses, including Crédit Foncier de France, which in 1996 announced losses for the previous year greater than shareholder capital.
Ghana (1983–89)	Government-owned banks, private commercial banks, and rural banks.	Forty percent of bank credit to nongovernment borrowers was nonperforming in 1989; one bank was closed and two were merged.
Hungary (1987–present)	State and private commercial banks.	Eight banks, accounting for 25% of financial system assets, became insolvent. At the end of 1993, 23% of total loans were problematic. There have been 2 depositor runs.
Indonesia (1992–present)	State-owned and private banks.	Nonperforming loans, which were concentrated in state-owned banks, were over 25% of total lending in 1993 but declined to 12% in September 1995. A large private bank was closed in 1992.
Japan (1992–present)	Commercial and saving banks, *jusen*, credit cooperatives, and life insurance companies.	In early 1996, the Ministry of Finance estimated problem loans at around 8% of GDP. A regional bank and several credit unions failed in 1995, and there were depositor runs at some of the credit unions. Many of the larger banks declared losses for 1995–96.

Table 3 *(continued)*

Country	Institutions Affected	Description of Problems
Kazakstan (1991–95)	Most private commercial banks, but especially formerly sectorally oriented banks.	Forty percent of assets are to be written off; 80% of banks would be insolvent if all loan losses were written off.
Kuwait (1990–91)	Entire financial system.	A large part of the private sector's loan portfolio became nonperforming due to the loss of property and collateral.
Latvia (1995–present)	Large and small private banks.	The publication of audited reports in April 1995 revealed that two thirds of the audited banks recorded losses in 1994. Eight bank licenses were revoked in 1994, and 15 more were revoked during the first seven months of 1995. The subsequent closure of the largest bank (with 30% of deposits) and 2 other major banks triggered a banking crisis in the spring of 1995. A decision has been taken to liquidate the largest bank (subject to court approval), and several banks, including a few large ones, have had their licenses revoked.
Lithuania (1995–present)	Large and small banks.	Of 25 banks, 12 small ones are being liquidated and 4 larger ones do not meet the capital adequacy requirements. The fourth largest bank was closed. The operations of 2 banks, which accounted for 15% of deposits, were supported in 1995. There were large-scale deposit withdrawals at the end of 1995 and beginning of 1996. A restructuring plan is under consideration.
Malaysia (1985–88)	Commercial and cooperative banks, finance and insurance companies, illegal deposit-taking institutions.	The largest domestic bank wrote off nonperforming loans equivalent to approximately 1.4% of GDP in 1983. During 1985–86, there were sporadic bank runs and a number of deposit-taking institutions failed. The authorities intervened in 3 banks, 4 finance houses, 24 deposit-taking institutions, and 14 insurance companies. Nonperforming loans were estimated at 32% of total loans in 1988.
Mexico (1994–present)	The entire financial system.	The ratio of nonperforming to total loans rose from 9% at the end of 1994 to 12% in December 1995. The authorities intervened in 2 banks in September 1994, and 4 of the remaining 35 banks (which held 17.5% of total assets at the end of 1994) in 1995. An additional 2 were taken under the administration of FOBAPROA (the deposit insurance agency). Several banks placed

Table 3 *(continued)*

Country	Institutions Affected	Description of Problems
		subordinated obligations of mandatory conversion with FOBAPROA to meet their minimum capital requirements and to repay external credit lines; the latter were fully amortized by September 1995. The government, through FOBAPROA, assisted the recapitalization of some banks by purchasing problem portfolios at their accounting value net of loan-loss provisions. At the end of 1995, 19% of the bank loan portfolio was restructured into long-term loans denominated in inflation-indexed units. The overall cost of the several programs to support the banking system is estimated at 6.5% of GDP.
Norway (1987–93)	Commercial and savings banks, credit cooperatives, and finance companies.	Six percent of commercial bank loans were nonperforming. Heavy losses and insolvencies led to a crisis at the end of 1991. The government became the principal owner of the 3 largest banks, whose share of total commercial bank assets was approximately 85%.
Pakistan (1980–present)	Mainly state-owned banks.	The banking system is financially vulnerable because of a high proportion of nonperforming loans—estimated to be 10% of bank assets.
Paraguay (1995–present)	Banks and finance companies and illegal deposit-taking institutions.	The authorities invervened in 4 private banks (out of 35), a savings and loan, and 3 finance houses, accounting for some 10% of financial system deposits, during the summer of 1995. There have been interventions in 6 other finance companies since then. Depositor restitution and operations to facilitate borrowing by distressed institutions cost an estimated 4% of GDP by the end of 1995.
Philippines (1981–87)	The commercial paper market, investment houses, commercial and rural banks, a development bank, and thrift institutions.	Rural and thrift banks accounting for 1.6% of banking system assets failed in 1981, owing in part to the effect of a confidence crisis sparked by fraud in the commercial paper market that also resulted in bank runs and the failure of several investment houses. Through the mid-1980s, 3 private commercial banks, 128 rural banks, and 32 thrift institutions failed; 2 other private banks were taken over by government financial institutions. The largest commercial bank, which was state owned, and the Development Bank were bailed out; their nonperforming assets, which were transferred

Table 3 *(continued)*

Country	Institutions Affected	Description of Problems
		to a government agency, accounted for nearly 30% of total banking assets. In 1986, 19% of loans were nonperforming.
Poland (1991–present)	State and private commercial banks, cooperative, and specialized banks.	Sixteen percent of loans were classified as losses, 22% as doubtful, and 24% as substandard in 1991.
Russia (1992–present)	Most domestic banks.	Over 2,500 banks have been established since 1992. In 1994, 110 banks were closed and 96 were closed in the first 8 months of 1995. Official estimates of loan arrears were 40% of total credit to the private sector at the end of 1995.
Spain (1977–85)	Small, medium-sized, and new commercial and industrial banks.	From 1978 through 1982, 110 banks, accounting for 20% of deposits, were rescued. In addition, in 1983 one group that controlled 100 enterprises and 20 banks was nationalized.
Sweden (1990–93)	Started at finance houses and spread to banks and mortgage institutions.	Eighteen percent of total unconsolidated bank loans were reported lost (on a consolidated basis the figure was 13%), although the loss is likely to be less than 10% after recoveries and the sale of collateral. The 2 main banks were assisted.
Tanzania (1988–present)	Domestic state-owned banks, and the local Meridien subsidiary.	State-owned commercial banks, accounting for over 95% of the system, were insolvent. Between 60% and 80% of all loans were nonperforming, and the losses of the largest bank were equivalent to 70% of deposits at the end of 1994. The government contributed to recapitalizing this bank and to the reorganization of the second largest bank between 1993 and 1995. There was a run on a small state bank in 1994, which subsequently failed in 1995. The Tanzanian subsidiary of Meridien BIAO also failed in 1995.
Thailand (1983–87)	Finance companies, securities companies, and commercial banks.	Fifteen percent of bank assets were nonperforming. There were runs during the crisis of 1983–85 and 15 finance companies failed. More than 25% of the financial system's assets were affected. Through 1987, 25 institutions were closed, 9 were merged, and 18 supported.
Turkey (1994)	State and private commercial banks, unlicensed fringe institutions, and stockbrokers.	Depositor runs in the spring of 1994 resulted in the closure of 3 medium-sized banks. To stem further runs, the government introduced full-deposit insurance in May 1994.

Table 3 *(concluded)*

Country	Institutions Affected	Description of Problems
United States (1980–92)	First thrifts and credit unions, then commercial banks.	During the period, 1,142 savings and loan (S&L) associations and 1,395 banks were closed; 4.1% of commercial bank loans were nonperforming in 1987.
Venezuela (1994–present)	Commercial banks and financial groups.	In 1993, 8.5% of loans were reported as nonperforming before the crisis started. The authorities intervened in 13 of 47 banks, which held 50% of deposits, in 1994. These included 3 of the 4 largest banks. An additional 5 banks were subject to intervention in 1995. Support by the government and the central bank to the banking system amounted to almost 17% of GDP in 1994–95.
Zambia (1994–present)	Domestic commercial banks, including local Meridien subsidiary.	One of the largest commercial banks, the local Meridien BIAO subsidiary, failed in early 1995 and received official support equivalent to approximately 1.5% of GDP. Two small banks failed in late 1995; 2 other small banks are experiencing liquidity, and possibly solvency, problems. Other banks are also considered to be fragile.

[1] Years in parentheses denote the period of banking problems.

in this volume in subsequent tables, which catalogue the factors (structural, macroeconomic, and microeconomic) that contributed to their banking sector problems, and the repercussions for monetary, fiscal, and exchange policies and the real economy.

Economic Conditions and Sound Banking

Banking system soundness reflects in large measure the health of the economy. In a weakening economy, there may be few new bankable projects. Business and household borrowers and even the government may have difficulty in servicing their existing loans. Financially and operationally fragile enterprises, with high debt, low profitability, and declining markets, will have reduced ability to service their loans and responsiveness to interest rates.[12] Thus fluctuations in real sector conditions, particularly in the enterprise sector, have an immediate impact on banking system soundness through the quality of loan portfolios; loan losses in turn reduce the level of bank capital and reserves (net worth). The country cases presented in Table 4 include many instances of recessions in the period leading up to banking sector problems.

[12] See Kneeshaw (1995) and Sundararajan (1995).

Table 4. Shifts in Macroeconomic Policy and Conditions[1]

Argentina (1980–82): Recession in 1980–82. Fast growth in money and credit occurred as the boom of the late 1970s matured. Substantial real appreciation of the peso and a loss of international reserves preceded the crisis. Inflation was reduced in the early 1980s from the high levels of the 1970s.

(1989–90): Recession in 1988–90. There were strong capital outflows and a sharp devaluation in 1989. The fiscal deficit was high and the government was unable to borrow. There was a hyperinflation from 1989 to July 1990, and a sharp devaluation in 1989.

(1995): Inflation ended abruptly when the exchange anchor was introduced in 1991. Growth started to slow in 1993 and there was a recession in 1995. The public sector borrowing requirement shifted from approximate balance in 1992–93 to a marked deficit in 1994. Strong aftershocks from the December 1994 Mexican crisis were experienced in the capital markets leading to large capital outflows and a loss of excess gross international reserves under the convertibility regime. Interbank interest rates rose from 10% in December 1994 to 65% in March 1995. Some political uncertainty preceded elections in May 1995.

Bangladesh (1980s–present): Droughts and floods were factors, as was political unrest. Inflation reached double digits, and interest rates became negative in the early 1980s. Inflation was reduced from 1988 to 1994.

Bolivia (1994–present): Hyperinflation in 1985, since reduced; the economy has since stabilized with moderate economic growth but rapid credit growth. Dollarization reached 90%. Interest rates doubled, while U.S. rates were falling, and spreads were high. There was a flight to quality, although the Mexican crisis had little effect.

Brazil (1994–present): Monthly inflation fell dramatically from an average of almost 45% a month during the second quarter of 1994 to 3.3% by August 1994 with the adoption of the Real Plan. Since then, the monthly inflation rate has remained low, averaging below 1% in the first quarter of 1996. Economic activity surged in the second half of 1994 and first quarter of 1995, but as a result of restrictive policy measures, growth was 4.2% in 1995 as a whole. Monetary and credit aggregates increased substantially in the second half of 1994 owing to remonetization in the economy as a result of the sharp fall in inflation rates. There was a strong spillover from the Mexican crisis that began in December 1994. There had been large capital inflows prior to and following the introduction of the Real Plan, but they reversed to strong outflows during the Mexican crisis. In May 1995, the inflows began to increase again and international reserves increased by US$13 billion in 1995. Monetary conditions tightened in 1995. Interest rates increased in real terms in the first half of 1995 reflecting the government's economic policies to cope with the overheated economy and the increase in risk following the Mexican crisis, but they declined throughout the second half of the year and continue to decline in 1996.

Chile (1981–86): From 1974, there was determined stabilization through tight monetary and fiscal policies and, from 1977, through a predetermined exchange rate that was eventually fixed in 1979. As a result, inflation declined sharply but the real exchange rate appreciated noticeably. Credit to the private sector rose sharply before the crisis. Beginning in 1979, massive capital inflows led to a substantial accumulation of private foreign debt. From 1981, the price of copper (Chile's main export) collapsed, while international interest rates rose. Imports surged and the current account deficit rose to

Table 4 *(continued)*

14% of GDP in 1981. In 1982 foreign capital inflows shrank to less than 30% of the amount received in 1981; there was a recession from 1982–83.

Czech Republic (1991–present): Inflation rose to 57% in 1991 but fell to 10% by 1994; there was a deep recession from 1991 to 1993. Capital inflows were spurred by bank inefficiencies in intermediation, which kept spreads high, and by an unwillingness on the part of domestic banks to lend long term.

Egypt (1991–95): The economy was initially overregulated; the move toward a decentralized and outward-oriented economic structure started from 1991. Gradual stabilization was achieved with a drop in the inflation rate and a reduction in the fiscal deficit. Exchange rate depreciation in 1991 contributed to significant commercial bank losses.

Estonia (1992–95): Trade with the Soviet Union was lost in 1990 and there was a terms of trade shock. Monetary policy was tightened and a currency board was instituted to end the posttransition inflation. There was a sharp recession in 1992 and the beginning of 1993.

Finland (1991–94): Lower interest rates and rapid credit growth led to a real estate bubble and overheating of the economy in 1988, during which monetary policy was constrained due to the exchange rate regime. Monetary tightening started in 1989. A tax reform that limited the deductibility of interest payments, coupled with high debt burdens, burst the bubble and caused a recession in 1990–93. Trade with the Soviet Union collapsed in 1990, and the economy suffered from a worldwide recession during the Persian Gulf war. The currency depreciated sharply in November 1991 and from September 1992 to early 1993, leading to defaults by businesses with foreign currency obligations.

France (1991–95): There was a real estate boom followed by an economy-wide recession in 1992–93; a real estate depression in 1992–95; and low inflation, but high unemployment and fiscal deficit.

Ghana (1983–89): Severe weather induced fluctuations in agricultural output (e.g., drought in 1982–83 and flooding in 1989). There is high exposure to price fluctuations in commodities such as gold and cocoa. Controlled interest rates were negative in real terms until 1983. An economic reform program was put in place from 1983, and there were sharp exchange and interest rate adjustments in 1983–87. Ad hoc monetary measures were implemented, including a demonetization of notes, a freezing of large accounts, and the recall of certain loans. Credit rose sharply before the crisis, then fell.

Hungary (1987–present): There was a severe recession in 1991–93. The current account deficit was almost 10% of GDP in 1993–94 and the external debt rose from an already high level. The high inflation that followed the transition was reduced. Strict bankruptcy laws were introduced in 1992. The fiscal deficit grew to 8% of GDP in 1994 and a crawling peg was introduced in March 1995. There was heavy foreign borrowing by enterprises in 1994–95 and strong capital inflows in the second half of 1995.

Indonesia (1992–present): Money and credit grew quickly after liberalization in 1988–89; they were severely tightened in 1991–92. Periodic surges in capital inflows complicated monetary management. The interbank rate rose from 10% to 16% in a strong reaction to the Mexican crisis in early 1995.

Japan (1992–present): Expansionary monetary policy in the late 1980s contributed to bubbles in the real estate and the stock markets. A tightening of monetary policy led to the bursting of the bubbles in late 1990 and a downturn in economic activity.

Table 4 *(continued)*

Kazakstan (1991–95): The economy was stagnant from 1986–90; there was a drought in 1991 and a sharp decline in the economy in 1991–95. The country exited from the ruble area in late 1993 and the exchange rate fell sharply in 1993–94. Fiscal and monetary policies were tightened in late 1994. Large subsidies to enterprises continued through the end of 1994; however, real interest rates became positive. There were capital inflows in 1995.

Kuwait (1990–91): Banks and the economy were hurt by structural weakness in oil prices. The Persian Gulf crisis from 1990–91 disrupted the economy and destroyed property, including bank collateral.

Latvia (1995–present): A terms of trade shock and a collapse of eastern markets occurred early in the transition. Banks' profit margins on trade financing declined as a result of price liberalization in Russia. Inflation was reduced from almost 100% in 1992 to 26% in 1994.

Lithuania (1995–present): The economy lost most of its Soviet trade in 1990 and experienced a sharp rise in energy prices to world levels. There was a recession in 1991–93. Expansionary monetary policy and supply shortages led to hyperinflation in 1992–93, which was reduced to 30–35% a year in 1995.

Malaysia (1985–88): Fast money and credit growth and a fiscal deficit of 20% of GDP in the early 1980s spurred inflation and price bubbles in the stock and real estate markets. The countercyclical policy led to a recession in 1985–86 and the bubble burst. Inflation was reduced to less than 1% in 1985. The slowdown resulted in a contraction of cash flow; corporate deposits fell by 19%. Oil and other commodity prices fell sharply in 1986. Real estate prices declined by 60–70% in 1986 relative to 1983. The terms of trade deteriorated sharply and the ringgit depreciated 17%.

Mexico (1994–present): During 1994, events such as the uprising in Chiapas in January, the assassinations of presidential candidate Colosio in March and of the secretary general of the ruling party in September, and a second Chiapas uprising in December, contributed to an environment of considerable political uncertainty. On December 20, 1994, the Mexican authorities widened the exchange rate intervention band that had been in place since late 1991. Two days later, as capital outflows persisted, the exchange rate was allowed to float. This was followed by a sharp depreciation of the peso and an increase in interest rates, accompanied by an abrupt downturn in the economy. The peso depreciated from MexN$3.94 per U.S. dollar (prior its floating) to MexN$7.60 per U.S. dollar in mid-March 1995. Short-term interest rates rose from 14% in 1994 to around 50% in 1995, reaching a peak of 85% in mid-March. GDP, which grew 3.7% in 1994, was expected to decline by about 6–8% in 1995. At the beginning of 1995, banks faced problems in rolling over foreign currency deposits and other short-term lines of external credit. The government had to amortize a substantial amount of short-term debt (Tesobonos) indexed to the U.S. dollar.

Norway (1987–93): Capital inflows were strong until the oil price decline in 1986. Tax reform occurred in the late 1980s. There was a credit explosion in the mid-1980s financed by foreign borrowing and central bank credit. A low interest rate policy was maintained. The exchange rate depreciated during and after 1986. Following the decline in oil prices, the bubble burst, and credit to the private sector fell in 1987. There was a recession from 1989–91.

Table 4 *(continued)*

Pakistan (1980–present): The economy has been highly regulated. Interest rates were decontrolled in 1995. There has been slow progress in fiscal consolidation. A recent devaluation caused losses on account of foreign exchange cover equivalent to 0.25% of GDP.

Paraguay (1995–present): No significant shocks.

Philippines (1981–87): The ratio of credit to GDP experienced a sustained increase before the crisis. The world recession from 1980–82 hurt bank borrowers. The balance of payments crisis of October 1983 spilled over to the banking system, with the announcement of a moratorium on external debt payments provoking panic and runs. The exchange rate depreciated during the crisis.

Poland (1991–present): The hyperinflation that followed the transition ended in 1990–91, and the fiscal deficit was reduced. There was a recession in 1990–91.

Russia (1992–present): Following the collapse of the former Soviet Union and the end of central planning, there was a sharp decline in economic growth and lax demand-management policies were adopted. The liberalization of prices in 1992 resulted in an abrupt jump in the domestic price level. The collapse of the ruble zone in early 1993 resulted in a sharp deterioration in the terms of trade and a collapse in trade flows. In 1994 and 1995, macroeconomic policies were tightened, resulting in a reduction in inflation and increased exchange rate stability.

Spain (1977–85): Oil price shocks in 1973 and 1980 hurt this oil importing economy. The death of General Franco in 1975 gave rise to some political uncertainty. Monetary policy was tightened to reduce inflation. Industrial production fell from 1975 to 1978 and again in 1981. Real interest rates rose to high levels after having been negative. Share and real estate prices fell from 1974–81.

Sweden (1990–93): There was a large increase in credit following liberalization in 1985. There were capital outflows from 1988 to 1992. Inflation was cut sharply early in the 1990s, ending a real estate boom; real estate prices fell up to 50% in a short period. Tax reform contributed to the decline in real estate prices. The ERM (exchange rate mechanism) crisis in 1992 led temporarily to very high short-term interest rates that hurt banks.

Tanzania (1988–present): The economy was highly controlled until the mid-1980s. The financial sector was nationalized after 1967. Inflation was high; the exchange rate became overvalued; and real interest rates were negative from 1971 until 1988. Stabilization and structural reform programs began in 1986.

Thailand (1983–87): Credit grew very rapidly until there was a slowdown in economic activity in the 1980s.

Turkey (1994): Several years of increasing macroeconomic imbalances contributed to banking losses. High and rising fiscal deficits and an appreciating real exchange rate resulted in a rapidly increasing trade deficit, buildup of foreign debt, high inflation, and high real rates of interest. There was an exchange and financial market crisis during the early part of 1994, followed by a major depreciation of the currency. In April 1994, the government introduced stabilization and structural adjustment policies.

United States (1980–92): The Federal Reserve shifted from targeting interest rates to reserves in October 1979, which began the process of curtailing inflation in the United States. Interest rate ceilings, phased out in 1978–83, contributed to poor banking

Table 4 *(concluded)*

practices. Interest rates, which had been negative in real terms, rose to high real levels and became volatile in the early 1980s. The thrift industry was rendered market-value insolvent almost overnight, and the international debt crisis affected major money center banks. Oil price fluctuations contributed to booms and collapses in oil producing and consuming regions. There were recessions in 1980, 1982, and 1990–92. A silver crisis in spring 1980 caused problems for some U.S. banks. The decline in commodity prices caused bank failures in agricultural states in the early to mid-1980s. The exchange rate appreciated until 1986, hampering exports; thereafter the dollar declined until 1995. Tax reform in 1986 limited the deductibility of interest payments, reducing incentives for borrowing. The Persian Gulf war accelerated the decline that was beginning in the property markets in the early 1990s, while hurricanes and floods presented additional challenges to banks in affected regions. Political and tax preferences for housing encouraged an overexposure to the real estate industry.

Venezuela (1994–present): Oil prices declined after the Persian Gulf war ended. There was political unrest in 1992–94. Fiscal deficits spurred high inflation in the early 1990s, but recession in 1993–95 led to a decline in the asset price boom. Expansive monetary policy allowed negative real interest rates in 1994–95, coinciding with a large fiscal deficit. The external situation deteriorated with capital flight and exchange rate depreciation in 1994. Confidence declined further following political disruption and bank failures. Spillover from the Mexican crisis that began in December 1994 hurt domestic banks.

Zambia (1994–present): Fiscal and monetary tightening in 1992 led to a reduction in inflation. Indirect instruments of monetary policy were introduced in late 1992. The exchange rate was allowed to float in 1993. Prolonged drought exacerbated economic problems.

[1] Years in parentheses denote the period of banking problems.

Bank difficulties associated with business cycles or other temporary effects can often be managed within the context of an appropriate cyclical macroeconomic policy. In some cases, however, the fundamental banking sector weaknesses exposed by a cyclical downturn are too severe to be redressed solely by an economic upturn. For example, recent banking problems in Japan were linked to the bursting of the asset price bubble in 1990 and exacerbated by the prolonged recession. The cyclical downturn helped to reveal, but was not the principal cause of, the weaknesses in bank balance sheets. It is now recognized that simply waiting for the economy to grow out of the problem is unlikely to be sufficient without additional measures to restructure and recapitalize banks. Asset price declines, particularly in real estate, also played a role in the Nordic countries, the United States, and Venezuela.

Beyond the general difficulties of operating in a weak economy, macroeconomic shocks often contribute to bank unsoundness. Table 4 summarizes economic shocks experienced by the 34 sample countries. Sharp changes in relative prices can present problems to enterprises and to their banks. Economies in transition have undergone dramatic shifts in relative prices, which contributed to enterprise insolvencies and bank unsoundness. The rise in oil prices in the 1970s and early 1980s damaged oil import dependent businesses and countries, and their banks; the decline in oil prices beginning in 1986 contributed to recessions and bank failures in oil exporting countries (e.g., Nigeria and Norway); and in 1981, the collapse in the price of copper contributed to bank problems in Chile.

Shifts in the terms of trade have contributed to banking difficulties in many countries, including Chile in the early 1980s, Malaysia in the mid-1980s, and the countries of Eastern and Central Europe, the Baltics, and the former Soviet Union in the early 1990s. Finally, major changes in an economic system can lead to the disappearance of markets or sectors, which will present problems for enterprises, traders, and their banks. The demise of the Council for Mutual Economic Assistance (CMEA) had severe effects on both member countries and their nonmember trading partners (such as Finland).

Noneconomic shocks, such as wars or severe weather (droughts, floods), may have an adverse economic impact. Table 4 indicates a number of instances in which such events have contributed to banking sector difficulties in the sample countries.

Monetary Policy Instruments

The monetary instruments used to implement policy will also have effects on the banking system. The absence of a properly functioning lender-of-last-resort facility can distort the smooth functioning of payments systems and drive illiquid banks into insolvency through a fire sale of assets. Credit or interest rate controls can compel banks to hold unremunerated excess reserves, constrain bank liquidity management, and result in disintermediation, reducing banks' client base and profitability. Required reserves that are not remunerated at market rates constitute a tax on the banking system, and a large increase in nonremunerated required reserves may force banks to execute sudden portfolio adjustments that might affect their solvency and liquidity.[13] Similarly, high liquidity ratios that are used as a means to finance budget deficits at below-market interest rates also constitute a tax on the banking system and can result in a widening of interest rate spreads, increased bank lending rates, and disintermediation.[14]

---

[13] See Marston (1996).
[14] See Gulde (1995).

In part reflecting the concern for soundness of money markets and banking systems, monetary operations typically strive to implement policy through smooth adjustments in instruments that avoid high volatility in interest rates. The development of market-oriented financial instruments, such as treasury bills, can facilitate liquidity management by banks, but, where treasury bills are widely held by nonbanks, may increase pressure on banks' deposit base and expose market risks. Thus, the management of bank soundness during a transition from direct controls to indirect monetary instruments, and during the subsequent operation of market-based instruments, poses unique challenges for each country.[15]

Fiscal Instruments

Fiscal policy instruments may affect bank profitability and incentives to recognize loan losses on the banks' books in a timely manner. Tax systems that do not allow banks to deduct loan-loss provisions or that define earnings to include interest accrued on nonperforming assets effectively tax nonexistent profits, decapitalizing banks. Systems that include bank-specific taxes, or taxes on bank-provided financial instruments and transactions (such as taxes on checks or on bank debits) impose a burden on intermediation that can both weaken banks and reduce their role in the economy. Sharp changes in taxation, such as rescinding the tax deductibility of interest payments, can affect asset prices and the ability of borrowers to service loans. Such fiscal innovations, if inappropriately sequenced, may jeopardize bank liquidity and solvency, as was the case in several Nordic countries and the United States.[16]

Governments frequently use banks as a source of finance, through reserve requirements or required holdings of government securities; if these assets do not pay market rates, bank earnings suffer. In addition, some governments have imposed quasi-fiscal roles on both the central bank and commercial banks, particularly state-owned banks, in the form of programs of directed credit at below-market interest rates, portfolio restrictions, and regulations covering credit allocation, interest rates, and bank branching. These typically weaken banks (and sometimes the central bank) and have contributed substantially to systemic unsoundness in many countries.

Exchange Rate Policy

The effects of exchange rate policy vary across sectors. A prolonged overvaluation will be detrimental to export sectors, while a prolonged

---

[15] See Alexander, Baliño, and Enoch (1995) and Sundararajan (1995).
[16] See Drees and Pazarbaşioğlu (1995), and Table 4.

undervaluation will negatively affect sectors reliant on imports. The primary impact on bank profitability of the level of the exchange rate will be through the performance of borrowers although there may be some impact on banks' foreign exchange services or trading.

Exchange rate shifts also have different effects across sectors. The impact of a significant change in the exchange rate will usually worsen the financial condition of some borrowers and increase the number of nonperforming loans. The impact on banks may be compounded if regulations and management practices have not limited banks' direct and indirect foreign exchange risk exposure. Exchange rate shifts played a role in many of the 34 countries in our sample (Table 4).

Exchange rate instability and high levels of uncertainty negatively affect bank operations. Uncertainty linked to the Mexican financial crisis of 1995 in turn triggered financial problems in several Latin American countries and placed stress on banking systems in other emerging markets far removed from the crisis.[17] Unstable or deteriorating conditions are often accompanied by sharp increases in real interest rates, reflecting increased risk premiums. Exchange rate policies, often coupled with political concerns, may induce capital flight and bank runs. Expectations of a devaluation can cause disintermediation as depositors shift to foreign currency. Dollarization, which reached 90 percent in Bolivia, for example, can limit the effectiveness of domestic monetary policy instruments. Furthermore, while extensive dollarization of domestic intermediation may appear to reduce exchange risk, this is often only at the expense of increased credit risk, which will surface when a depreciation impairs borrowers' ability to service their foreign-exchange-denominated loans.

Overall Policy Stance

The macroeconomic policy stance will affect banks directly and via the real sector. Restrictive policies tend to have an immediate negative effect on the banking system, particularly if banks are already unsound. A relaxed policy that accommodates inflation may improve bank profitability but carries its own risks. When stabilization is finally implemented, banks are likely to find the adjustment difficult.

While sound banks should have sufficient balance sheet flexibility to adjust to changes in liquidity conditions, a sharp monetary contraction could trigger liquidity crises among unsound banks, which in turn could lead to or reveal insolvency. For example, the U.S. monetary contraction beginning in 1979 sparked the savings and loan (S&L) crisis. Banks will also be affected by a rise in interest rates or a change in the slope of the

---

[17] See Folkerts-Landau, Ito, and others (1995), and Rojas-Suárez and Weisbrod (1995b).

yield curve, to the extent that the rates banks pay to acquire funds adjust at a different pace from the yields of the assets banks hold. Interest rate increases will eventually be passed through to borrowers, but this will increase banks' credit risk as some borrowers, particularly highly leveraged borrowers, will be less able to service their loans at the higher rates. To the extent that a monetary tightening slows economic growth, the cyclical effects discussed above will come into play.

Experience has shown that although a loosening of monetary policy could be to the advantage of banks in the short term, an excessively loose policy may contribute to asset price bubbles and inflation and to future banking system problems. Rapid expansion of domestic credit tends to result in increased lending to high-risk sectors and to distort asset prices. Rapid growth in banking system credit relative to GDP was observed prior to financial crises in Argentina (1981), Chile, Colombia, Finland, Japan, Mexico, Norway, Sweden, and Uruguay.[18]

Banks can usually mitigate the impact of high inflation on their own profitability by indexing lending rates and shifting into assets whose prices lead inflation, such as foreign exchange. However, bank income under such circumstances is often derived from the float on payments, from the inflation tax collected on nonremunerated demand deposits (net of reserve requirements), and from foreign exchange dealing. These earnings may be unsustainable, particularly when inflation declines. Furthermore, bank portfolio risk is likely to increase.

High inflation or exchange rate variability, or both, reduces the quality of information provided by interest rates and goods prices. High interest rates during inflation may exacerbate the moral hazard and adverse selection problems inherent in bank lending. Uncertainties associated with inflation also erode the information base for business planning and credit appraisal (see Appendix I).

Prolonged macroeconomic instability and persistently inflationary policies will exact a toll from the economy, by, among other things, distorting bank operations and eroding the real value of bank capital. However, the transition to a more stable environment may not be easy for the banking system. Stabilization preceded episodes of unsoundness in Chile, Malaysia, and Finland, among other countries.[19] Where previously expected inflation has been incorporated into investment decisions, a rapid reduction in inflation will leave those forecasts unmet and borrowers unable to service their loans. Furthermore, after banks have adjusted their operations to inflationary conditions, macroeconomic stabilization may have a significant impact on bank profitability. A decline in inflation

---

[18] Hausmann and Gavin (1995).
[19] Garcia (1995).

deprives banks of inflation-linked sources of earnings. Instead, banks must rely increasingly on traditional intermediation, focusing on loan and client assessment.

The required transition in bank operations takes time, is difficult to manage, and has contributed to systemic banking problems in a number of countries. High inflation in Russia resulted in underemphasis on credit analysis and overemphasis on foreign exchange speculation. Tightening of monetary conditions in early 1995 reversed the gains in foreign currency positions and made default by marginal borrowers more likely as loan principal was no longer eroded by inflation.[20] Banks in Brazil experienced similar difficulties in 1995 owing to the reduction in income associated with the inflation tax. Brazilian banks seemed to have successfully adjusted to a high-inflation environment; however, the recent decline in inflation revealed underlying weaknesses in some banks' balance sheets and credit assessment. A significant reduction in the rate of inflation appears to have been a factor in 21 of the problem cases listed in Table 4.

These observations do not constitute an argument to retain persistently inflationary policies. Rather, they show that the mix of policies to reduce inflation has implications for bank unsoundness. The type of monetary tightening and the mix between interest rate and exchange rate policies may affect banking soundness, depending upon initial balance sheet exposures. For example, a steep rise in interest rates (or reduction in domestic liquidity) can result in a sharp decline in asset prices. As noted above, significant declines in asset prices were contributors to banking problems in the United States, Japan, the Nordic countries, and elsewhere. On the other hand, operating through the exchange rate could achieve a tightening of monetary conditions with perhaps a more attenuated effect on domestic asset prices, but would negatively affect banks to the extent that they have uncovered foreign asset positions. Regardless of the specifics of a banking system's exposures, an adjustment program that relies too heavily on monetary restraint could place excessive demands for swift adjustment on banks. In particular, a policy stance in which tighter monetary policy is used to compensate for unconstrained fiscal imbalances is likely to strain the microeconomic foundation for monetary policy, the banking system.

---

[20] See Jaffee and Levonian (1995).

5

Macroeconomic Consequences of an Unsound Banking System

A banking system that is in distress can distort allocative efficiency and macroeconomic policy implementation, even though it can continue to function as long as it remains liquid. In addition to complicating monetary management, banking system unsoundness can also impose high costs in the form of fiscal obligations and other macroeconomic distortions.

Behavior of Unsound Banks

In analyzing the policy implications of bank unsoundness, it is important to bear in mind the behavioral patterns observed in unsound banks that affect the banking system's interactions with and responses to policy instruments. Banks that have lost most or all of their capital face a different incentive structure from sound banks, and competition from insolvent banks can pose threats to the financial soundness of their competitors. As owners and managers try to recoup their losses, moral hazard increases, particularly when managers or owners do not have their own funds at stake.[21] An unsound bank may offer higher interest rates than competitors to draw in deposits to pay operating expenses, may resort to outright gambling by choosing high-risk transactions, or may incur higher risk through adverse selection.[22] In many cases, unsound banks become captive to insolvent debtors or carry a portfolio of loans to related borrowers, who have no intention of repaying their debts. Unable to declare loans in default lest they acknowledge their own insolvency, such banks may continue to lend to nonperforming borrowers or to capitalize

---

[21] Moral hazard is the tendency for people to be less careful when they do not expect to bear the full cost of their behavior.

[22] To raise profitability, a bank would be inclined to charge higher interest rates to borrowers. Adverse selection occurs if it fails to adequately screen customers and attracts and selects only those customers looking to fund high-risk projects.

interest on these borrowers' loans (a process sometimes referred to as "evergreening"). As the situation deteriorates further and prospects for long-term employment are reduced, insiders may turn to fraud and theft.

Thus, banks that are desperate to raise income or that have become overburdened with nonperforming assets may spiral into insolvency with increasing speed. As an unsound bank searches for liquidity at any cost or is willing to assume any risk, it will tend to be less responsive to interest rates and other market signals, or may exhibit perverse responses. Such behavior, when sufficiently widespread, has important implications for the reactions of economic agents, the functioning of financial markets, the efficiency of financial resource use, the transmission of monetary policy, and the ultimate resolution costs. The degree of unsoundness at which these effects take hold will vary from situation to situation; where unsoundness is systemic, the macroeconomic effects are likely to be significant.

Impact on the Real Sector

A sound banking system contributes to economic growth by mobilizing financial resources and by channeling them to activities with the highest expected rates of return for a given level of risk. The banking system also provides transaction services and payment systems, which increase the efficiency of economic activities. In addition, banks provide expertise in project screening and corporate governance, which aids in the efficient use of resources.

A weak banking system is unable to intermediate savings effectively. Across a range of countries that experienced banking crises, growth and economic efficiency have suffered. It is often difficult to separate the effects of banking sector problems on the real economy from a decline in real economic activity that may have contributed to the banking sector problems in the first place. Nevertheless, the experiences of the countries in the sample, as shown in Table 5, suggest that episodes of fragility in the banking sector have been detrimental to economic growth in the countries concerned.[23]

The lack of a sound banking system is particularly severe in developing and transition economies in which equity and capital markets are underdeveloped and do not provide alternative financial instruments. The soundness of intermediation is as important as its volume. In several Latin American countries, despite a rising volume of intermediation, the reduced efficiency of investment intermediated by unsound banking and financial systems apparently contributed to a negative relationship

---

[23] See also Johnston and Pazarbaşioğlu (1995).

Table 5. The Impact of Bank Unsoundness on the Real Sector[1]

Argentina (1980–82): Interest rate spreads were high. Credit and payments systems were disrupted. Growth was reduced after the 1980–82 crisis. There was a substantial redistribution of wealth in favor of debtors.

(1995): The sharp growth in real GDP following convertibility was reversed to a recession in 1995.

Bangladesh (1980s–present): Spreads are wide and reduce intermediation.

Bolivia (1986–87): High interest rates and heightened caution on the part of liquid banks limited the access of small businesses to credit.

Brazil (1994–present): High interest rates and increased caution on the part of the banking system limited access to credit.

Chile (1981–87): Growth was reduced from an average of 8% a year in the five years before the crisis to 1% in the five years after it. The payments system was disrupted.

Czech Republic (1991–present): There were high spreads between domestic deposit and loan rates and between rates on domestic and foreign funds. High levels of nonperforming loans reduced banks' ability to extend credit.

Egypt (1991–95): Interest rate spreads were high.

Estonia (1992–95): There was already a severe recession before the banking crisis occurred; it is not clear whether the banking problems exacerbated the downturn.

Finland (1991–94): Growth averaged 4.5% in the three years before 1990, zero for 1990, and –4.0% in the following three years. Unemployment reached a peak of 18.4% in 1994.

France (1991–95): No apparent impact.

Ghana (1983–89): Low levels of intermediation, inadequate resource mobilization, and a large stock of nonperforming assets reduced banks' flexibility to lend to new customers. Favorable returns on risk-free investments also discouraged lending. Economic growth fell from 3% in the five years before the crisis to 2.5% in the three years after it.

Hungary (1987–present): Stabilization and growth were impeded. Despite enacting bankruptcy legislation, enterprise restructuring was hampered by inadequate reforms to bank lending policies.

Indonesia (1992–present): High spreads led to disintermediation and a growth in nonbank financial institutions.

Japan (1992–present): Weak bank balance sheets have tended to undermine public confidence and may have limited the speed of economic recovery. Loan rates rose relative to funding costs.

Kazakstan (1991–95): Real interest rates became positive. A lack of competition and perceived weakness in the banking system induced very high interest rate spreads.

Kuwait (1990–91): Banks' hesitancy to lend and uncertain domestic investment prospects reduced growth.

Latvia (1995–present): There was a decline in economic activity, but it was not as sharp as the 20% decline observed in the monetary aggregates.

Table 5 *(continued)*

Lithuania (1995–present): There was a credit crunch, especially in the agricultural and energy sectors.

Malaysia (1985–88): A secondary mortgage market to aid bank liquidity was established. The crisis caused high real interest rates as banks increased their margins to cover the cost of their nonperforming loans. This contributed to disintermediation and impeded investment.

Mexico (1994–present): Real interest rates are high and are affecting the repayment capacity of borrowers. It is estimated that credit to the private sector declined by about 20% in real terms during 1995.

Norway (1987–93): Growth fell from an average of 3.2% in the five years before the crisis to 1.7% in the two years after it, but not solely as a result of the banking crisis.

Pakistan (1980–present): High interest rates and credit shortages for the private sector diminish investment and growth.

Paraguay (1995–present): There was a flight to quality, reducing the availability of bank funding. Economic growth slowed toward the end of 1995 owing in part to the disruptive effects of the banking problems.

Philippines (1981–87): Real interest rates rose and there was a recession and a credit crunch. Growth fell from an average of 6% a year in the five years before the crisis to −1.25% in the following five years.

Poland (1991–present): Lending to enterprises was viewed as risky and banks preferred to lend to the government. Thus financing to the real sector declined sharply from 1991 to 1993. Banks raised interest rate spreads in an attempt to earn their way out of trouble.

Russia (1992–present): The weak banking system has not mobilized savings efficiently and has a limited ability to intermediate savings to private sector investors. Banks have focused on short-term investments in foreign exchange and government securities.

Spain (1977–85): Financial intermediation costs rose (both interest margins and operating expenses), imposing an increased burden on enterprises.

Sweden (1990–93): Small borrowers complained of high interest rates and restricted access to credit. There was an economic downturn, but it is difficult to separate the effects of the banking crisis from those of the currency crisis and the broader European recession.

Tanzania (1988–present): The cash-based economy has hindered growth. There is little intermediation. The deposit-to-GDP ratio declined from 1980–88 and much of those funds that were available were misallocated. The payments system is slow.

Thailand (1983–87): Bank spreads fell, and there was a sharp decline in finance company loans to the private sector. The effects are difficult to gauge but growth slowed in 1984–85.

Turkey (1994): Real rates are high and a flight to quality and tiering have occurred. Responding to a number of factors, output contracted sharply in 1994, but recovered quickly in 1995.

Table 5 *(concluded)*

United States (1980–92): The real estate markets in several areas of the country experienced a cutback in credit supplies as a result of the problems in the thrift industry, which may have contributed to the decline in property prices in the early 1990s. The credit crunch arising from weak bank capitalization slowed recovery from the 1990–92 recession.

Venezuela (1994–present): Interest rates turned sharply negative following the reintroduction of exchange controls; nevertheless, the fall in imports disrupted production. The demand for credit remained strong.

Zambia (1994–present): The wealth effect of deposit losses diminished demand and growth. There was a credit crunch for some borrowers, but intermediation in general and the payments system were not impaired.

---

[1] Years in parentheses denote the period of banking problems.

between growth and financial intermediation in the 1970s and 1980s.[24] In many economies in transition, private sector development and the transition process have been hindered by vulnerable banking systems.[25]

A sound banking system in a competitive environment provides financial intermediation at low cost. A competitive environment limits the ability of individual banks to increase spreads; banks would have little scope to charge higher interest rates except by lending to higher-risk borrowers. In the competitive U.S. system, troubled thrifts in the 1980s lowered spreads by aggressively bidding for deposits and reducing loan rates to attract customers. Excessively low spreads as institutions try to grow out of their problems by garnering market share at any cost are one manifestation of the pathology of unsound banks.

In other cases, especially in less competitive markets, weak banks may widen their spreads to cover the cost of nonperforming loans, penalizing depositors and discouraging investment. For example, in 1985–88 Malaysian banks did not reduce lending rates even when general liquidity conditions improved and deposit rates fell.[26] Attempts to compensate for loan defaults may explain the rise in loan rates relative to funding costs for Japanese banks beginning in 1990.[27] High interest rate spreads characterized periods of banking sector problems in most of the countries in our sample.

A widening of spreads and a rise in lending rates may occur even in a relatively competitive banking market if unsoundness is widespread or

---

[24] De Gregorio and Guidotti (1992).
[25] Borish, Long, and Noël (1995).
[26] Sheng (1992).
[27] Bank of Japan (1994), p. 50.

systemic. When most banks share the same problems, such as high levels of nonperforming loans, the interest spread reflects the high cost structure of banking throughout the sector. Montes-Negret and Papi (1996) provide illustrative calculations showing how break-even spreads rise with the ratio of nonperforming loans to assets. Wider spreads and higher lending rates allow banks to recover profitability, but they also deter the investment needed to support faster macroeconomic recovery. Galbis (1993) examined the role of banking market structure and financial fragility in bouts of high real interest rates following financial liberalization. That study found that unsound banking practices, particularly lending to companies in distress, contributed to high real interest rates in Chile and the Philippines following the liberalization of interest rates in those countries.

The stock of nonperforming loans in bank portfolios will also limit the amount of credit available for new and better borrowers. An unsound bank may continue lending to unprofitable enterprises with which the bank has had a long-term relationship, or to insolvent debtors to prevent defaults that would in turn result in open insolvency of the bank. This has been the experience in a number of countries in our sample, particularly formerly centrally planned economies.[28] If depositors shift their funds out of unsound banks into cash or other financial instruments, the availability of credit will be further reduced; a pronounced flight to quality occurred in several of the countries in the sample. As Calvo and Coricelli (1994) show, excessive credit contraction can shift the economy to a lower output path; this evidently contributed to the persistence of output declines in Poland and several other Central and Eastern European countries in the first stages of transition.

A bank with insufficient earnings may have to use deposits to cover its operating expenses, thereby distorting its role as an intermediary and decreasing its net worth. Unsound banks will have reduced incentives to avoid riskier projects, since any loss in excess of already depleted capital will be borne by depositors, the deposit insurer, or the public sector. The perverse incentive structure facing unsound banks can result in adverse selection of borrowers and further increases in real interest rates, hampering the efficient allocation of credit resources and contributing to high costs of intermediation and to output levels that are below potential.[29]

The magnitude of business cycles will depend in part on the soundness of the banking system; weak banks may be forced to call loans or sell assets and collateral into a declining market, further exacerbating a cyclic downturn.[30] In extreme cases, where unsoundness results in a financial crisis,

[28] See also Perotti (1993), Hinds (1988), and Calvo and Kumar (1994).
[29] See de Juan (1991).
[30] See Alexander and Caramazza (1994).

the resulting uncertainty lowers the expected rate of return on real assets, with consequent negative effects on asset markets and output.[31] It may also result in a breakdown of the payments system, reducing the efficiency with which almost all domestic and foreign trade transactions are conducted. Even where the banking system was not the key factor in precipitating a financial crisis, a weak and vulnerable banking system may impede recovery and jeopardize macroeconomic stability; the 1995 experience of the larger Latin American economies is a case in point.

In some economies, banks play an important role in helping assess the value of corporate projects, monitoring borrowers, and enforcing financial discipline, thus contributing to corporate governance.[32] When banks are poorly managed or are financially impaired, the economy is deprived of a key source of these services.[33] For example, systemic unsoundness in economies in transition has severely limited the role banks can play in reforming the operations and governance of the corporate sector in those countries.[34] This deficiency is of more significance in developing and transition economies that do not have well-developed credit monitoring agencies and lack a broad base of managerial talent. Even in industrial countries, some enterprises, particularly small and medium-sized enterprises, are likely to feel the impact of reduced bank contributions to financial discipline and corporate governance.

Monetary Policy Implications

The banking system is the primary conduit for transmitting monetary policy signals. Effective implementation of monetary policy requires that the banking system be able to expand and contract its aggregate balance sheet in response to policy initiatives without adversely affecting the efficiency of intermediation or depositor confidence. No matter what the specific objectives of monetary policy, an unsound banking system affects the instruments and results of monetary policy as well as the authorities' ability to formulate and conduct monetary policy. This is true regardless of whether quantitative monetary policy formulation focuses on the banking system as a whole or only on the central bank, since the effects on the macroeconomy of changes in the central bank's balance sheet are mediated through the banking system.

The importance of the competitive structure of the banking system for monetary policy has long been recognized and has been the subject of

---

[31] Brunner and Meltzer (1988).
[32] See Prowse (1994) and Aoki and Patrick (1994).
[33] See Berglöf (1995).
[34] See Fries and Lane (1994) and Dittus (1994).

analysis, although firm conclusions are difficult to draw because of the model-dependency of most studies.[35] On the other hand, the importance of soundness for monetary policy implementation has not received much analytical attention. Recently, the significance of banking system soundness for monetary policy was recognized by the June 1995 amendments to the European Union (EU) banking directives, which permit exchange of supervisory information with monetary and payments system authorities. The quality of the banking system portfolio affects the relationships underlying the monetary policy process, including the reliability of monetary statistics, and the effectiveness of monetary instruments and transmission mechanisms.

Relationships Underlying the Monetary Policy Process

The practical implementation of monetary policy usually requires the existence of relatively stable relationships between monetary instruments, operating targets, intermediate targets or indicator variables, and ultimate policy objectives.[36] Disruption of the financial system will affect these relationships; as a banking system becomes more insolvent, the links between operating targets, such as interest rates, intermediate targets, such as money or credit aggregates, and policy goals, such as price stability, will be altered.

In some operational frameworks for monetary policy, the focus is on established relationships between reserve money and broader aggregates or macroeconomic objectives. However, variations in bank reserve holdings and in public preferences for financial instruments, which often accompany increasing unsoundness of banks, can destabilize benchmark relationships such as the money multiplier. As shown in Table 6, money demand or monetary relationships were unstable in 15 of the cases studied (see also the quantitative studies in the annex to Part II). Money multipliers in Argentina, Chile, Ghana, the Philippines, and Uruguay increased during periods of unsoundness prior to crises. In contrast, the 1992 Estonian banking crisis precipitated a rise in the currency-to-deposit ratio and a fall in the base money multiplier. Even when the operational target is a narrow money aggregate that is under the central bank's control, the linkage to policymakers' ultimate objectives will be weakened by the same factors. The stability of the money multiplier process has broken down for many industrial countries because of financial innovation and consequent structural changes in the demand for reserve money. These were not always directly linked to banking sector problems. There is some

[35] See, for example, VanHoose (1988) and Faig-Aumalle (1987).
[36] For a discussion of the linkages between these variables, see Alexander and Caramazza (1994).

Table 6. Consequences of Bank Unsoundness for Monetary Policy[1]

Argentina (1980–82): Emergency credit to banks rose to 100% of their reserve holdings. Inflation increased rapidly after the problems of the early 1980s. The money multiplier rose before the 1980–82 crisis and became volatile in the 1980s, making monetary control difficult. Interest controls were reintroduced.

(1989–90): The excess reserve ratio became volatile, and central bank aid to troubled institutions rose to 110% of reserve money in 1992.

(1995): Reserve requirements were reduced to aid banks and the differential between buying and selling pesos was removed to reduce bank transaction costs.

Bangladesh (1980s–present): Capitalizing interest distorts the monetary statistics. Liquidity management is complicated by the recapitalization efforts.

Bolivia (1994–present): Problem banks requiring liquidity support from the central bank placed an excessive burden on open market operations to control overall credit. Bank support was sterilized by accumulating public sector deposits.

Brazil (1994–present): The central bank's results deteriorated as a result of the mismatch in interest rates on assets that were mainly denominated in foreign currency and on liabilities that were derived from sterilization operations.

Chile (1981–86): Inflation rose from 9.5% in 1981 to 20.7% in 1982 and to 26.5% in 1985, and remained above 10% until 1994. Because of massive support programs that were mostly financed through the placement of central bank paper, the central bank's operational losses surged to 18% of GDP in 1985 and declined only slowly in the following years. The money multiplier rose early in the crisis and became volatile, making monetary control difficult; credit to the private sector rose sharply before the crisis.

Czech Republic (1991–present): The transmission of monetary policy was impaired as unsound banks became less interest sensitive and the interbank market became segmented. Market-based central bank instruments had uneven effects across the banking system, as liquidity surpluses at some banks coexisted with liquidity shortages at other banks.

Egypt (1991–95): High interest rate spreads. Despite large fluctuations in the level of commercial banks' excess reserves, interest-rate stickiness persists, and inhibits market responses.

Estonia (1992–95): The currency board arrangement protected monetary policy from expansion as a result of the banking problems. The economy relied more heavily on cash payments, so the currency-to-deposit ratio rose and the money multiplier fell.

Finland (1991–94): The money multiplier rose sharply before the crisis. Continued multiplier volatility made monetary control difficult.

France (1991–95): No effects have been discerned.

Ghana (1983–89): Credit controls were ineffective owing to the rollover of nonperforming loans. Bank deposit and lending rates were unresponsive to open market operations. Mopping up excess reserves has proved costly. The high level of currency circulating outside banks limited the effectiveness of monetary policy. The money multiplier rose sharply from 1988 to 1992.

Hungary (1987–present): The use of indirect instruments of monetary policy was impeded by the rapid growth of nonperforming loans.

Table 6 *(continued)*

Indonesia (1992–present): Concerns over bank profitability affected the authorities' willingness to raise domestic interest rates for monetary policy purposes and may have been a factor behind the increasing use of moral suasion to curb the growth of bank credit.

Japan (1992–present): Monetary policy was eased and interest rates were reduced in 1995 to spur economic growth. The low discount rate has contributed to banks' current profitability, allowing massive loan write-offs. The Bank of Japan contributed some of the funds for bank and credit union resolution, and the Deposit Insurance Corporation can borrow from the Bank of Japan.

Kazakstan (1991–95): The interbank market is limited to banks that meet prudential standards. A broader set of banks has access to the central bank credit auction. Some small banks are excluded from both markets. This has resulted in a divergence of borrowing rates across banks.

Kuwait (1990–91): Credit to the private sector increased owing to the capitalization of interest on nonperforming loans.

Latvia (1995–present): The Bank of Latvia provided limited liquidity support to troubled banks. There was a sharp fall in the demand for money, and broad money declined by 20%.

Lithuania (1995–present): Liquidity support, under the currency board arrangement, was kept within the prescribed margins.

Malaysia (1985–88): Liquidity and reserve requirements were reduced during the crisis to aid bank profitability. Deposit rates were freed to give banks greater flexibility. Controls on interest rates were reimposed from 1985–87. There was a flight to quality and cash, which complicated the conduct of monetary policy.

Mexico (1994–present): Interbank interest rates rose to 90% in March 1995. At the peak of the crisis in April 1995, the Bank of Mexico had to provide liquidity in U.S. dollars in the amount of US$3.8 billion to banks that were unable to roll over their foreign currency obligations. These loans were repaid by September. Loans to banks that required intervention totaled MexN$32 billion (1.9% of 1995 GDP). The demand for base money declined more than expected, which complicated the setting of intermediate targets.

Norway (1987–93): The Norges Bank placed deposits with commercial banks at subsidized rates. The money multiplier rose before the crisis and then fell.

Pakistan (1980–present): Monetary policy has had to face a high volume of nonperforming loans and high spreads. Bank weakness is constraining a more aggressive use of interest rate policy to tighten monetary conditions.

Paraguay (1995–present): The central bank provided liquidity support to banks in difficulty; this support was largely sterilized.

Philippines (1981–87): Inflation increased and the money multiplier rose sharply during the crisis. Controls on interest rates were reintroduced during the crisis. The emergency credit that was provided conflicted with monetary policy and inflation spurted to 50% in 1984. The money demand function shifted downward.

Poland (1991–present): Policy effectiveness is hampered by the low level of monetization. (M2 was only 22% of GDP in 1993.)

Table 6 *(concluded)*

Russia (1992–present): The weak state of part of the banking system has led to market segmentation and contributed to the temporary collapse of the interbank market in August 1995, which required the central bank to inject liquidity temporarily.

Spain (1977–85): The central bank provided liquidity support to banks in distress and loans to the Deposit Guarantee Fund. The increase in central bank credit contributed to higher inflation.

Sweden (1990–93): No direct effect was observed; interest rates were raised sharply in an ultimately unsuccessful attempt to defend a weak currency, despite the impact on the banking sector.

Tanzania (1988–present): Banks' inability to meet reserve requirements in 1989–92 made the reserve base unpredictable and weakened monetary control. There was a poor response to indirect instruments and to interest rate signals. The effectiveness of credit controls was reduced owing to ongoing losses. The public relies heavily on currency for transactions.

Thailand (1983–87): The central bank had to sterilize its liquidity assistance. Nevertheless, monetary policy was eased, banks' reserves and liquidity grew quickly, and interest rates fell, which aided bank profitability. Money demand increased.

Turkey (1994): There is little stability in the intermediary targets. The exchange rate is probably the key variable for transmission, and it is not clear whether interest rates are an important channel for monetary policy. The central bank can affect the interbank market and uses reverse repos to mop up liquidity and counteract capital inflows.

United States (1980–92): Monetary policy was eased in August 1982 in response to the international debt crisis that seriously afflicted the banking industry. Some analysts claim that monetary policy was also eased in the early 1990s to aid banks, but that easing was also consistent with the need to counter the recession and with the lower inflation that was being experienced.

Venezuela (1994–present): Credit to the private sector as a share of GDP, which had been declining and volatile, rose immediately before the crisis, making monetary control difficult. The money multiplier rose sharply at the start of the crisis and then fell. Misinformation impeded policy. The use of reserve requirements is limited as they are unremunerated and costly for banks. The central bank eased policy to aid banks. Only half of the liquidity support was sterilized; the rest contributed to price and exchange pressures.

Zambia (1994–present): Liquidity support compromised monetary policy. Reserve requirements were high but were reduced early in 1995.

---

[1] Years in parentheses denote the period of banking problems.

evidence, however, that credit supply problems in the early 1990s reduced the usefulness of M2 and M3 as policy guides in the United States (see Akhtar, 1993–94).

In other frameworks, the focus may be on broader money supply and demand functions. However, as a banking system becomes unsound, the supply of broad money will be affected by changes in intermediation due to the instability or erratic performance of unsound banks. The demand for money will be altered by factors such as depositor flight to higher quality stores of value, both domestic and foreign, and the rise in uncertainty in payment systems and credit market conditions. Resulting portfolio shifts may change the interest elasticity of demand for currency and deposits, and the value of monetary aggregates as target variables may be reduced. Shifts in interest elasticities for currency (generally negative) and for M2 (generally positive) have been documented for Argentina, Chile, the Philippines, Spain, and Uruguay following banking crises.[37] Shifts in money demand were also observed. After the banking crisis of 1981, demand for real M3 in the Philippines declined, rendering movements in this aggregate unreliable as a policy indicator; central bank overestimation of actual M3 demand appears to have contributed to loose monetary policy and rising inflation in the subsequent years.[38]

As has been often pointed out, the impact of financial liberalization and a shift to the use of indirect instruments of monetary policy on the stability of monetary relationships will be affected by banking sector fragility.[39] Where banks are sound, a new set of relationships can be expected to emerge once agents and institutions have adjusted to the new environment following liberalization. This adjustment process, though, requires consistency in responses to economic signals, which cannot be expected from an unsound banking system.

Interest rate movements are often used as indicator variables reflecting supply and demand conditions in financial markets. Where banks have incentives (and, owing to limited competition, the ability) to widen margins or assume greater risk to generate short-term cash flow, it will be difficult to determine whether a rise in the level of market interest rates represents real changes in the supply of and demand for funds for productive investments. The relative contributions of the opportunity cost of funds and risk premiums in determining the real interest rate will be altered. Market segmentation between sound and unsound banks will make interest rate price signals still more difficult to interpret, as money market conditions and interest rates may reflect liquidity or solvency deficiencies at particular banks rather than the overall stance of monetary policy. For example, in Venezuela in 1994 the deposit rates at sound banks fell sharply while rates offered by unsound banks rose.

The data needed for the quantitative formulation of monetary policy may be inaccurate in unsound banking systems. There is often extensive overvaluation of loans and other assets, nonperforming loans are routinely

---

[37] Sundararajan and Baliño (1991).
[38] Nascimento (1991).
[39] See Hargraves and Schinasi (1993) for a discussion of the impact of liberalization on money demand.

misclassified and improperly provisioned, and interest is frequently capitalized. In many countries, loans that are renewed on the basis of capitalization of past unpaid interest are considered to be new loans. For example, capitalization of interest is estimated to have accounted for 100 percent of credit expansion in Poland in 1991.[40] Such practices, which result directly from poor accounting and loan valuation standards but are almost invariably associated with unsound banking systems, make it difficult to ascertain the true levels and rates of change of domestic credit.

These factors complicate monetary programming and may contribute to policy errors.[41] Because quantitative measures of net domestic assets include both domestic credit and other items that would be affected by improper accounting for loans and by bank losses, focusing on net domestic assets rather than net domestic credit may ease the task of quantitative targeting. However, distortions due to the behavioral effects of nonrepayment, rollovers, and loan restructuring introduce an additional wedge between the growth of net domestic assets and real sector effects.

Monetary Instruments and the Transmission Mechanism

As a banking system becomes increasingly unsound, normal relationships between policy instruments and targeted objectives become less predictable and may be perverse in some cases. This occurs because unsound banks that are less able to control their balance sheets are less sensitive to an increase in their cost of funds and are more willing to accept risky borrowers, who will pay high rates that discourage more creditworthy customers.

Regardless of whether monetary policy is transmitted through credit channels or interest rate channels, or both, the importance of the soundness of the banking system in shaping the effectiveness of the transmission mechanism will not be deminished. A credit channel for policy transmission will become less efficient, as effective credit demand becomes relatively less price-elastic; credit availability will tend to be more dependent on bank capitalization and less responsive to policy instruments.[42] For example, weak bank capital positions contributed to the credit slowdown in the United States in 1989–92. In the United States, monetary policy action to increase bank resources also failed to produce additional bank lending because banks were constrained by binding capital ratios.[43] Weak bank balance sheets in Japan limited the scope for strengthening the eco-

---

[40] See Thorne (1993).

[41] The basics of monetary programming are outlined in IMF (1987) and Swiderski (1992).

[42] The literature on the credit channel for monetary policy transmission is surveyed in Alexander and Caramazza (1994), Dimsdale (1994), and Gertler (1988), among others.

[43] See Akhtar (1993–94) for a summary of several studies.

nomic recovery in the mid-1990s. The process of bank recapitalization and loan consolidation in formerly centrally planned economies exacerbated output downturns during the transition by starving productive enterprises of credit.[44]

Transmission of monetary policy through the money supply and interest rates will be hampered by illiquid or insolvent banks, because of their inability to adjust their reserves or lending in response to monetary policy actions, and by the reduced sensitivity to and predictability of responses to interest rates. Banks that do not respond to market forces cannot be relied upon to transmit interest rate changes. Cottarelli and Kourelis (1994) studied the speed of policy transmission through interest rates in a sample of industrial and developing countries and found that less efficient policy transmission is associated with banking systems in which market forces are weak, particularly those dominated by state banks. In more extreme cases of unsoundness, the supply of credit may become less constrained by capital or interest rates, as banks ignore risk factors in their attempts to generate income. Credit demand and bank lending also become insensitive to interest rates when banks permit borrowers to capitalize interest payments or when borrowers do not expect to repay loans. For example, in Bangladesh, successive rounds of loan write-offs and an inefficient judicial framework have weakened some debtors' incentives to service their debts in a timely fashion, and in many economies in transition, expectations of future loan write-offs have fueled credit demand by state-owned enterprises.

Indirect instruments of monetary policy take effect through their initial impact on bank liquidity and interbank interest rates. Banks with limited balance sheet flexibility are unlikely to respond appropriately to policy impulses. For example, reserve requirements or clearing account overdraft limits will not be fully effective if unsound banks are not able to respond to an increase in the reserve ratio or meet interbank settlement obligations from their own resources. There is likely to be an increasingly imbalanced distribution of excess reserves among banks, with less sound banks being less liquid in part owing to a "flight to quality" in the interbank market. Official efforts to recycle surplus banks' excess reserves outside the central bank, as was done in Argentina in 1995, and decreed, but not implemented, in Venezuela in 1994, typically require official guarantees and may contaminate sound banks and ultimately prolong problems.

Unsound banks may maintain deficient reserves even at a penalty; shortfalls in required reserves despite liquidity support operations by the central bank and high penalties for reserve deficiencies have characterized problem banks in Bolivia, Latvia, and Tanzania, among other countries.

[44] See Calvo and Kumar (1994).

While banks that cannot satisfy reserve requirements should be unable to contribute to credit expansion, control over the supply of money and credit will be impaired to the extent that the central bank is forced to accommodate reserve shortfalls. Meeting a monetary target could require, other things being equal, a higher reserve ratio to compensate for non-compliance by unsound banks. An increase in reserve requirements to sterilize the liquidity effects of bank unsoundness is not optimal, as it would adversely affect the remaining sound banks.

Moreover, the money market cannot be expected to lend to unsound banks trying to make up reserve shortfalls. The resulting segmentation of markets can further impede systemwide monetary management and may eventually disrupt the functioning of the financial markets through which monetary policy is transmitted. The markets for money and securities, and the payment systems that support these markets, depend on banks being able to deal routinely and confidently with one another. The availability of suitable collateral, such as treasury bills, can help in integrating interbank markets. However, banks facing solvency or liquidity difficulties may not be able to acquire or retain such collateral. When a substantial segment of the banking system cannot be relied upon, interbank markets may send extreme signals or may rapidly break down.

Interbank rates in Venezuela in early 1994 diverged widely between banks perceived as unsound and those perceived as sound. In Paraguay in 1995, those banks (mainly foreign) that increased deposits at the expense of those perceived as vulnerable were reluctant to lend to the latter through the interbank market. Russian interbank activity was interrupted owing to concerns about counterparty soundness in August 1995.[45] Breakdowns in correspondent banking relationships were also observed during the problems experienced by the U.S. saving and loan associations.[46] In some cases, such problems have impeded the development of these markets altogether, limiting the authorities' ability to implement monetary policy effectively. The Croatian money market has failed to advance beyond central bank-guaranteed overnight lending in part due to the perennial illiquidity and potential insolvency of several large banks. In Zambia, a two-tier market has developed, with larger banks trading among themselves and smaller banks relying on central bank overdrafts.

Liquidity management through open market operations will be blunted when the banking system is unsound. The impact on credit expansion of open market sales will be reduced by the interest rate inelasticity of demand of high-risk borrowers, requiring a higher interest rate to absorb a given amount of funds. Open market operations in segmented markets

---

[45] See Rosett (1995).
[46] Clair, Kolson, and Robinson (1995).

may lead to unpredictable results. For example, in Venezuela in 1994, the market became segmented as sound banks reduced interest rates to avoid attracting deposits they could not deploy. The central bank sought to raise rates through the auction of its own securities, but rates dropped sharply nonetheless, as the sound banks placed their excess liquidity in central bank securities.

Instruments for injecting liquidity, such as open market operations, rediscount facilities, and credit auctions, also become less effective. Where unsound banks lack sufficient market instruments to participate in open market operations, attempts to provide liquidity to the banking sector may be stymied as liquidity will continue to accumulate at the sound banks and will not be dispersed across the banking sector due to interbank market segmentation; this was the experience in the Czech Republic, among others. Lender-of-last-resort accommodation may be provided to particular banks. However, operation of such accommodation could be problematic because of the difficulty in distinguishing between illiquid and insolvent banks.[47] A credit auction or similar market-based liquidity facilities may be distorted by adverse selection and moral hazard, since unsound institutions may be willing to borrow at any price to avoid illiquidity.[48] In such circumstances, the technical design and operation of market-based instruments, such as credit auctions, must limit access by unsound banks and promote collateralized transactions.[49]

With such adjustments, the desired liquidity impact of central bank market-based instruments can be achieved, but often at a price of much higher interest rates than would apply in a situation where banks are sound.[50] To minimize interest rate volatility, a mixture of instruments might be needed simultaneously to inject as well as absorb liquidity.

Although, in cases where indirect instruments have lost effectiveness, it may be desirable to employ direct instruments of monetary control on a temporary basis, direct instruments, in particular credit controls, are also less effective when applied to an unsound banking system.[51] Credit ceilings can become ineffective when banks roll over their portfolios of bad debts. For example, rollovers contributed to credit ceilings becoming ineffective in Ghana from 1983–86.[52] Credit ceilings also cannot be relied

---

[47] Where there is a financial and operational restructuring plan in place, special lender-of-last-resort lending can bridge the gap produced by segmentation of the interbank market, while moving toward a resolution of the banking sector problems.

[48] See Mathieson and Haas (1995).

[49] See Saal and Zamalloa (1995).

[50] A rise in interest rates could result in adverse selection of borrowers and credit expansion rather than credit rationing; see Dooley and Isard (1992).

[51] This is in addition to the difficulties encountered in applying direct controls even in a sound system, which include the possibility for evasion and the distortion of resource allocation (see Alexander, Baliño, and Enoch 1995).

[52] See Kapur and others (1991).

upon to halt the growth of broad money because insolvent banks' losses contribute to an expansion of net domestic assets of the banking system, the counterpart to broad money. As long as banks are liquid, net domestic assets can continue to grow, with losses rather than performing credit as the counterpart to increased deposits. Interest rate ceilings may exacerbate credit misallocation and contribute to disintermediation and capital flight; this applies to sound and unsound banks alike. In some circumstances, direct intervention in bank management may be required.

When banks are extremely fragile, the application of monetary instruments tends to become asymmetric; it will be easier to loosen monetary policy than to tighten. In some cases, appropriate monetary policy action may not be taken or sustained for fear that it will contribute to a banking crisis. For example, in 1994, Mexico's concern about the potential for banking system losses due to the effects of higher interest rates may have contributed to the authorities' failure to raise interest rates sufficiently to defend the exchange rate,[53] and in 1996 Mexico's inflation targets were apparently tempered in part by concerns that a faster reduction in inflation would have adverse consequences for the banking system in the short term. The Venezuelan banking crisis resulted in pressure on the central bank not to permit interest rates to rise enough to accomplish the absorption of sufficient liquidity to forestall international reserve losses in the first half of 1994. Contractionary Federal Reserve policies in the United States the late 1980s may have been constrained by fears of financial crisis,[54] and Thai monetary policy may have been relaxed in 1986–87 to improve bank profitability.[55]

In more extreme cases, monetary control may be suspended by giving unsound banks direct support through overdrafts on their central bank clearing accounts, reductions in central bank lending rates, or other means. Central bank support to ailing banks in Zambia in 1994–95 and Jamaica in the summer of 1995 resulted in liquidity expansion and contributed to exchange rate depreciation. The 1995 Paraguayan banking crisis resulted in net domestic credit and currency in circulation both exceeding their targets, in part due to the extension of central bank credit to banks that were subject to official intervention or that faced liquidity shortages.

In other cases, liquidity has been provided to the banking system as a whole. The Central Bank of Russia responded to the August 1995 interbank market crisis with large-scale purchases of short-dated treasury bills. Japan's principal response to banking problems in 1995 was to reduce the

---

[53] Calvo and Goldstein (1995).
[54] See Bosworth (1989) and Hausmann and Gavin (1995).
[55] Johnston (1991).

discount rate, resulting in rapid monetary expansion. On a wider scale, international monetary policy in the 1980s was strongly influenced by the perceived need to provide liquidity to debtor countries so as to prevent failures of the large internationally active banks.

Finally, the real sector effects of monetary policy adjustments will be determined in large measure by banking practices. Tighter monetary policies carry greater long-term negative effects, if banks do not allocate credit on the basis of the expected return of borrowers' projects and if reduced levels of credit are poorly distributed among borrowers. In this regard, distortions in the banking sectors probably increased the real costs of monetary austerity in economies in transition.[56] On the other hand, a loosening of monetary policy may increase credit availability, but if unsound banking practices result in misallocation of these resources, the real benefits of the policy stimulus will be reduced. For example, in Argentina, Mexico, and Peru, poor bank credit policies permitted an expansion of credit in the 1980s to accrue to government-related institutions. Instead of generating a corresponding expansion in real economic activity, the growth in credit contributed to severe inflation.[57]

Fiscal Impact

Banking problems can affect a country's overall fiscal balance from both the revenue and expenditure sides. Tax revenues from banks will be reduced to the extent that increased loan losses reduce banks' taxable income. The cost of sterilizing any central bank liquidity support to the banking system will involve direct costs for the government or reduced central bank profit transfers, unless unremunerated reserve requirements (which could further damage banks) can be increased. For example, in Paraguay, the annual cost of sterilization is expected to exceed 0.5 percent of GDP in 1995–96. Central bank profits will be reduced if the central bank takes over nonperforming loans or bankrupt institutions, as occurred in Chile, the Philippines, and Uruguay.[58] Revenue from the broader economy will also be reduced by lower levels of economic activity and output resulting from inefficient financial intermediation.

On the expenditure side, as unsound banks move to riskier assets and become less efficient in intermediating funds, the cost of financing any given deficit—and government debt-servicing costs generally—will be affected. The direction of effect would depend on whether or not the banking problems disrupt the government securities market and on the amount of bank financing that is used.

---

[56] Griffith-Jones (1995).
[57] See Rojas-Suárez and Weisbrod (1995b), p. 22.
[58] See Vos (1995) and Pérez-Campanero and Leone (1991).

More significant from the expenditure side is the buildup of direct liabilities arising from state ownership of insolvent banks and contingent liabilities arising from deposit or credit guarantees. In most cases of systemic unsoundness, the government will ultimately bear a large part of the cost of resolution. Among the countries in our sample, the recorded fiscal cost has ranged to almost 20 percent of GDP (Table 7). In some of these cases, the final cost has yet to be determined.

In fact, the exact size of the government's liability cannot be known with certainty until the contingencies fall due, and will depend on whether a separate fund has been set aside for deposit insurance or other guarantees, as well as on how a resolution of the banking problem is effected. The government may provide support directly to banks, to the banks' borrowers, or to depositors. It may arrange closure, merger, or recapitalization, which may entail full or partial write-downs of owners' capital. Some of the costs to the government may be covered by future asset recovery and the proceeds from subsequent reprivatization of banks (if they were initially state owned). The extent and form of government support to the banking system will, of course, also have implications for monetary control.

The direct fiscal costs will increase if government entities have placed funds with banks that failed. For example, many local and regional authorities in Latvia had deposits at Banka Baltija, which failed in 1995.[59] The Bank of Zambia maintained foreign exchange deposits at Meridien Bank, which failed in 1995; the loss of these deposits had balance of payments implications. The Venezuelan Deposit Guarantee Fund and the Social Security Fund of Paraguay both placed a large portion of their assets in insolvent banks.

External Sector Effects

An unsound banking system will have repercussions for exchange rate stability and the balance of payments. The experiences of the countries in our sample suggest that external balance and banking sector problems are intimately linked (see Table 8). It is often difficult, however, to determine whether the exchange rate or capital flows are responding to banking sector problems or to the same underlying macroeconomic events or imbalances that caused the banking sector problems. Kaminsky and Reinhart (1996) reviewed the experiences of 20 countries that experienced banking and balance of payments crises and found that in about half, the banking crisis preceded the balance of payments crisis. The causal pattern was

---

[59] Timewell (1995).

Table 7. The Fiscal Effects of Bank Unsoundness[1]

Argentina (1980–82): The direct fiscal cost in 1981 was 4% of GDP.

(1989–90): Data are not available.

(1995): Assistance to the banking system required disbursing $800 million from two trust funds established for this purpose; some recoveries are expected.

Bangladesh (1980s–present): Government bonds equivalent to 4.5% of GDP were provided to banks. The interest costs of recapitalization hurt the budget and increased government debt.

Bolivia (1994–present): The treasury's domestic interest expenditure is increased because it bears the interest cost of the central bank's taking over 4.2% of GDP in bad loans.

Brazil (1994–present): The restructuring of the banking system will require tax measures and quasi-fiscal costs, which have not been quantified yet.

Chile (1981–86): The quasi-fiscal losses of the central bank amounted to 18% of GDP in 1985, 8% in 1986, 2% from 1987–90, and 1% since then. The fiscal accounts shifted into deficit temporarily under the impact of recession and the government-financed support programs for banks.

Czech Republic (1991–present): 12% of 1994 GDP was spent on bank support through 1994.

Egypt (1991–95): The cost is that of servicing $2.1 billion of ten-year bonds at the London interbank offer rate (LIBOR).

Estonia (1992–95): The cost of restructuring was borne by the budget and equals 1.8% of 1993 GDP.

Finland (1991–94): By the end of 1994, funds had been dispersed to the extent of 8.4% of GDP and an additional 6.1% of 1994 GDP was committed in guarantees.

France (1991–95): $1.5 billion has already been spent and $10 billion (0.6% of GDP) more is expected to be necessary.

Ghana (1983–89): 3% of GDP has been expended, $170 million of which was borrowed from international sources.

Hungary (1987–present): 9% of 1993 GDP was spent between 1992 and 1995. Interest on the debt issued to support banks amounted to 1.75% of GDP in 1995.

Indonesia (1992–present): The recapitalization of state banks through the budget and the conversion of Bank Indonesia's emergency credit into equity or subordinated debt cost 2% of GDP.

Japan (1992–present): Initial proposals for the 1996/97 budget were for expenditures amounting to approximately 0.2% of GDP. The final cost is as yet undetermined.

Kazakstan (1991–95): The cost is between 3% and 6% of the average of 1994 and 1995 GDP.

Kuwait (1990–91): The cost consists of interest payments on the $18 billion in bonds that were issued to purchase problem loans and the $10 billion in principal (approaching half of GDP in 1992) that is not expected to be recovered.

Table 7 *(concluded)*

Latvia (1995–present): Compensation to depositors of failed banks had a negligible effect on 1995 budget outlays, but banking problems did reduce government revenue. The government has issued bonds to recapitalize the savings bank.

Lithuania (1995–present): Funds have not yet been expended, but costs are expected to be high.

Malaysia (1985–88): The cost was equivalent to 4.7% of GDP.

Mexico (1994–present): Most of the costs of the support programs for banks (consisting of the government's purchase of the loan portfolio, the Unidad de Inversión (UDI) loan-restructuring scheme, and assistance to debtors and highway concessionaires) will have a fiscal impact stretched over several years but no immediate cash impact. The support program for banking system debtholders (ADE) introduced an interest rate subsidy to final borrowers who for one year will pay a capped interest rate. The government has decided to pay in cash the cost of the ADE (about 0.4% of GDP in 1995 and 0.3% of GDP in 1996). The cost (present value) is estimated at 6.5% of 1995 GDP.

Norway (1987–93): Direct fiscal costs of 3.3% of GDP were incurred in 1993; a large portion of this has subsequently been recovered.

Pakistan (1980–present): None have been recognized.

Paraguay (1995–present): Not known, but the central bank has already lent 3.5% of GDP to troubled banks.

Philippines (1981–87): 13.2% of GDP was contributed to banks as equity.

Poland (1991–present): Bonds issued to recapitalize problem banks amounted to 2% of GDP in 1993–94.

Russia (1992–present): There is an unknown contingent liability that is expected to be significant.

Spain (1977–85): The net cost of the crisis is estimated at 5.6% of GDP, 77% of which was covered by the Deposit Guarantee Fund and the Bank of Spain.

Sweden (1990–93): 4% of GDP was expended on resolving the banks' problems; a large portion of this has subsequently been recovered.

Tanzania (1988–present): The costs include interest paid on government restructuring bonds and direct central bank contributions to the resolution of Meridien Bank and a small, failed state bank. Bonds equivalent to 14.5% of GDP were provided to 2 banks. The final cost is estimated at between 6% and 7% of GDP.

Thailand (1983–87): The assistance provided increased the deficit. The annual interest cost of the assistance was estimated at 0.2% of GDP.

Turkey (1994): Difficult to quantify, but below 1% of GDP.

United States (1980–92): The treasury made a small loan to the bank insurance fund, which was rapidly repaid. The estimated cost of the thrift industry bailout is currently $130 billion (2.4% of 1990 GDP).

Venezuela (1994–present): 13% of GDP in 1994 and 17% through 1995. In addition, FOGADE (the deposit insurer) has an unfunded liability of $2.3 billion (5% of GDP).

Zambia (1994–present): The cost of the Meridien crisis is estimated at 3% of GDP.

---

[1] Years in parentheses denote the period of banking problems.

reversed in only a few instances. Thus, there is support for the notion that bank unsoundness exerts negative effects on the external balance and the exchange rate.

The reasons for this are manifold. The banking system is a key partici-pant in international trade and capital movements; banks facilitate inter-national payments and transfers and are active in the foreign exchange markets. An unsound domestic banking system will be less capable of pro-viding an efficient foreign exchange market and of maintaining adequate correspondent relationships and external interbank credit lines. Where banks are major participants in the local foreign exchange market and pro-vide related payments services to other market participants, disruptions in the banking sector can destabilize the foreign exchange market and con-tribute to exchange rate volatility. For example, several large Tanzanian exchange bureaus that banked with Meridien Bank lost access to their funds when that bank collapsed in March 1995.

Worries about the soundness of the banking system can also lead to a flight to quality by domestic depositors and overseas investors. This often takes the form of an exchange of domestic for foreign assets, with consequent exchange rate effects. Concerns about the ability of Argentine banks to meet cash demands in the first part of 1995 led deposi-tors to shift to overseas banks.[60] In Israel, concerns about overvaluation of Israeli bank shares in October 1983 led to sales of domestic currency assets and bank shares; the price of bank shares collapsed and the cur-rency was devalued.

Flexibility in external sector policy—in particular the degree to which the mix of interest rate and exchange rate policy can be chosen—will also be influenced by the strength of the banking system. The ability of a cen-tral bank to withstand a speculative attack on the exchange rate depends in part on the strength of the banking system. A typical response when a pegged exchange rate is under pressure is to raise domestic interest rates. The authorities' ability to raise interest rates may be constrained, howev-er, by a fear that bank portfolios will deteriorate.[61] For example, Sweden's 1992 defense of its peg to the European currency unit (ECU) was limited by the fragility of the banking system.[62] These considerations imply that the type of exchange arrangement that is feasible may also be circum-scribed; for example, a pure currency board arrangement would be unlikely to be sustainable in an economy with a significantly weak bank-ing system.[63]

---

[60] Folkerts-Landau, Ito, and others (1995).
[61] See Rojas-Suárez and Weisbrod (1995) and Folkerts-Landau, Ito, and others (1995).
[62] Goldstein and others (1993, p. 16).
[63] Rostowski (1994) and Folkerts-Landau, Ito, and others (1995), pp. 123–25.

Table 8. External Sector Events and Effects[1]

Argentina (1980–82): The country lost international reserves. There was a sharp deterioration in the exchange rate in 1983–84 and it became volatile.

(1989–90): The policy of openness was reversed. Capital outflows rose and net international reserves fell.

(1995): The exchange rate peg held despite capital outflows.

Bangladesh (1980s–present): No effects have been observed.

Bolivia (1994–present): There is a high degree of dollarization. Capital inflows reversed to heavy outflows in 1995 because of banks' unsound offshore and off-balance-sheet operations.

Brazil (1994–present): Trade credit lines have been maintained, or even increased. The high interest rates attracted capital inflows, especially after the reduction in exchange rate uncertainty following the smooth introduction of the new exchange mechanism in March 1995.

Chile (1981–86): After two large devaluations, the fixed exchange rate was replaced by a crawling peg in 1982. The central bank established a preferential exchange rate to aid debt servicers.

Czech Republic (1991–present): High interest rates stimulated the supply of foreign capital, while the shortage of long-term domestic finance increased the demand for it.

Egypt (1991–95): Bank unsoundness led to the imposition of limits on banks' foreign exchange exposure.

Estonia (1992–95): The exchange rate, pegged to the deutsche mark, was not affected.

Finland (1991–94): The exchange rate depreciated sharply during the crisis.

France (1991–95): There was foreign exchange market turbulence in mid-1993. Net outflows of long term capital in 1994–95 were more than offset by short-term inflows, mainly in the banking sector.

Ghana (1983–89): The exchange rate depreciated during and after the crisis.

Hungary (1987–present): The large intermediation spreads necessary to provision against bad loans led to large direct foreign borrowing by enterprises in 1994–95.

Indonesia (1992–present): Capital outflows were avoided by interest rate differentials and an expectation of a public bailout.

Japan (1992–present): The premium on borrowing in the international interbank market rose in late 1995.

Kazakstan (1991–95): International reserves are growing despite the banking problems.

Kuwait (1990–91): The reduction in official external assets due to the fiscal deficit caused by assistance to banks greatly reduced the government's investment income. Outflows of private capital occurred because of the uncertain domestic prospects.

Latvia (1995–present): Capital outflows occurred in the wake of the banking crisis, but the exchange-rate peg was retained.

Lithuania (1995–present): There were widespread deposit withdrawals and large foreign exchange outflows through the currency board in early 1996.

Table 8 *(concluded)*

Malaysia (1985–88): The currency was allowed to depreciate and the central bank reformed its export credit refinance scheme and created an investment fund to shift bank lending to the tradable sector.

Mexico (1994–present): The foreign exchange market is very thin and sensitive to news about the condition of the Mexican banks.

Norway (1987–93): The exchange rate continued to depreciate during the banking problems.

Pakistan (1980–present): The need to boost international reserves led the central bank to offer incentives to induce capital inflows.

Paraguay (1995–present): The authorities continued to operate a managed-float exchange rate policy; there was a small nominal depreciation during 1995.

Philippines (1981–87): Capital fled and the exchange rate depreciated sharply during the crisis.

Poland (1991–present): Several exchange rate devaluations occurred through the period, although these were not linked directly or solely to banking sector problems. The exchange rate followed a crawling peg during the latter part of the period. There were devaluations in addition to the crawling peg in 1992 and 1993. More recently, foreign exchange reserves have been increasing.

Russia (1992–present): Banking problems may have contributed to the depreciation of the ruble.

Spain (1977–85): The currency was allowed to depreciate beginning in 1977.

Sweden (1990–93): Capital outflows occurred as the central bank defended the exchange rate until the krona was allowed to float in November 1992.

Tanzania (1988–present): Uncertainty and banks' foreign exchange losses may have affected the exchange rate and the availability of foreign exchange.

Thailand (1983–87): Monetary policy was relaxed in 1986–87 in part to support bank profitability, but with inflation low and the balance of payments in surplus, this appears to have had no significant effects on the external sector.

Turkey (1994): Spreads over the London interbank offer rate (LIBOR) were permanently raised; banks' losses on foreign exchange speculation temporarily decreased the central bank's foreign exchange reserves.

United States (1980–92): High interest rates in the early 1980s attracted capital inflows and raised the value of the dollar. Later rates were reduced, partly to aid banks, and the dollar fell.

Venezuela (1994–present): There was capital flight, the exchange rate depreciated sharply, exchange controls were reintroduced, and the exchange rate fixed in mid-1994. A further sharp depreciation was effected in December 1995.

Zambia (1994–present): There was a loss of foreign exchange reserves deposited with a failed bank.

---

[1] Years in parentheses denote the period of banking problems.

In addition, the degree of capital account liberalization that can be sustained may be limited by soundness considerations. Policy flexibility can be constrained insofar as banks lack the systems and skills in credit and risk management that are necessary to intermediate foreign capital flows efficiently and to control their own foreign exchange and liquidity exposure. Liberalization of the capital account would then allow unsound banks to look abroad for resources they cannot attract at home, particularly if disclosure, prudential standards and supervision are inadequate to the task of limiting banks' foreign exchange exposure. Such resources may be acquired directly, via affiliates, or through various offshore or derivative transactions. Once banks have built up large open positions by borrowing abroad to finance domestic assets, or through foreign exchange lending to residents supported by domestic resources, the authorities' room for maneuver through exchange rate depreciation may become limited. The effectiveness of a flexible exchange system or adjustment of a fixed rate will also be reduced if unsound banks continue to extend credit to weak borrowers so as to prevent defaults, since the resulting rigidity in resource allocation would tend to reduce the supply response to a devaluation.[64]

---

[64] See Hinds (1988).

Annex
Selected Case Studies—Quantitative Analysis

In order to analyze the implications of unsound banking systems for macroeconomic policy, a sample of eight countries that experienced banking sector crises was selected.[65] The sample includes Argentina, Chile, Finland, Ghana, Norway, the Philippines, Uruguay, and Venezuela.[66] In seven of these eight countries, an outright crisis occurred and provided evidence that the banking system was unsound—a condition that might otherwise not have been observed. We can posit, however, that in the period leading up to a crisis, there was a high degree of unsoundness. Thus, it is in the precrisis period that we can look to verify some of the macroeconomic effects discussed in this study.

While assessing the full range of interlinkages between policy and banking system soundness and between banking system soundness and macroeconomic performance is beyond the scope of this brief analysis, several trends do emerge. It is interesting to note that all of the sample countries had undertaken financial sector reforms prior to their banking crises.

Impact on the Real Sector

The evidence from the sample suggests that both output growth and efficiency decreased in the aftermath of banking crises (Table 9). However, causality cannot be attributed definitively to the banking crises. Causality often runs from a downturn in the real sector to unsoundness in the banking sector, and while the data in Table 9 suggest persistent lower growth after a crisis, which may be due to banking sector effects on the real economy, the factors leading to reduced output growth may have been the same factors that led to banking system fragility and crisis.

---

[65] This annex draws heavily on work done by Ceyla Pazarbaşioğlu. Able research assistance by Kiran Sastry is also gratefully acknowledged.

[66] Ghana was not identified in Table 1 as a crisis case; because the financial system was predominantly state owned and its assets were dominated by the public sector, no liquidity crisis or need for sudden intervention arose (see Sheng and Tannor, 1996).

Table 9. Impact of Banking Crises on the Real Sector[1]

	Argentina	Chile	Finland	Ghana	Norway	Philippines	Uruguay	Venezuela
Real GDP growth								
Mean_0	2.08	8.03	2.84	5.21	3.16	5.78	2.47	2.89
Mean_1	0.62	1.35	-4.07	2.60	1.66	-1.26	-0.23	—
Efficiency[2]								
Mean_0	0.38	0.40	0.28	0.47	0.27	0.50	0.34	0.31
Mean_1	0.29	0.34	0.20	0.31	0.21	0.34	0.29	—

Sources: Sundararajan and Baliño (1991), Drees and Pazarbaşioğlu (1995); IMF, *International Financial Statistics*; and World Bank Database.

[1]Mean_0 and mean_1 are the sample means for the five-year period before and after each banking crisis, respectively. For Ghana, Norway, and Finland, the postcrisis is taken as periods of three, two, and one year respectively. For Venezuela, postcrisis data are not available.

[2]Output-to-capital ratio, calculated as GDP at 1987 prices divided by capital stock at 1987 prices.

Monetary Policy Implications

The analysis of the conditions in the sample countries suggests that the relationships between monetary aggregates and the stability of interest rates were affected by episodes of banking system unsoundness. Greater volatility of the money multiplier was evident in all countries except Finland (Chart 1); in Argentina, Chile, Ghana, the Philippines, and Uruguay, the money multiplier increased sharply prior to or during the banking crisis. Most of the sample countries experienced sharp increases in interest rates after the crises, and interest rates exhibited a high degree of volatility prior to the crisis episodes (Table 10).

All of the sample countries except Venezuela experienced a sharp expansion of credit to the private sector prior to the crisis (Chart 2), consistent with the observation that rapid credit expansion can be a factor in poor lending decisions that ultimately contribute to unsoundness.

Except for Ghana and Finland, interest rate spreads were very high in the period leading up to the crisis (Table 10), reflecting lack of competition, inefficiency, and the need to cover increased expenses due to loan losses.

Fiscal Policy Implications

Since the crises are over in these countries, most of the difficulties in assessing the likely fiscal impact of unsoundness have been resolved. Recorded fiscal costs are provided in Table 11, along with the year in which the estimate was made. It should be noted, however, that in some cases, the final costs will continue to change as loan recoveries proceed, asset prices recover, or banking system problems continue.

External Sector Effects

Significant exchange rate volatility and currency crises took place in the aftermath of banking crises in Argentina, Finland, Norway, Uruguay, and Venezuela (Chart 3). The degree to which exchange rate effects contributed to the banking crisis or were a result of banking system unsoundness cannot be stated with certainty, however.

Chart 1. Money Multiplier[1]

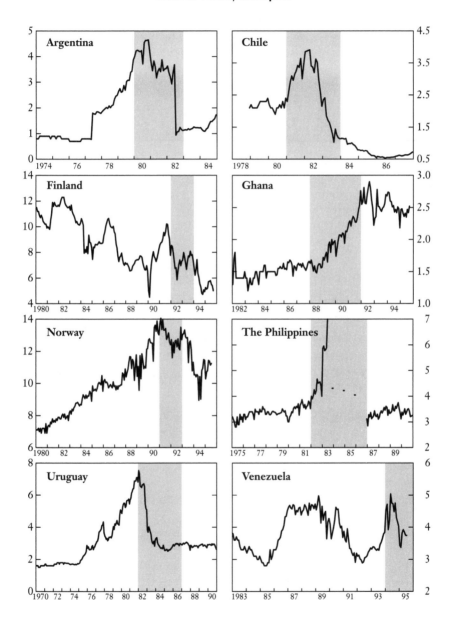

Source: IMF, *International Financial Statistics.*
[1]Seasonally adjusted monthly data, except for Chile and the Philippines. The shaded area indicates a crisis period.

Table 10. Interest Rate Developments Surrounding the Banking Crises[1]

	Argentina	Chile	Finland	Ghana	Norway	Philippines	Uruguay	Venezuela
Real interest rate[2]								
$Mean_0$	-4.55	-6.41	0.28	2.10	2.95	4.49	9.57	-8.61
$Mean_1$	-0.87	1.02	3.64	7.33	5.56	13.80	21.24	—
$Sdev_0$	0.73	0.51	0.39	0.73	0.29	0.49	0.53	0.10
$Sdev_1$	0.28	0.26	—	0.21	—	0.13	0.09	—
Gross interest margins[3]								
$Mean_0$	16.15	18.40	2.86	3.40	8.61	7.87	28.53	5.44
$Mean_1$	7.49	12.20	4.71	8.10	4.47	3.93	15.49	—
$Sdev_0$	0.62	0.56	0.82	0.68	0.73	0.59	0.30	0.41
$Sdev_1$	0.59	0.38	—	0.31	—	0.15	0.16	—

Sources: Sundararajan and Baliño (1991), Drees and Pazarbaşioğlu (1995), and IMF, *International Financial Statistics*.

[1] $Mean_0$ and $mean_1$ are the sample means for the five-year period before and after each banking crisis, respectively. $Sdev_0$ and $Sdev_1$ are the mean-weighted standard deviations for the five-year period before and after each banking crisis, respectively. For Ghana, Norway, and Finland, the postcrisis is taken as periods of three, two, and one year respectively. For Venezuela, postcrisis data are not available.

[2] Calculated as the nominal short-term interest rate minus the inflation rate.

[3] Lending rate minus deposit rate.

Chart 2. Claims on Private Sector/Nominal GDP[1]
(In percent)

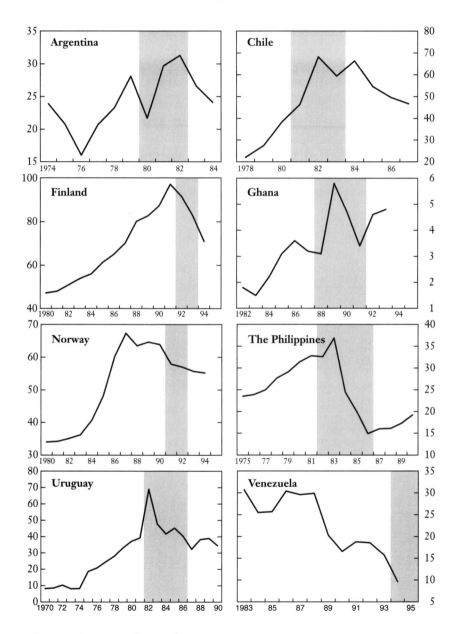

Source: IMF, *International Financial Statistics.*
[1]The shaded area indicates a crisis period.

Table 11. Direct Fiscal Impact of Banking Crises

	Argentina	Chile	Finland	Ghana	Norway	Philippines	Uruguay	Venezuela
Nonperforming loans as a percentage of total loans	9	19	13	40	6	19	11	9
Year recorded	1980	1983	1992	1989	1991	1986	1982	1993
Direct (immediate) fiscal costs as a percentage of GDP	4	5	8	3	3	6	—	17
Year recorded	1981	1985	1993	1990	1993	1985	—	1995

Sources: Sundararajan and Baliño (1991) for Argentina, Chile, Philippines, Uruguay; Drees and Pazarbaşioğlu (1995) for Finland and Norway; Sheng (1996) for Ghana; and for Venezuela, Central Budget Office (OCEPRE) and Deposit Insurance Agency (FOGADE).

Chart 3. Exchange Rate

(Currency per U.S. dollar, end of period)[1]

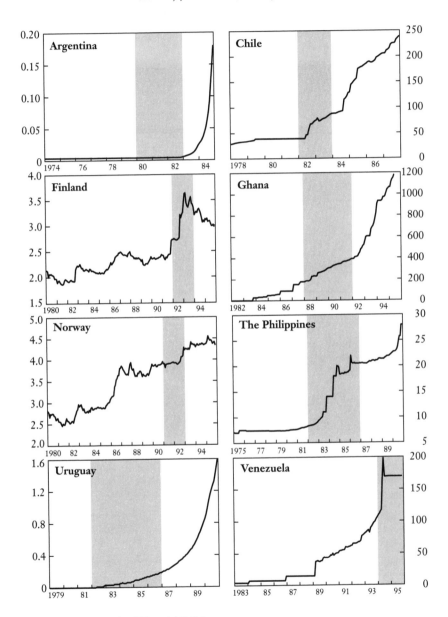

Source: IMF, *International Financial Statistics.*
[1]Unless otherwise indicated. The shaded area indicates a crisis period.

Part III
Maintaining a Sound Banking System

6

Operating Environment

The analysis and case studies that have been presented in Chapter 5 make a compelling case that a sound banking sector is critical for macroeconomic stability. The effects of systemic banking failures have been dramatic not only in the countries studied in detail in that chapter, but also in most of the 140 countries listed in Table 2. When an outright crisis occurs as the result of extensive banking sector problems, the impact on the real economy is usually immediate and obvious. Even when an outright crisis has been averted, the cost of distortions in resource use and of restructuring and recapitalizing the banking sector will burden the economy for years to come. Particularly where such costs are borne by the public sector, the implications will haunt economic management for an extended period of time.

Preventing such problems, or, more positively, maintaining a sound banking system, is therefore a legitimate and necessary goal of economic policy. Clearly this goal has microeconomic dimensions, and policies that affect the structure, conduct, and performance of the financial industry directly affect the achievement of this objective. The following chapters present a framework for sound banking that comprises a supportive operating environment, internal governance, external discipline provided by market forces, and external governance provided by regulation and supervision at the domestic and international levels. No single one of these elements is sufficient by itself; each is subject to failure, or may be underdeveloped in a given economy.

The economic environment, the quality of internal governance of banks, and the structure of the markets in which banks operate will all affect bank behavior and their soundness. A sound banking system requires an appropriate infrastructure to support the efficient conduct of banking business and a stable macroeconomic environment, which is conducive to efficient savings and investment decisions.

Economic Infrastructure

There are two important elements of economic infrastructure: the institutional framework, which includes the legal, administrative, and political structures that guide economic and financial transactions, and the structure of financial markets, which provides the immediate operating context for banks.

Institutional Framework

Banking requires a legal system that facilitates the enforcement of financial contracts, loan recovery, and realization of collateral. Banks must be able to collect what is due to them. If they have no recourse against borrowers who default, borrowers will have reduced incentives to repay their loans. Poorly defined bankruptcy procedures can further reduce incentives to repay and impair asset recovery. Similarly, where banks cannot rely on collateral, the value of their portfolios may be in jeopardy; problems in establishing full title to and realizing collateral have exacerbated bank weakness in a number of countries. Thus, the legal framework should include adequate corporate, bankruptcy, contract, and private property laws.

There must also be an administrative structure capable of enforcing the laws. The judicial system must be impartial, honest, and knowledgeable regarding financial transactions so that banks can rely on fair and speedy enforcement of economic rights and obligations. In addition, governing political structures must respect legal procedures and property rights, and not interfere in the operations of banks or in the administration of laws and regulations, including the enforcement of loan recovery. Inadequate legal frameworks characterized most of the developing and transition economies in our sample (Table 12), and many of the banking systems suffered from political interference in lending.

The structure of the banking industry also influences its soundness. A competitive banking system is essential for long-term efficiency and soundness. While a concentrated banking industry may enjoy economic rents, it often becomes inefficient and unable to respond innovatively to charges in the economic environment. This phenomenon is prevalent in banking systems dominated by state-owned banks. A significant number of countries with concentrated but inefficient systems have had banking problems, including 23 of the countries in our sample (Table 12). Competition and a well-functioning market for corporate control can potentially remove inefficient or unprofitable banks before they become insolvent. An open and competitive banking market exerts its own form of discipline against weak banks while encouraging well-managed banks.

Table 12. Financial and Legal Framework[1]

Argentina (1980–82): The financial system was bank dependent and dominated by publicly owned banks.

(1989–90): There were still few alternatives to banks, and state-owned banks still dominated the system with 64% of bank assets. The system was moderately concentrated at the top with 5 banks holding 36% of banking sector assets. Banking groups were important.

(1995): There were still few alternatives to banks, and state banks still dominated, although their share had fallen to 40%. Foreign competition comprised 16.5% of system assets. However, the system was overbanked with smaller banks because entry was easy.

Bangladesh (1980s–present): There was insufficient competition. The contract and credit laws were antiquated and an anti-repayment and anti-enforcement culture within a weak judicial system made obtaining judgment in loan-default cases virtually impossible. Bank exit is a problem as the central bank, Ministry of Finance, and the courts are all involved.

Bolivia (1994–present): The banking system is somewhat concentrated—two banks own 30% of assets. Laws and regulations and their implementation and enforcement are inadequate. Judgments are delayed.

Brazil (1994–present): Weaknesses in the regulatory and supervisory structure are being addressed by the authorities.

Chile (1981–86): Increasing concentration of bank and corporate ownership led to the emergence of unregulated conglomerates that practiced oligopoly pricing.

Czech Republic (1991–present): The money, credit, and capital markets are thin, but developing. The banking system is concentrated—5 banks own 73% of bank assets.

Egypt (1991–95): Competition exists but remains limited.

Estonia (1992–95): At the start of the crisis, the financial markets were still underdeveloped, and were in transition to a market economy. The state still owned the savings bank. The banking system was concentrated. There was no direct foreign competition—only joint ownership was permitted.

Finland (1991–94): The money and capital markets were undeveloped until the late 1980s. Competition was limited in terms of the number of credit institutions and new entrants in the late 1980s. The banking system was highly concentrated.

France (1991–95): There is an adequate legal framework; however, the system includes several significant state-owned institutions, and the regulatory system did not eliminate the unequal advantages and constraints that differentially affected public and private institutions.

Ghana (1983–89): The government wholly or partly owned virtually all banks. Money market development was hampered by an inadequate operational framework. Competition was limited: the largest bank accounted for 44% of total assets and the 7 largest banks, for 70%. There was an inadequate legal, regulatory, and supervisory framework.

Table 12 *(continued)*

Hungary (1987–present): State ownership of large banks had fallen to 38% by the end of 1991 but rose again to 70% in 1994 owing to recapitalization. The system is concentrated (5 banks owned 84% assets in 1989 and now hold 64%). Foreign competition is important and increased further in 1995 with the privatization of one commercial bank and the partial sale of the large savings bank. New financial sector legislation is expected to be enacted in 1996.

Indonesia (1992–present): The financial markets are bank dominated. Liberal licensing in the late 1980s and the growing number of private banks have increased competition, and the market share of state banks has declined.

Japan (1992–present): There are deep and broad financial markets, but they are bank dominated and there is high concentration. Foreign competition is weak and entry is difficult. Some banks are segregated by region and industry. Foreclosures are difficult.

Kazakstan (1991–95): The banking system is concentrated, with 4 banks owning 80% of the assets. Many new licenses have been issued and competition is increasing, but foreign banks have difficulty entering the market, which is segregated by industry. The bankruptcy and collateral laws were inadequate. An improved banking law is now in place, but accounting is still weak and the courts are unreliable.

Kuwait (1990–91): There is a high degree of competition among domestic banks and other financial institutions, although the regulations prevent the entry of foreign banks.

Latvia (1995–present): The financial sector is dominated by banking institutions and is highly concentrated and segmented. Lack of collateral laws and poor enterprise accounting resulted in high credit risk.

Lithuania (1995–present): The banking system was highly concentrated and state dominated, with 5 banks accounting for about 70% of total assets, and 3 of the 4 largest banks state owned. Banking laws and accounting practices were inadequate.

Malaysia (1985–88): The financial markets were broad and deep and foreign ownership was strong (16 of 36 banks). The court system provided fast and stern judgments.

Mexico (1994–present): Between 1991 and 1994, the Mexican financial system was reprivatized and grew considerably. The number of commercial banks increased from 20 to 35, although foreign participation in the financial system was limited. Credit-rating bureaus did not exist until 1995.

Norway (1987–93): There was no foreign ownership until 1984. Finance companies were unlicensed until 1978. The securities markets were thin.

Pakistan (1980–present): Despite some entry, there is still little competition. The legal procedures for recovering bad debts are generally very protracted.

Paraguay (1995–present): Licensing is lax, despite legislation on minimum entry capital. Liquidation is carried out through the courts.

Philippines (1981–87): Segregation of commercial and development banks weakened competition as did high concentration at state banks and financial groups.

Poland (1991–present): The banking system is somewhat concentrated (5 banks own 50% of assets). Needed laws and regulations have been introduced, but they are not yet fully effective.

Table 12 *(concluded)*

Russia (1992–present): Competition exists but the market is segmented. The legal infrastructure is weak and, in some cases, contradictory.

Spain (1977–85): The thin financial markets were bank dependent. Entry had been severely restricted, so concentration was relatively high, although foreign entry was permitted after 1963. The licensing laws became relaxed and many of the 35 new banks quickly failed.

Sweden (1990–93): Thin financial markets were bank dependent. The banking system is an oligopoly with little foreign competition. After entry was eased in 1985, several new banks (both domestic and foreign) entered the market.

Tanzania (1988–present): The financial system is concentrated and bank dependent with little competition—1 bank holds more than 75% of assets. Foreign banks were allowed only in 1992.

Thailand (1983–87): There was a lack of competition and heavy concentration—3 banks owned 57% of assets. The foreign banking presence was minimal.

Turkey (1994): Competition exists, but many banks have close linkages to business groups both domestically and internationally and banks are specialized by industry.

United States (1980–92): The financial markets were deep and broad and bank concentration was low. Interstate restrictions forced banks to be undiversified, however. Entry restrictions for banks were relaxed in the mid-1980s and many of the new banks subsequently failed.

Venezuela (1994–present): The banking system was concentrated (6 banks held 57% of bank assets) and foreign competition was limited until 1995. Laws, regulations and enforcement were weak.

Zambia (1994–present): The financial system is bank dependent and concentrated, with 5 of 19 banks holding 85% of the assets. 12 new licenses are outstanding.

---

[1] Years in parentheses denote the period of banking problems.

Therefore, an appropriate structure of antimonopoly laws and competition policies can make an important contribution to the long-term soundness of a banking system.

Financial Markets

The financial markets define the operating context for banks and the set of opportunities available to them. Banks that are part of a financial system with well-developed interbank and money markets will have available a wider range of investments and sources of liquidity and face different forms of competition than banks in less-well-developed markets. In general, this would be expected to enhance systemic soundness, by providing banks with greater opportunities to diversify risk and increase efficiency in resource use. It may, however, also result in more competitive pressure, and in greater risks of contagion and domino effects when banks fail to control their interactions with unsound banks.

Perhaps the most important aspect of banks' market interactions is their central role in the payments system. Operating within the payments system exposes participants to various forms of risk. The most pervasive among these are credit risk and liquidity risk. Credit risk is the risk that one party in a transaction may not be able to meet its obligation because of insolvency; liquidity risk is the probability that the counterparty will not be able to settle on time. Another risk is operational risk, which arises when payments are delayed as a result of a technical problem. The most worrisome risk, however, is systemic risk. This occurs when the failure of one or more institution(s) to meet its (their) settlement obligations has a domino effect throughout the system, leading to liquidity or solvency problems in other institutions.

Steps can be taken to reduce risk in the payments system. Making transactions irreversible and as simultaneous as possible is one approach. Sometimes this is done by channeling settlement through the central bank, particularly for large-value payments, and by specifying finality rules. Real time gross settlement also reduces payments risk but is not cost-effective in all situations and may leave the system susceptible to gridlock unless accommodated by appropriate liquidity support. Retail, high-volume/low-value payments are usually cleared through clearing houses, which often have sought to control risk by removing from the settlement the transactions of any bank that cannot fulfill its obligations. Such arrangements could create systemic problems, however, as withdrawing one bank's transactions could cause other banks to be unable to settle their obligations. Thus, increased emphasis has been placed on other solutions, such as explicit loss-sharing arrangements to enable settlement to occur and having banks control bilateral exposures to each other. While progress has been made on modernizing and standardizing laws and practices governing payments across countries, much remains to be done to create a legal framework that will support payments systems that can reduce international payments risk.

The broader financial markets also have important influences on bank soundness. Banks must compete with debt and equity markets as sources of finance for enterprises. Banks may also engage in securities market operations on behalf of customers or for their own accounts. These activities provide opportunities for profit, but also present additional risks. Securities markets that are themselves poorly regulated or subject to wide fluctuations can adversely affect bank portfolios and thus the soundness of banks. For example, several banks operating in India incurred large losses in 1992 due to irregularities in trading in Indian equities, government securities, and public sector bond markets. In Japan, banks holding large equity positions were adversely affected by the sharp decline of the Japanese stock market after 1990.

Economic Conditions and Noneconomic Shocks

An adequate infrastructure is not sufficient to ensure that the banking system remains sound. As discussed above, the banking system mirrors the health of the economy as a whole. If the economy has experienced recession, policy shocks, or other disruptions, the banking system will reflect these events in its balance sheet (see Table 4). When the economy weakens, banks in general may find that their capital, based on earlier expectations of loss, is no longer adequate. A sound banking system will have the capital and reserves necessary to weather normal business cycles; however, events in many countries have shown that existing minimum capital standards have not been sufficient to withstand substantial or prolonged economic crises.

One factor contributing to this is that loan values may decline rapidly owing to the simultaneous actions of individual distressed banks. For example, if several banks have extensive real estate exposures, problems at a few banks that result in distress sales of collateral may drive down prices, resulting in further deterioration of other banks' positions. Individual banks may not have the information necessary to assess ex ante the interlinkages between their portfolios and those of other banks and to monitor the potential impact and feedback effects of broader economic trends.

Banks may also be affected by a variety of noneconomic shocks such as political unrest or interference, or natural disasters (see Table 4). These are occasionally predictable or preventable, but often banks have little opportunity to protect themselves. Political unrest reduces confidence in the economy and the financial system and can contribute to the disappearance of markets, sudden shifts in prices or exchange rates, or episodes of capital flight. Wars affect banks in the conflicting countries but their effect may be more widespread. For example, the Falklands war adversely affected banks in Argentina, Chile, and Uruguay in 1982. The Persian Gulf war resulted in the Kuwaiti government's taking over a large portfolio of bad loans from the banking sector in that country. Several Croatian banks that might have weathered the economic aspects of the disintegration of Yugoslavia became insolvent because of war-related defaults.

Natural disasters can impair borrowers' ability to repay, as well as banks' ability to function. Insofar as natural disasters are recurrent, they should be anticipated by banks and their borrowers, with additional cushions of capital and liquidity built up for contingencies. Events like flooding in areas that are prone to inundation are sometimes used as an excuse for debt forgiveness, eroding bank soundness, engendering moral hazard, and creating the basis for a culture of nonrepayment in the future. This was the case in Bangladesh.

Political interference in banking for quasi-fiscal purposes is perhaps the most common form of noneconomic disturbance. For example, governments in many countries direct banks to make loans to certain sectors or industries often without regard for proper credit evaluation criteria or at subsidized interest rates. Such interference contributes to bank fragility and is addressed further below in the context of internal governance and regulatory failure.

Financial Sector Liberalization

In recent years, many countries have implemented programs of financial sector liberalization, often as part of a broader program of stabilization and economic opening. While the long-term benefits of such programs are clear, liberalization is a form of policy shock. Deregulation permits banks to enter into new and unfamiliar areas of business, where they may incur increased exposure to credit, foreign exchange, and interest rate risk. For example, formerly regulated banks may lack the necessary credit evaluation skills to use newly available resources effectively, and rising asset prices may be relied upon for repayment, rather than projected cash flows. Deregulation often opens the domestic banking market to other financial institutions and to foreign competition; this will put pressure on the market share and profitability of domestic banks, at least in the short term.

Unless properly overseen, liberalization can result in too rapid growth of bank assets, overindebtedness, and asset price bubbles. Market participants and supervisors, as well as banks, face challenges in managing the liberalization and adjusting to the new environment. Since radical changes in banks' operating environment can be expected to increase banking risks and affect banking soundness, liberalization should be accompanied by prior or concurrent measures to strengthen the oversight framework.

Some form of liberalization was under way in most instances of banking sector problems experienced by the sample countries (Table 13). Although there is no direct connection between financial liberalization and financial crises, many banking systems have experienced significant problems following liberalization, particularly where adequate internal controls had not been developed and prudential regulation and supervision failed to contain the increased risk of new or expanded activities. Examples include Argentina (early 1980s), Finland, Thailand, the United

Table 13. Financial Sector Liberalization[1]

Argentina (1980–82): In 1977, before the crisis, the financial sector grew faster than GDP. After the removal of controls on interest rates, real rates became positive, doubled and became volatile. Entry barriers and branching restrictions were removed in 1977. The economy was opened to trade and capital flows in 1976 and 1981. The exchange rate was devalued and then allowed to float in 1981.

(1989–90): Prices and the exchange rate were freed in 1989.

(1995): Capital flows were completely liberalized under the Convertibility Law of 1991 and the Argentine peso was pegged to the U.S. dollar. Industry is being privatized.

Bangladesh (1980s–present): Two state-owned banks were privatized; credit controls were terminated; and interest rates were largely deregulated in late 1984; foreign exchange markets were unified in 1991–92; restrictions on current transactions were lifted in 1994.

Bolivia (1994–present): Liberalization was not a factor, although permission for dollar deposits and transactions contributed to capital inflows.

Brazil (1994–present): During the second half of 1994, there was a consumption boom. The disinflation process was accompanied by rising real wages and a lower inflation tax. Credit to individuals increased by 91% in the third quarter of 1994 relative to the previous quarter, and by nearly 14% in the fourth quarter of 1994.

Chile (1981–86): Comprehensive liberalization of the economy included the removal of price controls, privatization of most state-owned enterprises, trade liberalization, and financial reform. Domestic interest rates remained high, however, in both nominal and real terms.

Czech Republic (1991–present): In transition from a controlled to a market economy. Enterprise privatization is ongoing and 80% of assets are in private hands; banks have been privatized, but the state retains an important ownership interest in the largest banks.

Egypt (1991–95): The liberalization of trade, interest rates, and prices is under way; limited privatization is ongoing.

Estonia (1992–95): In transition from a controlled to a market economy.

Finland (1991–94): Capital controls and restrictions on lending were removed and credit rationing was ended in the mid-1980s. An asset-price boom followed. Foreign banks were allowed to enter in 1982. The banking industry engaged in very heavy competition for market share after deregulation in the mid-1980s. In this process, banks' margins were reduced and interest rates did not compensate for banks' risk exposure.

France (1991–95): Regulatory reforms were undertaken from the mid-1980s.

Ghana (1983–89): The exchange system was liberalized in 1986–87. Most interest rates were decontrolled in 1987. Most controls on sectoral credit allocation were abolished in 1988. The agricultural lending requirement was lifted in 1990.

Hungary (1987–present): The economy is in transition from a controlled to a market economy. Interest rates were deregulated in 1990. Banks are being privatized and competition increased.

Indonesia (1992–present): The financial sector was deregulated in the late 1980s, and reserve requirements were reduced.

Table 13 *(continued)*

Japan (1992–present): Interest rates were deregulated and capital movements were freed. The authorities continued to exercise some moral suasion, however.

Kazakstan (1991–95): In transition from a controlled to a market economy. The liberalization of prices has been completed; for interest rates and trade, it is under way. Privatization is also under way.

Kuwait (1990–91): There has been a relaxation of financial and interest rate policies and limited divestiture of public ownership.

Latvia (1995–present): In transition from a controlled to a market economy. Beginning in mid-1992, directed and subsidized credits and interest rate controls were ended. The current account became convertible and all restrictions on capital movements were removed.

Lithuania (1995–present): In transition from a controlled to a market economy.

Malaysia (1985–88): Interest rates were deregulated in 1978–82, but moral suasion continued and controls were temporarily reimposed during the crisis. The exchange rate floated with intervention. Capital flows were fairly free, but approval was needed to borrow foreign exchange.

Mexico (1994–present): Most interest rates and quantitative credit controls were eliminated in 1989. In 1991–92, banks were reprivatized. Financial liberalization and the strengthening of public finances (which reduced the public sector's resort to bank credit) resulted in a shift of lending in favor of riskier borrowers. Total loans increased in real terms by about 25% a year between 1991 and 1994.

Norway (1987–93): The financial sector was initially heavily regulated. Interest and exchange rates were deregulated in the 1980s and credit restrictions were removed. Asset prices subsequently rose sharply.

Pakistan (1980–present): The economy was overregulated, but interest rates were decontrolled in 1995 and some state banks were privatized. Bank borrowers were successful in delaying necessary reforms and also in thwarting their implementation. Slow progress in fiscal consolidation contributed to delays in liberalizing the financial system.

Paraguay (1995–present): Liberalization began in the late 1980s and was mostly completed by the early 1990s.

Philippines (1981–87): Liberalization began in the 1980s. Interest rates were freed in 1980–81. Foreign entry was eased. Universal banking was permitted, giving banks and thrifts new activities to conduct. Capital markets were fairly free.

Poland (1991–present): In transition from a controlled to a market economy. Interest rates were deregulated in 1990. Nine state banks were commercialized in 1991 and 4 of these banks had been privatized by the end of 1995.

Russia (1992–present): In transition from a controlled to a market economy. Broad-based liberalization was begun in 1992. By 1995, most prices had been decontrolled and both interest rates and exchange rates were market determined. Many state-owned banks have been privatized, as have 90% of all small and medium-sized firms, but the Savings Bank, with 40% of ruble deposits, remains state owned.

Table 13 *(concluded)*

Spain (1977–85): Interest rates were liberalized gradually between 1974 and 1981. Bank licensing and activity restrictions were eased in 1974. Capital flows were freed and exchange rate determination was based on a managed float.

Sweden (1990–93): Lending restrictions and interest rate controls were lifted in 1985. An asset-price bubble followed.

Tanzania (1988–present): Sharp exchange rate adjustments occurred from 1986–90. Interest and exchange rates were substantially deregulated in the early 1990s.

Thailand (1983–87): Most lending rates, but not deposit rates, were freed. Capital flows became fairly free and prime companies borrowed heavily abroad. Exchange rates were fixed in relation to a basket of currencies.

Turkey (1994): Liberalization and reforms in the banking sector were ongoing throughout the 1980s. Interest rates were deregulated and the lira was made convertible.

United States (1980–92): Interest rates were deregulated in the late 1970s and early 1980s. Legislation in 1980 and 1982 gave thrifts powers to engage in new activities, and bank licensing was temporarily eased in the mid-1980s.

Venezuela (1994–present): Interest rates were deregulated and credit controls eased in the late 1980s. There was a shift to indirect instruments of monetary policy.

Zambia (1994–present): The economy was excessively controlled until liberalization began in the late 1980s when controls on external payments, interest rates, and exchange rates were removed.

---

[1] Years in parentheses denote the period of banking problems.

States, Venezuela, and most economies in transition.[67] As a result, it is now well recognized that, in addition to adequate stabilization policies, timely implementation of prudential and bank restructuring policies is essential to avoid major disruptions to growth and stability during financial liberalization.[68]

This, however, raises the question of how best to design and implement prudential regulations and supervisory systems to ensure successful liberalization of financial markets and transition to market-based instruments of monetary control. Insofar as the initial condition of the banking system is marked by significant portfolio weaknesses and inadequate capitalization, rapid liberalization of interest rates and a strengthening of prudential norms will be difficult to implement, unless a program of bank restructuring is put in place in parallel with the liberalization package. In practice, policies to restructure banks (and enterprises) and strengthen

---

[67] See also Sundararajan and Baliño (1991), Johnston and Pazarbaşioğlu (1995), Fischer and Gueyie (1995), and Kaminsky and Reinhart (1996).

[68] See Galbis (1995).

prudential supervision can be phased in to support the interest rate liberalization process.

Country experiences suggest that the scope of official oversight systems needs to vary with the state of market development and the institutional environment, and to continuously evolve as markets evolve. Appropriate sequencing of prudential and bank-restructuring policies can serve to establish a critical mass of reforms in supervision and of bank balance sheets, which in turn would help to speed up the adoption of market-based monetary instruments and enhance their effectiveness.[69] Operational considerations suggest that reforms of accounting standards for banks and loan-valuation systems should begin early in the reform process, as these strengthen supervisors' ability to monitor banks, increase the efficacy of oversight by bank owners, and provide a basis for market discipline. Financial market discipline can be strengthened by improved data disclosure, a careful design of the regulatory framework, and policies regarding deposit guarantees, last-resort lending, market entry, and market exit that do not inhibit market discipline.

A program of systemic restructuring of banks, where necessary, should be combined with appropriately strong prudential policies—phasing in prudential regulations, bringing about balanced application of off-site analysis, on-site inspection, and external audits—and with policies to establish institutional arrangements for loan recovery and enterprise restructuring. Such a comprehensive package, encompassing both official oversight and restructuring options, is necessary to avoid adverse incentives toward excessive risk taking by banks. Moreover, reforms of commercial bank accounting systems and implementation of effective internal monitoring systems can support stabilization objectives and facilitate the task of financial restructuring of banks.

Prudential policies to strengthen the banking system should, therefore, be an integral part of any liberalization program; however, standards should not be set at levels that few banks can meet. The implementation of new or more stringent prudential standards also must be undertaken with due regard to both macroeconomic trends and the strength of the banking system. Introduction of new prudential standards may require phasing in over several years, sometimes taking into account the pace at which problem banks and their debtors can be restructured and the associated fiscal adjustments can be made.

---

[69] For a detailed discussion of issues in sequencing prudential reforms during financial liberalization, see Sundararajan (1995).

7

Internal Governance

The primary responsibility for keeping individual banks sound lies with each bank's owners, directors, and managers. Together they must establish a framework of internal controls and practices to govern the operations of the bank and ensure that it functions in a safe and sound manner. As indicated in Table 14, poor internal governance was a factor in virtually all the instances of unsoundness in our sample.

Public policies must aim at limiting the negative externalities associated with bank failures. However, maintenance of a sound banking system depends on numerous factors, only some of which are directly influenced by policies. Public policies can reinforce incentives and market forces that encourage individual banks to remain sound. At the same time, such policies should not normally focus on individual banks but rather on the banking system as a whole. There may be cases in which a bank is considered "too big to fail," that is, it cannot be removed without damaging the system. Such a bank may be preserved and restructured, but its owners and managers should not be bailed out. It should be noted that the potential systemic repercussions of the failure of a large bank are often overstated; the case of Continental Illinois in the United States is an example (see Kaufman, 1990).

Ownership

The owners of a bank, and the directors they appoint, normally make every effort to see that the bank is well run and remains sound. A bank's owners are responsible for capitalizing the bank with sufficient resources to operate and to withstand reasonable losses. Owners with their own capital at risk have strong incentives to appoint competent directors and managers and to make every effort to see that these officers maintain the bank's profitability and solvency. An active market for corporate control will place pressure on owners and managers to maintain the bank in sound

Table 14. Deficiencies in Internal Governance[1]

Argentina (1980–82): Banks knew little about their clients and allowed speculative and distress borrowing. Accounting was weak.

(1989–90): Portfolios were not diversified, and banks lent heavily to the public sector. Public sector banks were inefficient and had very high levels of employment. Accounting was still weak. Banking was subject to political direction.

(1995): State banks were still weak. Banks were not diversified or automated and they made a large share of their loans in dollars. Accounting improved only in 1994.

Bangladesh (1980s–present): There is poor corporate governance with weak accountability and extensive insider lending. State-owned banks that account for two-thirds of deposits have very weak management and accounting systems. Political interference in lending occurred throughout the period.

Bolivia (1994–present): Troubled banks have several problems: concentrated ownership, extensive insider and related-party lending, weak internal controls, a lack of a clear division of internal responsibilities, low efficiency, and high costs.

Brazil (1994–present): Management was poor at some state banks that were not run on a commercial basis. The same applied to some private banks that did not diversify risks well. Some banks did not adjust quickly to the postinflationary environment.

Chile (1981–86): Banks were undercapitalized with respect to their historic averages. Loans to controlled companies were used to finance speculative asset purchases. From 1980, there was a sharp increase in "distress borrowing," rolling over bad loans, and capitalizing interest due.

Czech Republic (1991–present): Banks are inefficient and overstaffed, and shareholders exert pressure to obtain loans on preferential terms. Some small banks funded their loans in the overnight interbank market.

Egypt (1991–95): Domination of banking activities by 4 state-owned commercial banks is a problem.

Estonia (1992–95): Banks were not diversified and extended insider loans to owners. Credit-assessment skills were undeveloped and banks had weak accounting systems and inadequate classification and provisioning systems for bad debts.

Finland (1991–94): Banks had low capital, were not diversified, and engaged in aggressive, concentrated lending. Management focused on gaining market share rather than on risk analysis. Corporate lending to a large extent was in foreign currency. Auditing was lax.

France (1991–95): Internal controls have improved markedly in recent years and are broadly appropriate, although increased separation of back-office operations is still desirable. More generally, state shareholding in several banks (e.g., Crédit Lyonnais) poses specific problems.

Ghana (1983–89): Inadequate management, information, and internal control systems led to high operating expenses and even fraud. Loan losses were not recognized. There was no uniform system of asset classification or provisioning. Accounting standards were not uniform or were inappropriate.

Table 14 *(continued)*

Hungary (1987–present): Fraud occurred at 2 failed banks. Banks have too many branches and are overstaffed. There is adverse selection of borrowers at state-owned banks.

Indonesia (1992–present): State banks have been poorly managed in the past and have been subject to political interference. Industrial ownership of private banks has sometimes led to intragroup lending in excess of the legal limits on large exposures.

Japan (1992–present): The main bank system has led to selected lending. Accounting systems and internal controls were weak at some banks (e.g., Daiwa Bank). Banks' financial technology lagged behind their growth. They were not diversified, made inadequate provisions for problem loans, and grew rapidly in a quest for market share.

Kazakstan (1991–95): Management has no clear strategy. Speculation in foreign exchange produced profits but banks have no concept of how to grant and manage credits. Loans are rolled over and interest is capitalized. Lending is often concentrated or extended to related parties.

Kuwait (1990–91): Internal governance appears to have been adequate.

Latvia (1995–present): Risk-assessment skills are lacking; management is poor and accounting systems are weak. Major problems have been high foreign exchange exposure, insider lending, and fraud.

Lithuania (1995–present): The country's banks suffered from political interference in lending, inherited from Soviet times. Management is poor at state-controlled banks and private banks alike. In some cases, shareholders have seriously misused their rights.

Malaysia (1985–88): Banks were often under family control. Some smaller institutions lacked a code of ethics, internal controls, audit committees, and Chinese walls, so that fraud occurred. Institutions engaging in new activities (such as finance companies) often lacked professional expertise and fast growth overstretched their managerial resources. Risks increased rapidly (the loan-to-deposit ratio reached 90%) and distress borrowing was permitted. Management was not used to dealing with bad loans in an expanding, inflationary economy.

Mexico (1994–present): After many years of nationalized banking (from 1982 to mid-1992), commercial banks lacked the experience and organizational and information systems to adequately assess credit and other market risks and to monitor and collect loans. Accounting practices did not follow international standards. Concentration of loans and loans to related parties was a problem in those banks that were subsequently subject to official intervention.

Norway (1987–93): There were problems with high leverage, fast and concentrated growth in risky assets (especially in real estate), and lax auditing.

Pakistan (1980–present): State ownership has been a problem—state banks have been subject to political pressure to lend and to withhold debt-recovery efforts. Political interference in lending and weak collection have hurt banks.

Paraguay (1995–present): Insider lending and risk concentration was high and there was excessive illegal (off the books) deposit taking by banks.

Philippines (1981–87): There were weak banking and accounting practices and portfolios were not diversified. State banks owned 36% of banking assets. Commercial ownership through groups was high, leading to connected lending, interlocking directorships, and excessive risk taking.

Table 14 *(concluded)*

Poland (1991–present): Political interference has occurred at some state banks. Banks were overstaffed and had poor management and information systems. New accounting standards were introduced in 1995.

Russia (1992–present): Weak internal controls and management practices have contributed to falling profitability and fraud. Accounting standards are weak. The central bank has introduced improved reporting requirements but the underlying chart of accounts is inadequate.

Spain (1977–85): Banks were not diversified, and credit was politically directed, which discouraged the development of credit-evaluation skills. Accounting was not consolidated.

Sweden (1990–93): Loan administration was poor and systems for credit monitoring were lacking. Pricing did not adequately reflect risk. There was an undue concentration of bank portfolios on real estate, and competition to lend to the real estate sector was destructive.

Tanzania (1988–present): Management and internal controls at state banks were weak. These banks were inefficient, overstaffed, and not run for profit. There was political interference in bank structure and lending for most of the period from 1967 to 1994. Accounting, auditing, reporting, and credit assessment were weak.

Thailand (1983–87): Banks were run by a few families, who were not professional bankers. Management weaknesses were pronounced especially at finance and securities companies. Ownership was concentrated, with little outside shareholder discipline. Internal controls were inadequate and there was heavy insider lending and high expenditure on banks' offices. Accounting was weak.

Turkey (1994): Industrial owners of banks pressured for subsidized loans. Accounts were not adjusted for inflation. There were deficiencies in risk analysis and risk management especially regarding foreign positions, leading to speculation. Banks had poor (unaudited) information on their borrowers. Banks are overstaffed and overbranched. There has been fast growth, especially in the off-balance-sheet activities.

United States (1980–92): In general, management and internal controls were adequate at the banks that survived, but they were seriously deficient at many banks and thrifts that failed. Savings-and-loan regulators encouraged "phony" accounting to hide net worth deficiencies. There was also political interference in lending in the thrift industry. Accounting even at banks ignored off-balance-sheet activities until the late 1980s and was slow to acknowledge the importance of market valuation.

Venezuela (1994–present): Banks had inefficient operations with high costs and extensive branch networks and offshore operations. There was weak accounting, extensive insider lending, and rampant fraud.

Zambia (1994–present): Banks had weak management and internal controls. They engaged in risky activities, including derivatives, and experienced very fast growth (assets quadrupled in two years). There has been political interference in banking, and incentives for performance at the large state bank are weak.

---

[1] Years in parentheses denote the period of banking problems.

condition.[70] The threat of losing their capital or forfeiting control of their bank through bankruptcy, corporate takeover, or official intervention should compel most owners to exert good internal governance.

The incentive structure is usually different for state-owned banks, which may have other operational objectives than profitability and soundness. Governments do not face market pressure for corporate control and taxpayers do not monitor their stakes in state-owned banks as well as shareholders in private banks monitor theirs.[71] Special efforts need to be made to ensure that incentives for directors and managers to keep a state-owned bank operating on a sound commercial basis are in place. In practice, this is difficult to accomplish; in many cases, full or partial privatization is the only way to insulate bank management from political interference and to ensure also that capital markets can discipline the owners. Banks that are, or were recently, state owned were a factor in most of the instances of unsoundness in the sample (see Table 14).

Private ownership per se does not guarantee good governance, however. Some private bank ownership structures can result in incentives to operate the bank in an unsafe and unsound manner. Banks may be misused, for example, as captive sources of finance for owners who are reluctant to service their loans. Insider lending or lending to related enterprises has been a principal factor contributing to banking sector problems in numerous countries. In many of the cases illustrated in Table 14, banks were part of financial groups that were able to engage in insider lending through complex off-balance-sheet and offshore transactions that made it difficult to track the loans and enabled the banks to hide their losses. When private owners' motivation for owning banks is essentially to rob them, internal governance will be insufficient to ensure the soundness of these banks. It should also be noted that in some environments, private ownership does not insulate a bank from political pressure for directed lending.

Management

Banks assume risk in the course of their business and the role of their managements is to assess and manage that risk. Among privately owned U.S. banks, most bank failures may be traced to poor management.[72] Among state-owned banks, failures often are due to political interference, but management failures are an important factor as well. Lax manage-

---

[70] See Prowse (1995).

[71] See Kane (1995) for a discussion of this aspect of state ownership.

[72] Evidence on this for the U.S. case is discussed in U.S. Office of the Comptroller of the Currency (1988), Siems (1992), and Barker and Holdsworth (1993).

ment can result in failure to institute appropriate procedures and controls to limit risk exposures and to ensure that the bank carries out its principal functions in a safe and sound manner.

Management should strive to maintain the value of the bank by ensuring that the asset portfolio is sound and produces sufficient income. Loans constitute the most important class of bank assets; despite the increase in other types of business, the most common reason for bank failures remains losses from bad credit decisions. It should be recalled that credit losses at Crédit Lyonnais in France alone are estimated at around $10 billion, while all the recent well-publicized, derivatives-related losses worldwide only amount to some $15 billion. It is the responsibility of a bank's management to ensure that credit appraisal and valuation are handled properly and that the asset portfolio is properly diversified. It becomes more difficult to distinguish good from bad borrowers when bank loans are growing rapidly (see Hausmann and Gavin, 1995); management must ensure that growth in loans is not so rapid that credit quality is sacrificed. Many loans that are sound at their inception develop into losses because of lax credit administration. Good management will institute appropriate policies and procedures for internal loan review and for early intervention in problem asset situations.

The valuation of the asset portfolio should take into account borrower-specific credit risk and overall economic risk factors. Bank management also needs to ensure that the bank is not exposed to excessive liquidity risk. While maturity transformation is a key function of banks, a sound bank holds sufficient liquid assets to enable it to meet reasonable levels of deposit withdrawals without forced liquidation of portfolio assets. Thus, good bank managers assess their bank's liability structure, project how liquidity would be affected by adverse events, and determine if the bank's asset position is appropriate.

Banks encounter risks from abrupt shifts in exchange rates or interest rates. Exposure to foreign exchange losses depends on the relative balance of foreign exchange assets and liabilities in the bank's portfolio. When banks convert borrowed funds into domestic currency, they face foreign exchange risk; if they on-lend the foreign currency, their borrowers may default as a result of foreign exchange exposure. In some markets, exchange risk can be hedged; in any market, it can be limited through appropriate exposure management. Interest rate risk arises from a maturity mismatch between assets and liabilities and may be managed through appropriate liquidity matching or interest rate adjustment practices. Exchange rate and interest rate exposure may be explicit in the balance sheet or may be implicit in off-balance-sheet transactions, such as swaps and other derivatives. Off-balance-sheet transactions also involve credit risk, which must be evaluated like the credit risk in regular lending. For all these risks, it is the responsibility of management to monitor the port-folio and to ensure that exposures remain within the limits determined by the owners and top management.

Banks are increasingly exposed to risks stemming from their participation in securities, commodities, and derivative markets. Many of these risks can be readily broken down into constituent interest rate, exchange rate, or credit risk elements. However, the complex nature of some of the positions now being taken by the trading desks and investment arms of banks places greater demands on management to understand, monitor, and limit the risks assumed.

Finally, banks continue to be subject to operational and reputational risks linked to the fact that they are, after all, organizations designed and operated by humans. The danger of direct financial loss or loss of reputation (and clients) due to errors and fraud will therefore always be present. Here, too, the primary onus is on a bank's management to ensure that personnel and operating policies minimize the organizational hazards.

Internal Oversight

Owners and managers normally have a common interest in establishing internal systems to provide accurate reporting on the bank's condition and to monitor and control risk. Such systems must include accounting procedures that adhere to generally accepted standards, but extend also to reporting systems that properly value the bank's asset portfolio and indicate its risk exposure, and internal procedures to ensure that risks are not assumed unintentionally or inappropriately. Internal control systems should also provide managers with the information necessary to monitor the bank's compliance with laws and regulations, and to follow up on any corrective action being taken. Lax accounting or audit were identified as contributors to more than half the instances of unsoundness in our sample (see Table 14).

Banks are particularly exposed to internal risk in the form of incompetence, dereliction of duty, or fraud. Thorough internal and external audits and written policies and procedures help control these risks. Managers and directors must possess a full understanding of the financial instruments and markets in which the bank does business, be able to monitor their subordinates' activities, implement internal controls, and understand audit and other data depicting the bank's position. Where there is a clear potential for problems, rules and procedures are needed to control behavior. For example, it may be difficult to apply objective standards to loans to insiders, so rules are needed to limit such lending and to subject insider loans to special oversight.

Governance Failures

Internal governance may fail to ensure the soundness of a bank for a number of reasons, most of which relate to conflicts of interest and information asymmetries. Bank creditors' earnings are typically fixed or independent of the return generated by the actual use of their funds, so owners and managers may attempt to garner higher profits by making riskier investments, whose benefits accrue solely to them. Furthermore, owners whose main goal is to use the bank as a captive source of funding for other enterprises may not be concerned with the safety of the bank, since a collapse harms depositors and other creditors more than the borrowers or owners (see Garcia and Saal, 1996).

Similarly, while capital provides a bank with a cushion against losses, owners have incentives to put as little capital at risk as possible. Income recognition and loan-valuation rules are prone to manipulation by banks wishing to show higher profits or capital. By manipulating the classification of nonperforming loans, restructuring nonperforming loans without classifying them, including as income the interest accrued on nonperforming loans, or rolling over principal and interest into new loans ("evergreening"), banks can show accounting earnings and inflate asset values even when in fact they are incurring losses. In many Latin American countries, accounting standards were so lax that banking systems were reporting positive net income even during a banking crisis (Rojas-Suárez and Weisbrod, 1995). For example, evergreening contributed to the banking crisis in Chile in the early 1980s (Brock, 1992). The problem is not limited to less-developed economies; U.S. banks with low capitalization have apparently been able to manipulate accrual estimates so as to reduce loan-loss provisions (Kim and Kross, 1995) and appear to choose their charge-offs and provisions to manage the level of bank capital rather than to reflect loan quality (Beatty, Chamberlain, and Magliola, 1993).

Assuring that banks are well managed may be made more difficult by conflicts of interest between owners and managers. Owners may not have the information necessary to prevent managers from furthering their own interests rather than pursuing the objective of maximizing the value of the bank. The ownership structure can also be a problem if shareholdings are so fragmented that the widely dispersed owners are unable to exercise effective control. Managers may take on excessive risk, since it is the owners whose capital is at stake, not the managers.[73] Managers may make excessive outlays on headquarter offices, equipment, furnishings, salaries, and benefits, which can dissipate earnings and may lead to loss of capital

---

[73] One factor contributing to the increase in risk inclination in recent years may be the rise of managers with market trading rather than traditional banking backgrounds.

and eventual insolvency. Where managerial income is related to earnings, managers may attempt to hide problems by overvaluing assets or showing improperly accrued earnings. These problems may be ameliorated by strong internal controls, which allow directors and owners to monitor manager behavior, by incentive contracts aligning managers' personal benefits with owners' goals, and by an active market for managerial services, which puts pressure on managers to maintain their reputations. In this regard, treating managers of state-owned banks as civil servants, with the attendant job security and salary scale, may blunt managers' performance incentives.

8

External Governance: Market Discipline

When internal governance fails to ensure the soundness of banks, private and public sector creditors of banks must themselves strive to ensure that their interests are not jeopardized. Creditors can reinforce bank's incentives to operate safely and soundly by providing oversight, exerting discipline on banks' activities, and driving poorly managed or unsound banks out of the market. Such market discipline helps prevent isolated problems at individual banks from contaminating others and building into systemic unsoundness.

Private Sector

Private capital markets impose discipline through creditors who monitor a bank's financial data and respond to signals of unsafe or unsound practices by requiring higher interest rates or by withdrawing resources from the bank. This could take the form of a run but it need not be an abrupt process, provided that the market has sufficient—and regularly available—information to distinguish weak banks from strong ones; it may involve weak banks being forced to pay higher rates for funds, or the gradual transfer of funds from weaker into stronger banks, and ultimately exclusion from the interbank market. An example of market discipline was provided in late 1995 by the premium charged to Japanese banks in the international interbank market. In response, Japanese banks sought to reassure markets by increasing their disclosure of nonperforming loans.[74]

Faced with the potential of higher costs or being forced out of business, shareholders and boards of directors will be cautious about allowing high-risk banking practices, because negative market reactions to such practices would damage their stake in the bank and ultimately force its exit from the market. The exit of weak individual banks is critical for

[74] See "Japan," November 1995.

the maintenance of a strong banking system. The prolonged operation of unsound banks permits them to spiral into deeper insolvency, and possibly to damage competitors through market practices that, although not viable in the long term, might enable short-term survival. Experience has shown that unsound banks are invariably in worse condition than their financial statements indicate and that the least intrusive and cheapest way of keeping a banking system sound is to force the early exit of nonviable banks.

Such market discipline requires that creditors—at least the larger ones—have funds at risk in the market (i.e., that their claims not be not fully protected) and have sufficient information about the banks in which they have placed their funds, so that they can avoid risk. Large and well-informed creditors, including other banks, typically are most effective in exercising market discipline because they have more resources with which to monitor and influence banks. Well-developed interbank, securitized debt, commercial paper, and money markets are usually capable of providing such discipline. Small-scale depositors cannot generally be expected to provide external discipline because they lack the necessary financial analysis skills; they may also lack incentives to do so because their deposits may be insured. Even so, smaller depositors may manifest their discomfort with individual banks or with the broader stability of a banking system through bank runs and capital flight. In addition to creditors, deposit insurance schemes, credit-rating agencies, credit bureaus, external auditors, and market analysts, all develop and express opinions on the soundness of banks. These contribute to market discipline by providing information not only to creditors but also to banks' owners and potential owners.

When market discipline is working, banks are forced to correct their deficiencies or exit the market before they become insolvent. One would not expect creditors to wait until their claims can no longer be fully covered by bank assets. Similarly, it is in the interest of a private deposit insurance scheme to force the early exit of a bank before it becomes insolvent and results in losses for the deposit insurer. Exit pressure is greater in a competitive market, where an individual bank is more dispensable, than in a highly concentrated market. Where the fact that a bank is not too big to fail is common knowledge among depositors, other creditors, owners, managers, regulators, and politicians, depositors will have no incentive to rely on official assistance for the ailing bank.

Exit pressure also may be exerted through the market for corporate control. While creditors exert discipline by depriving the bank of liabilities, shareholders can exert discipline by selling their ownership stake, and driving down the value of the bank. Where there are concentrated ownership stakes, shareholders will use the signals provided by market participants (creditors, auditors, analysts) to guide their oversight of the bank and its management.[75]

Public Sector

Public sector creditors can also structure their involvement with banks (private or public) so as to provide oversight and external discipline for bank activities. Insofar as the government or other state-controlled entities maintain deposits at commercial banks or guarantee credits, they can act as any large, well-informed creditor to impose market discipline by withdrawing their deposits or guarantees. The most common public creditor is the central bank, which may provide credit to commercial banks generally for monetary policy purposes or temporary liquidity to individual banks as lender of last resort.[76] The central bank can restrict unsound banks' access to its credit facilities and thus force their market exit.

When deposit insurance is publicly provided, it is important to design the insurance system so as not to reduce the incentives for other market participants to exert discipline. Market discipline can be retained by creating an explicit deposit insurance system with clearly defined, credible rules that make insurance compulsory and confine guarantees to small depositors. Market discipline may be further reinforced by placing responsibility for funding deposit insurance on the banking industry rather than the government. A well-defined deposit insurance system can enhance market discipline by making the closure of insolvent banks more politically acceptable and therefore more likely to occur quickly.[77]

Public sector owners can play a role in disciplining state-owned banks parallel to the role played by markets with respect to privately owned banks. Responsibility for ownership oversight of state-owned banks must be clearly allocated to a particular ministry or agency that will monitor directors and managers of state-owned banks, and replace them if their performance is inadequate.

Market discipline has the benefit of avoiding unduly strict and costly official regulation and supervision. It also avoids creating the impression that the government vouches for the banking system through its regulatory and supervisory policies. Market discipline will create incentives for banks to keep themselves sound, and the occasional exit of weak banks

---

[75] This points to the potential importance of large shareholders. Poland recognized this in its approach to bank privatization, which attempted to ensure the presence of strategic shareholders with significant ownership stakes (see Bonin, 1995). In other systems, it is assumed that if the bank is poorly managed a corporate raider will emerge to assume this role.

[76] In some countries, the central bank also provides long-term credit to key sectors to meet development objectives.

[77] See Garcia (1996).

reinforces those incentives, by emphasizing that market discipline is working.

Failures in Market Discipline

Market discipline may fail if there is inadequate information, inconsistent incentives, or a lack of informed market participants. The experience of the sample countries, shown in Table 15, suggests that market discipline was not able to contribute to maintaining a sound banking system in almost all of the cases. It must also be recognized that market discipline may impose some negative externalities, and it may not be appropriate to rely on market forces in all circumstances. Even when market discipline against a particular bank does take hold, there is the danger of undesirable systemic or welfare repercussions.

Insufficient Effectiveness

Market discipline will fail if there is insufficient information available to market participants, or if the incentive structures are inadequate.[78] This was a factor in most of the cases in the sample. Effective market discipline requires that financial information be disclosed promptly and that it presents a true picture of the value of the bank, based on generally accepted accounting standards and on proper loan-valuation procedures. Where banks operate as part of larger financial groups or have overseas operations and do not report their consolidated position, they may operate with losses hidden in other operating units and their true condition undetected by the market. Failure to consolidate the different activities within conglomerates with off-balance-sheet, offshore, and foreign subsidiaries made it difficult to detect weaknesses in the condition of Bank of Credit and Commerce International (BCCI) and Meridien Bank before those banks failed. As discussed above, banks may have incentives to withhold or distort information. At the same time, market participants cannot be given access to all bank data because some information may be commercially sensitive. While accounting standards and practices may vary from country to country, certain common objectives, definitions, and valuation practices can be identified (see Appendix I).

Even when information is disclosed, the opacity of bank assets limits the ability of markets to fully assess the information disclosed, even in the most advanced markets where the best external auditors and third-party credit ratings of borrowers are available. Market discipline exerted by large depositors, particularly in the interbank market, typically will come

---

[78] Lane (1993) discusses the conditions for effective market discipline.

Table 15. Deficiencies in Market Discipline[1]

Argentina (1980–82): The state bore the full cost of deposit insurance until 1979, when a new, limited, voluntary scheme was introduced, although state banks remained fully guaranteed by the government. Borrowers were subsidized to the equivalent of between 11% and 13% of GDP. Foreign exchange exposure was guaranteed.

(1989–90): Deposit insurance ended in 1989. Depositors suffered significant losses when banks failed. The culture was anticreditor.

(1995): There was no deposit insurance until April 1995.

Bangladesh (1980s–present): Insolvent banks continue to operate. Weak accounting and information availability impede the markets. Politically directed and insider lending that flourish in opaque environments are blamed for most of the nonperforming loans.

Bolivia (1994–present): Two banks have been liquidated and 3 of 4 problem banks have new owners. The central bank compensated small depositors of the liquidated banks, but depositors with more than US$5,000 incurred losses.

Brazil (1994–present): There was no deposit insurance, except for saving accounts, until November 1995.

Chile (1981–86): An implicit government guarantee on deposits weakened market discipline. A dual deposit insurance system was introduced in 1986, providing full coverage for demand deposits and coinsurance for limited amounts of time and savings deposits.

Czech Republic (1991–present): The problem of moral hazard has been worsened by the resolution of pre-reform debts via transfer to a separate bank and the repeated bank recapitalizations that occurred until late 1994.

Egypt (1991–95): State-owned banks dominate the system.

Estonia (1992–95): There was no system of deposit insurance during the banking problems in the early 1990s and depositors suffered losses when banks failed. However, the authorities have subsequently been reluctant to liquidate banks and have supported them instead.

Finland (1991–94): A full guarantee of the savings banks and full deposit coverage weakened market discipline. Moreover, the underfunding of the deposit insurance schemes inhibited closure. The culture was antiregulation.

France (1991–95): Information is generally good, but there are unequal advantages and constraints between public and private institutions, which distort competition and allow risky operations. Crédit Lyonnais had an implicit state guarantee as a state bank and its portfolio was explicitly guaranteed in 1993.

Ghana (1983–89): The government guided credit allocation and interest rates, which, along with government ownership of banks, impeded market discipline.

Hungary (1987–present): There were repeated government-funded recapitalizations. Extensive preferential and guaranteed loans that were granted in 1994 further undermined incentives for market discipline.

Indonesia (1992–present): Disclosure is weak and the markets' perceptions that distressed banks will be bailed out limit market discipline. However, the interbank market is responsive to information.

Table 15 *(continued)*

Japan (1992–present): The "too-big-to-fail" philosophy applied to the 21 major commercial banks and the full deposit guarantees extended in mid-1995 may weaken market discipline. Deposit insurance is underfunded. The postal savings bank's deposits have long been fully government guaranteed. Poor disclosure prevents the public from distinguishing weak from strong banks.

Kazakstan (1991–95): Banks not meeting prudential standards are excluded from the interbank market. Bank closures are taking place. Past subsidization of large loss-making enterprises (which has now largely disappeared) weakened incentives in the past. The Housing Bank's deposits are fully guaranteed.

Kuwait (1990–91): Although there was no formal system of deposit insurance, there was an implicit guarantee, which was honored by a bailout of the system in the mid-1980s.

Latvia (1995–present): There is no system of deposit insurance and compensation to depositors of failed banks has been minimal.

Lithuania (1995–present): Market segmentation according to type of borrower (agricultural, energy, interbank) has reduced competition. The state-controlled banks' deposits are fully guaranteed. A new deposit insurance law limited the compensation received by depositors of failed banks in 1996. However, some banks have been provided with full deposit insurance under special laws.

Malaysia (1985–88): The lack of transparency, arising from poor accounting and reporting, delayed the recognition of, and impeded the markets' responses to, the problems that were building up. Audits were sometimes two years overdue at nonbanks. There was no deposit insurance and depositors were permitted to lose money.

Mexico (1994–present): Although the explicit deposit guarantee by FOBAPROA (the deposit insurance agency) is limited to the resources available in the deposit guarantee fund, official announcements indicate that FOBAPROA guarantees all banks' obligations, except for subordinated debt. In addition, there are debtors' organizations that contest the repayment of bank loans. Interest rates were lowered after a borrower defaulted, giving an incentive to default.

Norway (1987–93): Debt was subsidized by the tax system, which consequently discouraged equity issuance. The deposit insurance scheme, which offered a full guarantee, was underfunded.

Pakistan (1980–present): Competition from the poorly run state banks is destructive. The pro-debtor culture allows customers to avoid meeting their obligations.

Paraguay (1995–present): Competition from unlicensed institutions is destructive of the soundness of other banks.

Philippines (1981–87): The underfunded deposit insurance scheme was unable to meet all of its obligations or to improve depositor confidence. (Only 52% of depositor claims had been met by 1987.) The culture was pro-debtor and the bank closure process was slow. There was political interference in the banking sector.

Poland (1991–present): State banks have an unlimited guarantee through 1999. Limited deposit insurance was introduced for other banks in 1995. Data reporting and disclosure are weak.

Table 15 *(concluded)*

Russia (1992–present): Requirements that enterprises hold deposits in only one bank, the existence of government guarantees on household deposits in the Savings Bank, and inadequate disclosure of financial information have all severely limited market discipline. Because of risks, top-rated banks trade only among themselves.

Spain (1977–85): Lending was directed. Deposit insurance was instituted in 1977 but the system was revised in 1980. Weak disclosure discouraged market discipline.

Sweden (1990–93): Depositors expected to be bailed out even before a blanket guarantee was granted for the duration of the crisis.

Tanzania (1988–present): Repeated recapitalizations, loan guarantees to state banks, and the practice of exceeding deposit insurance limits have all weakened incentives and rewarded bad managers. Inadequate accounting rendered disclosure meaningless. Minimal market discipline is now imposed by clearinghouse practices; however, until recently there was no interbank market and the central bank provided overdrafts to cover shortfalls in payments.

Thailand (1983–87): Although there was no formal system of deposit insurance, depositors were bailed out, which reduced market discipline. The culture was pro-debtor, disclosure was weak, and there was political interference in the banking system.

Turkey (1994): Disclosure is impaired by weak accounting standards. Guarantees impede incentives; for example, the blanket guarantee for all household deposits, extended in early 1994, is still valid and loans to state enterprises are considered implicitly guaranteed.

United States (1980–92): The "too-big-to-fail" doctrine and the practice of merging banks rather than closing them protected depositors above the insurance limit until the FDIC Improvement Act of 1991.

Venezuela (1994–present): Depositors in failed banks were paid in full from 1978 through 1985 and again in 1987. Nonstandard accounting practices hid losses from depositors and the Superintendency of Banks.

Zambia (1994–present): Competition from unregistered and insolvent banks harmed their competitors.

---

[1] Years in parentheses denote the period of banking problems.

into play in an active sense only after there is clear indication of weakness. This is often too late to fully protect the failed bank's creditors.

The private sector also cannot be counted upon to discipline banks efficiently if it is known or expected that the government or central bank will bail out institutions that run into trouble. The possibility of lender-of-last-resort (LOLR) support creates a potential for moral hazard; banks may be less careful in managing their assets and liabilities given the availability of a such a lender. The LOLR becomes subject to adverse selection—it lends to banks that cannot obtain funding elsewhere and may not be able to identify which of the illiquid banks are also insolvent. To the extent that funds are provided at below market rates, LOLR lending may subsidize the operation of weak banks and encourage them to gamble with public funds in an attempt to recoup previous losses.[79] LOLR credit that is not limited to providing liquidity to solvent banks so as to discourage unwarranted runs by uninsured depositors can contribute to delays in remedial action. Similarly, when governments place deposits of state entities in unsound banks specifically to shore them up, market discipline is undermined and government funds placed at risk.

Excessive deposit insurance coverage can remove the incentives for the market to impose discipline on banks that are weak or take excessive risks. Partial coverage would retain creditors' incentives to press for early closure of weak (but not yet insolvent) banks. Where it has not been properly designed to combat the risks of adverse selection and moral hazard attendant on the guarantee, deposit insurance can diminish market discipline and foster incentives for poor internal governance. In particular, deposit insurance that provides excessive coverage can increase resolution costs and harm competitors by creating opportunities for owners and managers to continue to operate a troubled bank that would otherwise be closed by market discipline. Government loan guarantees carry a similar moral hazard risk; banks will have reduced incentive to be careful in loan assessments if the government bears the credit risk.

Governments may have public welfare and political incentives to provide deposit or credit guarantees that may undermine private sector market discipline. In particular, during a systemic banking crisis the authorities may be tempted to issue a blanket guarantee. The advantages of such short-term measures must be weighed against the direct cost as well as the future difficulty of re-establishing an incentive structure that will be compatible with a sound system over the long run. Similarly, banks are sometimes declared to be "too big to fail" because it is considered that closing them would carry systemic risks. Although this is occasionally a valid consideration, too often it serves as a convenient excuse to postpone needed actions. Policies that foster an open and competitive banking market can help to create a banking system in which no single bank is too big to fail.

A strong framework regarding bank exit (mergers, closure, and liquidation) is at least as important to a market system as allowing competitive entry, if not more important. In many systems, however, there are few market participants (creditors) capable of forcing exit. This is particularly true when wholesale deposit markets are underdeveloped, as participants in those markets tend to be more sophisticated than the average individual depositor. In systems with less-developed capital markets or concentrated and closely held banking systems, there may be few outside investors capable of influencing bank owners and managers through a

---

[79] This appears to have been the case in the United States; see U.S. House of Representatives (1991).

market for corporate control. The legal and political systems may also prevent creditors' attempts to force the exit of unsound banks; for example, in some countries, the closure of a bank requires the consent of the shareholders. In many countries, bankruptcy procedures are excessively long or are biased against creditors.

Potential Negative Externalities

Exit imposed solely by market forces may produce negative externalities. While an effective withdrawal of funds by the market can result in closure, it will not be a smooth process. A liquidity shortage due to segregation in the interbank market, or a run by depositors, may force the disorderly failure of a bank, with potentially dangerous repercussions. A fire sale of assets may further decrease the bank's net worth. The sequential servicing of deposit withdrawals may impose a socially inefficient distribution of losses and could result in a domino effect if other banks remain exposed. As exposed creditors scramble to cover their positions, depositor confidence may be shaken. If depositors are unable to distinguish problems in an individual bank from systemic conditions, a crisis of confidence and widespread runs may result. Uncertainty will linger until the situation is resolved and may spread throughout the system. As noted above, most markets have difficulty assessing the quality of opaque bank assets, which may lead to pressures on sound banks as well.

Market preferences for liquidity and profit over stability do not take into account the public policy concern for banking system stability. Furthermore, the distribution of losses attendant on a market-led closure may not accord with public preferences. Thus, in most countries there are both limits to how much reliance can be placed on market discipline and limits on the extent to which unfettered operation of market forces is desirable. Additional forms of external oversight and methods to ensure that individual banks fail with minimal systemic impact are required.

One country planning to rely almost entirely on market discipline is New Zealand. The Reserve Bank of New Zealand is moving from a system of detailed rules and monitoring by the supervisor to a system of improved public disclosure of financial information, relaxed supervisory regulation, and enhanced market discipline.[80] It should be noted, however, that only around 10 percent of bank assets in New Zealand are held by locally owned banks. Thus, in this case, even if the authorities did pursue detailed official bank supervision and regulation, it would have little bearing on the risk profile of the banking sector.

---

[80] See Reserve Bank of New Zealand (1995).

9

External Governance:
Regulation and Supervision

The previous chapters have described how the primary responsibility for the oversight of banks lies with their owners and managers; there is no substitute for adequate internal governance. External forces provide additional discipline through financial markets, forcing the exit of poor owners and managers or of the entire bank. There are limits, however, to the efficacy of market forces. To complement internal governance and market discipline, most countries institute some form of official regulatory and supervisory oversight. Particularly in developing and transition economies, where financial market participants are ill-equipped to monitor banks and where the alternatives to domestic banks for payments, savings, or finance are limited or nonexistent, discipline in the form of official supervisory oversight is critical to compensate for failures in internal governance and market discipline.

Banking Regulation

The failures in internal governance and market discipline described above suggest that the standard corporate legal framework is insufficient to ensure that the banking system operates soundly and that any disruptions are handled smoothly. Risk is inherent in banking. Prudential policies, while not panaceas, can attempt to limit risk and make sure that it is managed properly. Many countries therefore have adopted a separate regulatory framework to govern the entry, operation, and exit of banks.[81]

[81] In this discussion, the term "regulation" is used to encompass laws, decrees, regulations, and administrative rules that are intended to regulate (control) bank behavior. Countries' practices with respect to what is established by statute and what is delegated to administrative regulation differ substantially. In general, features considered either fundamental or controversial are established in the law, while rules covering technical and relatively noncontroversial aspects are issued as needed and changed as circumstances require.

Such regulations establish the authority of supervisors to regulate banks and set such detailed requirements as may be necessary to oversee and control bank behavior. They should be structured so as to foster cooperation between regulators of banks and of nonbank financial intermediaries and limit the potential for regulatory arbitrage. Although specific regulatory practices will vary across countries, several broad categories are used to reinforce banks' operating environment, internal governance, and market discipline.

Regulations Reinforcing the Operating Environment

Prudential regulations typically control entry into the banking industry and the scope of banking. Rules governing entry into the industry are needed because some forms of competition from new entrants can be destructive. While liberal entry rules may increase competition and result in lower costs to customers, new banks that are inadequately capitalized, or poorly governed or managed, often offer above-market deposit rates to attract resources and then cover their higher costs with riskier loans. Examples include Spain in the 1970s, Malaysia in the 1980s, and Estonia, Kazakstan, Latvia, Lithuania, and Russia in the 1990s.

At the same time, excessively restrictive entry rules may also result in unsound banks. While concentrated banking systems might be expected to generate significant economic rents, restricting competition rarely improves soundness, as poor corporate governance and management thrive in protected environments. Protected banks become vulnerable to loss and insolvency when faced with unexpected financial developments or when introduced to competition. The appropriate goal of entry regulations is not to protect individual banks by providing them with monopoly rents but to bring about a banking system that efficiently serves the economy and the public interest.

Well-designed licensing procedures ensure that banks entering the system are sound and are operated in a safe and prudent manner, by requiring that a business plan be in place and that owners, directors, and managers be "fit and proper."[82] The ownership structure of a bank as well as its ties to financial or industrial groups must be carefully defined. Furthermore, the bank must have sufficient capital to finance start-up expenses, conduct its intended business on a profitable scale, and safeguard it against unanticipated developments. If the licensing conditions are not met initially or subsequently, the supervisors must have the authority to reject the application or revoke the license.

---

[82] In this context, "fit" refers to technical expertise while "proper" refers to the character and integrity of the individuals.

Regulations also define the industrial structure of banking and the scope of activities that banks may conduct. Rules regarding entry and scope of activities will determine the competitive structure of the banking industry. These will legitimately vary across countries, depending on economic factors, such as the size and diversity of the economy, and institutional factors, such as prevailing industrial structures and attitudes toward antitrust regulation.

Inappropriate restrictions on banking may reduce the soundness and efficiency of the banking system. The more concentrated are bank portfolios, either by client base or region, the more exposed is the banking system to cyclical fluctuations at the sectoral or regional level. For example, the U.S. ban on interstate branching exposed its banks to periodic regional recessions. Agricultural banks failed in the earlier 1980s when commodity prices fell; banks in Texas, Oklahoma, and other states failed when oil prices plummeted; and banks in New England and California became insolvent when the recessions occurred in these regions (in the late 1980s and early 1990s) and property prices fell sharply. Canada, on the other hand, with a more diversified banking sector, survived both the Great Depression and the oil price decline in the mid- to late 1980s without widespread trauma.

Permissible banking activities need to be defined so as to allow adequate diversification of credit risk and the conduct of appropriate related businesses. At the same time, banks' ability to assume excessive risk, for example, through potentially damaging involvement in nonbanking businesses, should be limited. Banks that are permitted to hold large equity positions may become more vulnerable to asset price shocks and exposure to concentrated enterprise risk. There is no basis, however, for an a priori assumption that systems of universal banks are more or less prone to unsoundness.[83]

Regulations Reinforcing Internal Governance

Prudential regulations can provide assurance that owners and managers are fit and proper, that owners share the risks to which they expose their depositors, and that bank portfolio quality and risk-management standards are high. Not only do such regulations provide a formal control over bank behavior, but they also provide a basis for the production of additional information that can be used by owners, supervisors, and the market in disciplining banks.

Because sound banking begins with sound bankers, countries have increasingly adopted regulations designed to assure fit-and-proper

---

[83] The arguments for and against universal banking are beyond the scope of this book. Saunders (1994b) discusses the issues and provides references.

bankers and to improve corporate governance structures. Such regulations require that the roles and responsibilities of boards of directors and senior managers be clearly specified and that the persons appointed be competent to carry out those responsibilities. In this regard, regulators should be authorized to approve shareholders with a controlling interest, directors, and top management of a bank before the bank is licensed and, subsequently, whenever there is a change in significant ownership stakes or in key officers.

The corporate governance of banks is improved, and the potential conflict of interest with depositors is ameliorated, when regulations require that owners put their own capital at risk. Capital adequacy regulations ensure that, as a bank becomes less sound, its owners are required to recapitalize it and that, as the bank becomes undercapitalized, owners lose both their control of the bank and their investment in it. Capital standards must ensure that bank capital is sufficiently great, so that owners have an incentive to do their best to protect their stake and avoid a potential loss. Regulators normally require a certain minimum level of capital for a bank. Supervisors must verify that the capital is real, does not consist of borrowed funds, and is actually paid up in liquid form. Owners should also have incentives to limit the risks they assume. Accordingly, capital adequacy is established increasingly in relation to a risk-weighted asset portfolio, with more capital required against riskier assets.

In 1988, the Basle Committee on Banking Supervision (Basle Committee)[84] agreed to require large internationally active banks to hold capital equal to at least 8 percent of risk-weighted assets, thus preventing banks from unduly increasing credit risk through greater leverage; many countries other than those of the Group of Ten have also adopted the Basle standard. For each bank, owners and managers remain responsible for maintaining adequate capital and reserves and for structuring the bank's portfolio so as to withstand the adverse shocks inherent in the banking business. Most well-managed international banks hold capital substantially in excess of the 8 percent minimum.[85] Comparable resilience in countries where economic volatility is higher than in the Group of Ten countries would require capital considerably higher than 8 percent of risk-weighted assets.

Critical in implementing capital standards is the parallel implementation of appropriate loan-valuation and classification practices and supporting accounting standards. Effective capital standards require proper

---

[84] The Basle Committee members represent the central banks of Group of Ten countries, as well as Luxembourg and Switzerland. The Committee works under the auspices of, but is distinct from, the Bank for International Settlements (BIS).

[85] See "World's 100 Largest Banks," August 1995.

evaluation of a bank's asset quality, which implies that its loan portfolio, contingent commitments, and other off-balance-sheet activities are correctly valued. There are numerous instances of banks being insolvent, despite reporting adequate levels of capital "verified" by external audits, and of banks reporting positive accounting earnings, despite extensive economic losses. Inadequate loan classification and provisioning were factors in at least 11 of the countries in the sample. For example, the audited accounts of the Tanzanian National Bank of Commerce showed positive earnings and capital until 1993/94, despite massive losses that accumulated over seven years, but were only recorded as of the end of 1993/94 (National Bank of Commerce, 1995). Failures of external audit related to the U.S. savings and loan crisis have resulted in lawsuits and judgments against accounting firms that had conducted the external audits of institutions that later failed. Thus, capital standards must be combined with proper valuation standards and requirements that banks classify their loan portfolios and make adequate provisions for nonperforming loans. Whenever such basics are not in place, nominal adherence to international capital adequacy standards will not be meaningful.[86]

Policies restricting insider lending, foreign exchange exposure, and maturity mismatch help check bank management's ability to assume excessive credit, exchange rate, liquidity, and interest rate risk; these policies are described in more detail in Appendix II. Regulations may set specific levels for key indicators (such as credit exposure to insiders and single borrowers, liquidity mismatches, or foreign exchange open positions). Alternatively, regulations may explicitly permit banks' internal risk-management systems to set the appropriate level of exposure, where such systems are in place. For example, in late 1995, the Basle Committee introduced an amendment to its 1988 Capital Accord, recommending that banks be required to hold additional capital according to their exposure to market risk. Market risk may be measured using either a standard model or banks' own risk-assessment models. This approach, along with new disclosure standards, recognizes that financial innovation has made it increasingly easy for banks to radically alter their risk profiles with a few transactions and that new techniques are needed for the official oversight of risk management. Rather than focus on limitations on each type of risk or on the use of each financial instrument, the trend is toward a more comprehensive approach to risk management, stressing the importance of internal governance and the role of market discipline.

The role of prudential policy in supporting internal governance is to ensure that banks institute appropriate internal control procedures, and that managers are knowledgeable about and involved in the risk-

[86] See Dziobek, Frécaut, and Nieto (1995) and Kane (1995).

assessment process. Regulations may set specific standards for internal control, or may allow banks to organize their control systems as they see fit, provided such a system is in place. It is typically required that there be clearly defined internal audit functions and that annual accounts be subjected to external audit. Accounting and audit standards are critical to the ability of managers and owners (as well as the market and supervisors) to detect and correct weaknesses. Certain internal control principles, such as the need for at least two managers (the "four-eyes" principle) or the separation of dealing and back-office functions, may also be regulated. Most details of internal control, however, are usually left to banks' own discretion.

Regulations Reinforcing Market Discipline

Banking laws and regulations can enhance the soundness of, and confidence in, the banking system by ensuring that market participants have as much information as possible to judge the soundness of banks, and that the sanctions imposed by the market can take effect.

Prudential policy can support market discipline by fostering enhanced public disclosure of bank financial information. Adequate disclosure rules can decrease systemic risk by helping to distinguish good from bad banks. Even where corporate laws already require the publication of audited accounts for both financial and nonfinancial enterprises, banking regulations may need to make further specifications as to the standard and form of these accounts, and the specific rules for disclosure. The balance sheets of bank subsidiaries and other related entities should be consolidated so as to make bank activities more transparent; such consolidation should include both international affiliates and domestic groups and companies. With a view to encouraging improvements in reporting on off-balance-sheet activities, the Basle Committee recently has issued recommendations regarding public disclosure of banks' trading and derivatives activities.

A country's legal framework for banks and other companies defines the rights of bank owners, the obligations of banks as debtors, and the rights of banks' creditors. These laws facilitate market discipline by allowing creditors to apply credible pressure and by allowing a market for corporate control to drive out owners and managers who are not maintaining a bank's value. Clear definitions of creditors' rights also facilitate exit of unsound banks; transparency allows bank customers and other creditors to protect their interests during the resolution process. The banking law should establish rules governing the distribution of losses of a failed bank, so as to reduce conflict and speed the liquidation. For example, laws in some countries provide that all creditors share pro rata in the assets of a failed bank. Others establish a hierarchy of priorities for different classes of creditors, in which collateralized claims and depositors' claims usually must be satisfied before those of other creditors.

There is a public policy concern to foster the smooth exit of individual banks to protect the payments system, enhance systemic stability, and avoid negative externalities exerted by the continued functioning of weak banks. Where closure policies are weak and unsound banks are permitted to compete against sound banks, the former often have incentives to survive in the short term by undercutting competitors in an unsustainable way, which can ultimately weaken currently sound banks and increase resolution costs. Therefore, the banking law should also authorize the supervisor to monitor, intervene in, close, and possibly liquidate unsound banks, as discussed below. To carry out their roles and responsibilities successfully, supervisors need to operate in an institutional framework that provides them with access to the information they require to monitor bank condition.

Supervision

Bank supervisors ensure that regulations are enforced, that markets have information at their disposal, and that there is a backstop to internal governance and market discipline. As discussed in Appendix II, supervision is conducted both off-site, by monitoring reports that banks submit to the supervisory authority, and on-site, by actually verifying the adequacy of asset valuations, the accuracy of prudential reports, and the quality of internal controls. Supervisors strive to analyze the financial condition of banks, evaluate management, restrain unsound practices, and force the exit of insolvent banks.[87]

Supervision to Reinforce Internal Governance

Supervision confirms that bank managers are complying with regulations, provides information that owners can use to monitor managers, helps ensure that bank owners and managers are fit and proper, and provides a means for enforcing compliance with banking regulations.

A principal task of on-site supervision is to evaluate the accuracy of a bank's reports and the quality of the bank's asset-valuation systems and ensure that the balance sheet accurately reflects the bank's net worth. On-site inspection should also address the quality of a bank's earnings,

---

[87] Some supervisors use formalized rating systems such as CAMEL (capital, assets, management, earnings, liquidity) or ROCA (risk management, operations, capital, assets) as a summary for this process; see Appendix II.

which are a source of cash flow and liquidity and an indicator of the bank's viability. As mentioned above, profitability and capital provide a reliable picture of total earnings only when adequate provisioning for nonperforming assets has been made and the improper accrual of interest on past-due loans has been removed. While off-site analysis can provide some indications in these areas, only on-site analysis can provide the verification.

Similarly, bank compliance with prudential regulations is monitored by the supervisors through off-site analysis and on-site inspection. The accuracy of reported capital adequacy can only be verified on-site. Exposure to credit, liquidity, interest rate, foreign exchange, and off-balance-sheet risks and adherence to insider lending limits may be revealed by prudential reporting, but it also needs to be verified by audit or inspection. Such supervisory oversight ensures that bank managers and owners have incentives to comply with regulations, and to accurately value assets and off-balance-sheet exposures.

It is increasingly recognized that evaluation of the quality of management and the adequacy of internal controls and internal audit requires on-site inspection, since the market usually cannot adequately assess these aspects of bank operations. Supervisors provide an independent outside assessment. On-site inspection provides supervisors with a view of how management monitors credit, liquidity, market, and foreign exchange risk. Where deficiencies exist, supervisors may require that adequate systems be established to monitor and manage risk and will advise bank managers and owners. In this way, internal governance is supplemented by providing additional monitoring of staff on behalf of managers and of managers on behalf of owners.

Given banks' increasing ability to rapidly change the composition of their portfolios and their risk exposure, it is virtually impossible for any single person within a bank, let alone anyone outside the bank, to accurately value a bank's asset portfolio. Oversight by management, owners, and the market is becoming increasingly dependent on a bank's own internal control systems. The supervisors' contribution to this process is to assess both the quality of management and the adequacy of the policies, procedures, and systems that are used internally to assess, limit, and report on risk. In addition, supervisors are well placed to take a systemic view, and to notice where behavior that may appear rational to each individual bank, such as rapidly growing credit to a particular "hot" sector or credit expansion due to capital inflows, may have heightened systemic risk. In such cases, the supervisor can question banks' asset allocations, call for increased collateral, and encourage managers to take a more careful look at investment decisions. The Hong Kong Monetary Authority (1994) and the U.S. Comptroller of the Currency (Ludwig, 1995), for example, each recently issued a general warning to their banks that bank quality was declining.

Bank owners and managers have a responsibility to ensure that bank operations are consistent with all relevant laws and regulations. However, the law must establish the enforcement authority of supervisors for cases in which bank owners and managers are not in compliance. The law must provide supervisors with the authority they need, including the ability to act without political approval to impose a range of enforcement actions, which might include cease-and-desist orders, fines, removal orders of senior management and directors, and placement of the bank in conservatorship or liquidation. Their authority should enable supervisors to encourage voluntary compliance, punish noncompliance, and compel corrective action.

Supervision to Reinforce Market Discipline

Supervision strengthens market discipline by helping to ensure that accurate information is disclosed to market participants and that weak banks are forced to exit the market. Supervisors may disclose information directly to the market, by releasing aggregate data on the condition of the banking system or on individual banks, or indirectly by verifying the information provided to the market by the bank and its external auditors.

External audits can complement the supervisory process, but they cannot substitute for it. External auditors can evaluate the consistency of accounting methods, the accuracy of financial reports, and the adequacy of internal risk-management systems. This information enhances the ability of the market to judge the soundness of the bank. External auditors, however, are usually hired by, and in some senses beholden to, the bank itself. They may be reluctant to make strong negative statements about an asset or a procedure. Moreover, bank management may not heed the auditors' warnings. For example, Barings's external auditors notified management of deficiencies in internal controls relating to derivatives activities during the 1992 audit.[88] In addition, auditors may not be permitted to report unsafe and unsound practices to the supervisory agency, much less to the markets. In this regard, the International Accounting Standards Committee recommends giving auditors responsibilities to convey adverse information to supervisors, and in recent years, many authorities, including those of the EU, have increased the responsibilities of external auditors.[89] In some cases, supervisors may hire external auditors to provide an independent assessment of a bank.

[88] See the United Kingdom (1995), paragraphs 10.33.
[89] See International Accounting Standards Committee (1995) and the European Union (1995), Article 5.

The type of evaluation done by auditors tends to be backward looking; it assesses whether procedures were followed and repayment schedules met. Few external auditors can be counted upon to have the information or skills to do the forward-looking asset valuation, including projections for particular businesses and the economy as a whole, which is necessary to assess a loan portfolio and evaluate the future prospects of the bank (see Appendix I). On-site supervision can monitor the quality of external auditing and its consistency with the supervisors' assessment of the value of the bank and its assets; however, since supervisory reports are not published, the market can only infer broad supervisory concurrence from the fact that revisions to published audit reports have not been required.

Ideally, a system of prompt corrective actions will prevent banks from becoming insolvent. For example, in 1991, the United States introduced legislation (FDIC Improvement Act) that required supervisors to take prompt corrective action once a bank reaches certain levels of undercapitalization. Regulation and supervision, however, will not prevent banking problems from occurring, and, as explained above, the market will not always respond quickly enough to incipient insolvency.

Supervisory arrangements then must focus on preventing individual bank failures from becoming systemic problems. The continued operation of weak but solvent banks presents systemic dangers, including the potential for destructive competition that could weaken other banks. If a bank does become insolvent, it should be quickly closed and resolved; when this occurs without systemic disruptions, the process of prudential oversight can be deemed to be functioning properly in support of market discipline. As noted earlier, market-led exit involves a first-come, first-served distribution of assets, which may run counter to desired liquidation priorities. Furthermore, a precipitous withdrawal of resources from a single bank could incite a crisis of confidence, which might spread throughout the banking and payments systems.

Thus it is particularly important for supervisory action to be taken to initiate or at least control closure. Closure should certainly occur when a bank becomes insolvent; preferably it would occur earlier, when the bank becomes seriously undercapitalized. Supervisory data often provide the basis for such action. If closure has been initiated by market forces, supervisors should be empowered and prepared to oversee and smooth the process, for example, by closing a bank that is experiencing a run, so as to put in place an orderly liquidation process.

Rapid closure and liquidation usually requires the ability to act outside the standard corporate bankruptcy procedures and without political approval. The banking law should provide the supervisors with the authority to close a bank and to liquidate it. A system of limited deposit insurance can assist the authorities in maintaining some stability and in disposing of insolvent banks, promoting consolidation of creditors by replacing dispersed depositors with the insurance fund as the principal creditor. It can also provide political cover for closure decisions. The desirability of prompt action to enforce corrective measures or initiate the conservatorship, restructuring, or liquidation of troubled banks on strictly technical grounds without political interference reinforces the need for adequate supervisory capacity, authority, and independence, discussed below. Orderly bank failures should be viewed as powerful reminders to other banks that the market system works and that they need to remain sound. Implementing strong exit policies, including intervention before a bank is formally insolvent, would require a change in attitude in many countries. Often the authorities consider bank failures to be evidence of a political or supervisory failure and go to considerable lengths to avoid closure; however, the closure of individual banks without systemic repercussions can be viewed in most cases as evidence that supervision is indeed functioning.

Supervisory Authority and Independence

To function properly, the supervisory agency must have sufficient capacity, authority, and independence. Supervision covers a range of activities and requires adequate human and financial resources. The supervisory agency must have the capacity to provide inputs into legislation, design regulations, evaluate owners and business plans of banks applying for licenses, assess existing banks' net worth and loan-valuation procedures, and analyze the management functions and internal controls of banks. To accomplish these and related tasks, the supervisory agency must be able to attract and retain high-caliber employees and to provide them with the necessary facilities, equipment, and training.

Beyond this basic capacity, the supervisory agency must have sufficient authority, established by law, to carry out its duties. Necessary powers include the authority to request data from banks, to conduct on-site examinations at the supervisor's discretion, and to enforce corrective actions ranging from informal agreements, to cease-and-desist orders, to closure. Supervisors must be able to act against banks without the delays and subversions that result from a need for political approval; their authority to this end must be firmly established, along with legal protection for supervisors who are properly discharging their duties. In cases where the judicial system does not allow a speedy or impartial response, administrative summary procedures may be required.

The efficiency and integrity of the oversight process is hampered when the supervisory agency is not independent. Supervisory actions are often unpopular. The supervisory agency should be institutionally structured to have sufficient independence to carry out its day-to-day operations without interference. In many countries, this also means that the supervisory agency should have its own source of funding so that it cannot be held hostage to politically motivated budget battles; such funding may come from levies on banks being supervised. To ensure institutional independence, provide adequate information flows between the supervisory agency and the lender of last resort, and assure proper consideration of banking system soundness objectives in the broader policy mix, the supervisory agency is most commonly located within the central bank.

Alternative arrangements that constitute the supervisory agency as a separate administrative unit of government can also be appropriate; to a great extent, the location of the supervisory agency in different countries depends on historical, social, and political factors. Countries with different institutional structures have been able to construct effective supervisory systems. It should be noted, though, that supervisory agencies subordinated to a government ministry have often lost their ability to act independently, particularly when the government stands to bear the costs of bank closures or other supervisory actions. Supervision generally has greater independence of action if it is not a part of the government.[90]

Regardless of its institutional location, it is clear that the supervisory agency must develop a close working relationship with the central bank. This is necessary because the central bank requires supervisory information to back its decisions as lender of last resort and because the central bank should provide the supervisor with information on macroeconomic policy and overall conditions in the banking system.

The concept of supervisory independence should encompass prudential regulations, the application of which should be independent of monetary management. Prudential regulations are not monetary instruments to be varied over the business cycle in an effort to control domestic liquidity or to promote recovery from a general or sectoral economic slowdown. Using them in such a way could result in conflicts between supervisory and monetary authorities, reduce the long-term safety of the banking system, and create the mistaken impression that flexibility in the compliance with prudential regulations is acceptable. Rather, minimum regulatory standards should be established so as to keep banks sound regardless of the phase of the business cycle.[91]

Should a decline in general economic conditions cause a particular bank to have difficulty in complying with regulatory standards, the authorities may deem it appropriate to agree on a compliance program with that

---

[90] See Tuya and Zamalloa (1994).

[91] The initial implementation of prudential regulations may have short-term macroeconomic effects; the need for phasing in such regulations is discussed below.

bank; in so doing, they would closely supervise the bank's operations and monitor its progress toward meeting the regulatory standards. This need not imply a generalized relaxation of such standards. On the other hand, in periods of rapid growth in bank assets, increased monitoring of lending to high-risk sectors is in order. This may result in calls to stabilize or reduce exposure to such sectors, or in stricter collateralization rules. Such a tightening of prudential oversight is fully consistent with the supervisor's responsibility to take an overall view of banking sector developments and to act to maintain soundness when necessary.

10

Challenges Confronting Regulation and Supervision

The design and implementation of regulatory and supervisory policies for banks present a number of challenges, including the need to carefully direct policy toward legitimate and achievable objectives and the potential for conflicts of interest at a number of levels. All too often legislators, regulators, or supervisors fail to meet these challenges adequately. For example, politicians may be tempted to use the banking system to achieve social objectives they are unwilling to fund overtly in the budget, but which may prejudice bank soundness. Poorly designed incentive structures may encourage bank supervisors to pursue career interests that detract from bank soundness. Furthermore, bank regulations frequently have a macroeconomic impact. The authorities may legitimately phase in significant escalations of regulations to moderate their impact and give banks time to adjust to the new environment. It is not appropriate, however, to adjust prudential regulations in an attempt to use them as macroeconomic policy instruments.

Regulatory Failure

Regulations may fail by being too lax, too intrusive, poorly designed, or inadequately implemented. Regulatory failure in some form was a factor in all of the countries in our sample, with the possible exception of Kuwait (see Table 16). Where regulations are insufficiently strict or comprehensive, the solution is clear. Correcting a situation of regulatory capture, which occurs when regulators or legislators are allied with banking interests, is likely to be difficult, but here too the prescription is clear. On the other hand, banking regulations may also be too intrusive, raising the cost of compliance and reducing bank efficiency and the scope for innovation.

Bank behavior is often dictated by regulations that are more quasi-fiscal than prudential. For example, laws in some countries require banks to

Table 16. Deficiencies in Regulation and Supervision[1]

Argentina (1980–82): Changes in the regulatory framework lagged behind liberalization, and certain favored loans were excluded from capital requirements. Prudential regulations were fairly comprehensive, but the supervisory agency lacked resources to keep up with the growth in the financial sector. Supervisors checked compliance rather than credit quality, ceased conducting on-site inspections in the years before the crisis, and lacked strong exit powers.

(1989–90): Supervision remained weak and allowed banks to grow rapidly before the crisis. Reserve requirements were very high.

(1995): The system had too many smaller banks because entry was easy. Supervisors allowed banks to grow rapidly before the crisis.

Bangladesh (1980s–present): Prudential oversight needs many improvements; monitoring compliance with loan classification and provisioning rules is especially weak, as are exit policies.

Bolivia (1994–present): The supervisory agency has adequate information; however, the implementation and enforcement of regulations are inadequate, especially the requirements regarding liquidity and loan classification and provisioning.

Brazil (1994–present): The central bank's powers to remove management and apply corrective actions were limited until November 1995, when new legislation was enacted. Weaknesses in the regulatory and supervisory structure are being addressed by the authorities.

Chile (1981–86): Lax supervision allowed interlocking ownership patterns (with connected lending accounting for 21% of outstanding loans at the 5 largest banks in 1982) and facilitated excessive risk taking and unsound lending practices (including the fast accumulation of short-term debt and "distress borrowing"). Prudential regulations were also weak—loan classification and financial ratings were only introduced in 1980–82.

Czech Republic (1991–present): Following the transition from a monobank system, prudential regulations were put in place, but their implementation had to be tightened in 1994.

Egypt (1991–95): Banking supervision and regulation have improved substantially since 1991.

Estonia (1992–95): Licensing was weak—the capital requirements for new banks were inadequate and other prudential regulations were lacking. Supervision was inadequate and allowed fast growth, risky portfolios, insider lending, and inadequate loan classification and provisioning.

Finland (1991–94): Supervision under the Ministry of Finance lagged behind deregulation and, until 1991, lacked authority and resources. The supervisory agency checked compliance with rules rather than risk management and did not supervise savings or cooperative banks.

France (1991–95): Although the laws, regulations and enforcement powers were adequate, and although the supervisor (the Commission Bancaire) has the authority, skills, and resources it needs, its effectiveness is being questioned. The supervisor was aware of Crédit Lyonnais's problems in 1991 but did not disclose them until the first rescue in 1993 and then allowed them to continue so that a second rescue was needed

Table 16 *(continued)*

in 1995. For example, Crédit Lyonnais was allowed to grow rapidly and to assume risky exposures in real estate and to a few large borrowers. In general, however, there is no political interference in supervision.

Ghana (1983–89): There was an inadequate legal, regulatory, and supervisory framework that did not include capital adequacy, loan provisioning, and other key requirements. The insufficient supervisory capacity left most banks unexamined and allowed one bank to operate with an unclear legal status.

Hungary (1987–present): A prudential and regulatory system has been established but is hampered by weak accounting and fragmentation.

Indonesia (1992–present): Prudential regulations broadly conforming to Basle standards were introduced in 1991, but enforcement is uneven and a system for resolving failed banks has yet to be developed. For example, shareholders' consent is needed to close a bank.

Japan (1992–present): Foreclosures are difficult; the authorities lack the power to close failing banks without shareholders' consent or a court order. Credit cooperatives were supervised by the authorities in the prefectures, but supervision was inadequate. The Ministry of Finance applied forbearance between 1993 and 1995 to insolvent credit cooperatives.

Kazakstan (1991–95): Too many new licenses have been issued. Bank closures are taking place, but supervision is understaffed, loan classification and provisioning is very recent, and provisions are not tax deductible. There is a lack of standards for risk diversification and connected lending.

Kuwait (1990–91): Bank supervision was strengthened following the banking collapse associated with problems in the informal stock market in 1982 and was further strengthened in 1993–95.

Latvia (1995–present): Liberal licensing requirements and lax supervision allowed a proliferation of unsound banks. Enforcement of prudential regulations and exit policy was inadequate.

Lithuania (1995–present): There is insufficient implementation of all prudential regulations, particularly capital adequacy. Enforcement of exit policies has been difficult.

Malaysia (1985–88): Supervision was slow in dealing with the problems that developed, partly because responsibility was split between the Ministry of Finance and the central bank. There was a lack of regulations dealing with loans to single and connected borrowers, suspension of interest, loan classification and provisioning, reporting consolidated positions and authority to effect exit and take enforcement actions. Supervision was much weaker for nonbank financial institutions and illegal deposit-taking institutions were allowed to operate.

Mexico (1994–present): Supervisory and regulatory standards were weak. There were no limits on credits to related parties, until they were introduced in 1992 and 1994.

Norway (1987–93): Capital regulations were weak. Supervision lacked resources and lagged behind deregulation; it monitored compliance with reserve requirements rather than credit quality and avoided closing banks. The situation worsened when the supervisory agency was merged with the insurance regulator in 1986, in a process that preoccupied the staff and diverted them from on-site inspections, which almost ceased. There were also problems with staffing because of low salaries.

Table 16 *(continued)*

Pakistan (1980–present): Supervision, which has staffing problems, focuses on formal compliance with legal and administrative issues. Prudential analysis remains embryonic.

Paraguay (1995–present): Rules for loan classification and provisioning have been partially implemented but they were long delayed. The supervisor has inadequate exit powers, and there is political interference in the supervision process.

Philippines (1981–87): Prudential regulations regarding capital adequacy, connected lending, and relations between a bank and its subsidiaries were relaxed and, even then, were not enforced in the years before the crisis. Reforms were delayed and regulations were not enforced because of the political climate. Fast loan growth and heavy insider lending resulted. Accounting standards, loan classification and provisioning rules, and exit policies were inadequate.

Poland (1991–present): Too many new licenses were issued. Improved laws and regulations have been introduced, but they are not yet fully effective. There is now both off- and on-site supervision.

Russia (1992–present): An adequate supervisory framework exists although improved coordination between on-site and off-site supervision is needed and some further modification in prudential regulations is necessary. For example, restrictions on insider lending, correspondent banking, and foreign exchange exposure are inadequate. Enforcement of supervisory regulations is lax and exit legislation is inadequate.

Spain (1977–85): Licensing was relaxed. Supervision was antiquated and had not kept up with deregulation; it checked compliance with regulations rather than credit quality. Prudential regulations were inadequate and yet were eased before the crisis. Those that remained were not enforced.

Sweden (1990–93): The large exposure regulations on loans to one borrower were insufficient and there were no regulations to restrain foreign borrowing. Bank closure was subject to the general corporate bankruptcy code. Bank supervision lagged deregulation and it allowed fast growth and risky asset portfolios.

Tanzania (1988–present): Prudential regulations were weak; supervision was lax and concentrated on compliance with credit allocation plans rather than financial condition. There was inadequate loan classification and provisioning.

Thailand (1983–87): The regulatory system was inflexible and subject to political influence. Inadequate licensing practices allowed concentrated ownership with conflicts of interest and undiversified portfolio composition. Supervisory responsibility was split between the central bank and the Ministry of Finance. The Ministry of Finance lacked strong exit and enforcement powers. There was lax oversight of capital adequacy and loan classification and provisioning. Unpaid interest was capitalized. Bank regulations were relaxed before the crisis and, even then, they were not enforced. There were no on-site inspections and no consolidated oversight.

Turkey (1994): Problems of coordination between the Ministry of Finance and the central bank impeded effective prudential oversight. Regulations on open foreign exchange positions and accounting standards were inadequate. The supervisory system needed improved instruments for dealing with problem banks and was unable to enforce rules on connected lending, which was often hidden in subsidiaries.

Table 16 *(concluded)*

United States (1980–92): Regulation and supervision were adequate for banks for the most part although prompt corrective action requirements were lacking until 1991. Prudential regulation and supervision lagged deregulation in the thrift industry and were seriously deficient, encouraging savings and loans to hide their insolvency and continue operating in the hopes that they would "grow" out of their problems by taking more deposits and undertaking newly provided activities. There was political interference in the supervision of the thrift industry.

Venezuela (1994–present): Laws, regulations, and enforcement, especially regarding capital, loan classification, and provisioning were weak. Supervision lacked resources and basic tools, checked compliance rather than solvency, and did not conduct consolidated oversight, with the result that financial groups were able to hide problems. Under the 1995 Financial Emergency Law, most key supervisory decisions, such as revocation of licenses and requiring recapitalization, must be approved by the Financial Emergency Board, which is outside the supervisory agency.

Zambia (1994–present): An inadequate prudential framework was improved in 1994. Licensing requirements, however, continued to be deficient. Supervisors lack authority to discipline or close problem banks.

---

[1] Years in parentheses denote the period of banking problems.

---

extend loans that would otherwise not be extended, by designating priority sectors or mandating "community reinvestment" requirements.[92] Liquid asset ratios and similar portfolio regulations may require banks to lend to the government or other entities that issue eligible assets, often at below-market yields. Sectoral lending priorities or creating a particular type of banking system (e.g., a system composed of small local banks) is usually politically dictated, with the intent of achieving some social objectives. Interest rate controls may also be imposed in pursuit of certain resource allocation goals. These objectives may be achieved, but often at the expense of distorted prices, impeded market development, and increased bank fragility. Government development and social welfare policies are better handled transparently through budgetary allocations rather than by imposing regulations that could impair bank soundness.

The pursuit of economic efficiency along with banking system stability requires careful review of regulatory and supervisory policies to see that they are in line with the environment and enhance, rather than reduce, bank soundness and market discipline.[93] The international trend toward deregulation and financial liberalization reflects the experience that macroeconomic and allocative controls on bank behavior tend to be inef-

---

[92] Priority sectors may be favored domestic industries, or classes of citizens (as in Malaysia); for a discussion of community reinvestment requirements in the United States, see Benston (1986).

[93] This has been referred to as "market-friendly supervision" (Padoa-Schioppa, 1995).

fective and inefficient.[94] However, microeconomic efficiency (and private profit) may at times usefully be traded for stability (and public benefit) through prudential or consumer protection regulation; such stability enhances overall market efficiency. At the same time, these regulations should not remove the market's incentive to monitor bank behavior, by creating excessive deposit guarantees or by interfering so strongly in banking activities that the public infers an implicit government backing for the banks. Similarly, regulations must not shelter banks from healthy competition or from the market for corporate control. For example, Prowse (1995) presents evidence that the effectiveness of board intervention and of hostile takeovers as disciplinary mechanisms was reduced for U.S. banks relative to manufacturing companies and attributes this in part to banking regulation.

In many jurisdictions, different parts of domestic financial conglomerates are supervised by different authorities. Which institutions and activities are subject to banking laws needs to be carefully defined, so that the possibility for regulatory arbitrage among domestic regulators of banks and other financial institutions is limited.

Supervisory Failure

Supervisory failure usually takes the form of forbearance—an adjustment in the interpretation of rules to accommodate problem banks or a failure to act in a timely manner to prevent or address unsound banking. This can occur for a number of reasons. Supervisors may not have the ability to act independently, because of inadequate organizational structure or direct political interference. Where the political will to enforce regulations and supervisory standards is missing, supervision is unlikely to succeed in keeping the banking system sound. Some form of supervisory failure was a factor in almost all of the sample countries (Table 16).

Supervisors in some countries develop longstanding relationships with the banks they oversee. Such supervisors are subject to regulatory capture, a process in which the supervisor identifies more closely with the banking industry than with the public interest, and may see his role as protecting, rather than disciplining, the banking industry.[95]

Because the public often perceives the supervisor's only role as preventing bank failures rather than as ensuring the exit of weak banks so as to maintain systemic soundness, supervisors may be reluctant to close banks.

---

[94] See Vittas (1992).

[95] In countries where supervisors routinely find employment in the banking sector after leaving the public sector, regulations must be in place to address potential conflicts of interest. Williams (1996) indicates that this was a problem in Japan.

Supervisory accountability may be lacking, particularly when supervision is part of a bureaucracy in which responsibility for taking tough decisions is not clearly allocated. In addition, political interference may prevent intervention in a bank.

A common reaction to the emergence of banking distress is for the authorities to adopt a "wait-and-see" attitude, hoping that the difficulties are temporary, that no serious threat to the financial system is posed, and that any problems will either resolve themselves or remain submerged until after someone else takes office. This can occur where supervisory systems are not sufficiently independent or are underfunded and lack qualified staff; consequently, authorities are wary of taking potentially controversial decisions. Forbearance, delay, or cover-up may be abetted by ambiguous assignment of responsibility and a lack of accountability. It can also occur in well-developed systems where authorities have become more concerned about their reputation for overseeing a system with no visible difficulties than about resolving banking problems. Deposit insurance may further exacerbate the problem by removing pressure from depositors as a potential spur to action.[96]

Delay in addressing unsound banks is rarely effective and usually detrimental. Unsound banks continue to operate, weakening initially sound competitors and increasing the likelihood of systemic difficulties. Furthermore, unsound banks tend to take on even more risk or may be looted by insiders, which ultimately increases resolution costs.

Supervisory failure may also result in weakened effectiveness of regulation. Supervisors, sometimes under political pressure, may try to keep a banking system afloat by lowering capital standards, by allowing continued unfettered operation with less-than-adequate capital, or by permitting increased risk exposure. This in turn may delay corrective actions until after a bank has become insolvent. Despite this, supervisors in several countries have relaxed or failed to strengthen valuation and accounting standards when banks were weak, ostensibly to give the banks time to grow out of their problems. For example, U.S. regulators adopted accounting standards that disguised insolvency during the savings and loan debacle (United States, General Accounting Office, 1985). Accounting procedures obscured the true condition of Japanese banks and thrifts; corrective measures were first promised by the Bankers' Association, rather than the supervisors ("Japan," November 1995). In these and other cases, delay exacerbated unsoundness.

Systems in which supervisors either do not promulgate regulations independently or enforce those regulations unfailingly often result in the

---

[96] See Allen and Saunders (1993).

continued operation of weak, undercapitalized banks. Banking laws can be written, however, so as to limit the possibility of supervisory failure. The law should be flexible enough to allow the supervisors to apply successively more stringent corrective measures, while being firm enough to limit supervisory forbearance. It should also protect supervisors acting professionally, and limit lawsuits or other actions against them. Rules governing prompt corrective actions to be taken against banks that are not complying with the laws and regulations should be established in the law. Even with such provisions in place, there are limits to what regulation and supervision can accomplish.

Market participants will always be changing and innovating, and testing the limits of legality and prudence. Regulators and supervisors will almost always be a few steps behind, trying to adapt rules and supervisory procedures to the latest financial products and developments in financial markets. Innovation and capital market liberalization have made it easier for banks to circumvent existing regulations on net foreign exchange positions and leverage. Liberalization also makes it possible for banks to blind supervisors to their risk taking by engaging in complex offshore activities especially when conducted through derivative instruments. For example, Mexican banks' use of structured notes and other offshore transactions to weaken the impact of domestic financial regulations is often cited as a factor contributing to the pressure on the peso in late 1994.

In general, supervisors will not be able to anticipate sufficiently to outengineer the financial engineers. At the same time, other market participants will often have insights that supervisors lack. Supervision and regulation must therefore work alongside, and encourage, dynamic market and internal forces. Thus prudential regulation and supervision should be viewed as just one part of a comprehensive system of guidance and incentives influencing bank behavior; the system must also include market discipline and strong internal governance.

Macroeconomic Effects of Prudential Regulations

As explained earlier, bank activities affect macroeconomic conditions, particularly in the monetary area. Prudential policies and regulations that delimit bank activities will therefore have macroeconomic implications. Much of the concern in this area has been over strengthening capital requirements, which, it has been argued, could reduce bank lending and slow economic growth. Other prudential regulations, however, may also have a macroeconomic impact. This does not represent a form of regulatory or supervisory failure and does not argue for suspension of such regulations. The macroeconomic impact of prudential policies can be anticipated, and implementation of such policies can be adjusted accordingly.

Capital Standards

A frequently cited example of the influence of prudential policies on monetary and macroeconomic conditions is the impact of the 1988 Basle capital standards on credit conditions in the major industrial countries. There was a slowdown in credit growth in a number of countries during 1988–91, which appears to have lengthened or worsened cyclical downturns. It is likely the case that this slowdown, referred to as a "credit crunch," was in part the result of the increase in capital that banks were required to hold against assets. Banks apparently responded to the new capital requirements by reducing the volume of credit extended or by increasing their interest margins to build up own capital.

It is difficult to fully substantiate whether capital constraints contributed to the credit slowdown, however, since the demand and supply schedules for loans are not directly observable.[97] While the contribution of capital adequacy requirements to the U.S. credit crunch of 1988–91 cannot be isolated,[98] some studies have found evidence that growth in lending by U.S. banks that were constrained by the new capital standards was slower than the growth of lending by better capitalized banks.[99] On the other hand, the Bank of England concluded that the U.K. credit slowdown resulted from decreased borrowing capacity and banks' concern to tighten standards and improve profitability, rather than from problems in meeting the international capital adequacy standard.[100] Japanese banks widened their margins and adopted a more restrictive lending stance from 1988 to 1991, but observers differ as to whether or not wider bank margins reduced the macroeconomic impact of looser monetary policy, and whether the reduction in credit was due to a capital constraint or was mainly demand driven.[101] Thus the evidence is mixed, but there is some theoretical and empirical support for a capital-induced credit crunch.

Capital adequacy requirements can affect credit expansion in two distinct ways: they compel banks to build up sufficient capital at the time when ratios are initially imposed, and they compel banks to reduce risk assets when the capital constraint becomes binding. To some extent, these rules reinforce what should occur naturally. Banks should maintain adequate capitalization to support the risks they assume. A credit crunch surrounding a rise in capital requirements should be transitory, and may reflect other distortions (such as a real estate bubble) that have resulted in overextension that is difficult to reverse to meet a higher capital-to-asset

---

[97] See Goldstein and others (1992), Chapter III.
[98] See for example, Cantor and Wenninger (1993).
[99] Brinkmann and Horvitz (1995).
[100] Bank of England (1991).
[101] See Fairlamb (1994) and Shinagawa (1993).

ratio. If default rates rise in an economic downturn, capital will be reduced. Total assets will also decline as loans are written off, but the loss in asset-carrying capacity will be greater owing to the leveraging of bank capital—if a loan of 100 is written off, minimum required capital would decline by 8 but actual capital would decline by the full 100.

The effects of an economic downturn on bank assets will result in reduced capital due to loan write-offs. Thus the effects of minimum capital ratios tend to be procyclical, binding during recessions and asset price depressions;[102] however, capital adequacy ratios will also dampen volatility in the longer term. Thus, discussion of the effects of the Basle Capital Accord needs also to take into account the timing of implementation. Had stricter capital standards been applied in the early 1980s, a larger capital cushion would have been available to absorb losses later in the decade, and capital might not have become a binding constraint on credit growth.[103]

Other Prudential Instruments

Concern for macroeconomic effects extends also to other regulatory and prudential instruments, including liquidity, interest exposure, foreign exchange exposure, loan limits, and other prudential standards. These may constrain banks' asset allocation, resulting in higher costs or reduced income, and increasing interest rate spreads. For example, a number of historical periods of tight money in the United States have been linked to regulatory action, in particular to actions regulating interest rates.[104] If prudential regulations require banks to hold more liquid assets, and these yield less than other assets the bank might have chosen, the reduced income will be reflected in wider spreads.[105] Loan-loss provisioning will similarly increase bank expenses and contribute to wider spreads.

Excessively stringent regulations may be cause for concern. However, to the extent that prudential regulations merely force a recognition of the true costs of doing business safely, the higher price paid by borrowers and the lower yield to depositors do not mean that regulation has created additional costs for banks. Rather, wider interest rate spreads reflect a shifting of costs from the deposit insurer or lender of last resort and to the consumers of banking services.

[102] See Goodhart (1995) and Blum and Hellwig (1995).

[103] In addition, the asset price inflation that resulted in those losses might not have occurred to the same degree; see Alexander and Caramazza (1994). Cantor and Wenninger (1993) present views that the regulatory failure lay in not containing the excesses of earlier years.

[104] Romer and Romer (1993).

[105] Reserve requirements may also have an impact on both banks and the macroeconomy (see, for example, Chari, Jones, and Manuelli (1995) and Spiegel (1995)); however, reserve requirements should be considered monetary rather than prudential instruments, even though they overlap liquidity rules to some extent.

Regulations may have spillover effects on other financial instruments. Prudential rules on liquidity management by commercial banks typically also affect the demand for, and yield of, liquid assets such as treasury bills and commercial paper. In addition to the possible impact of systemwide regulations on bank lending and interest rates, actions taken to limit the activities of certain banks may also have an impact. For example, supervisory intervention to limit deposit acquisition by weak banks may remove a source of upward interest rate pressure and reduce credit growth. The actual effects of prudential regulations will ultimately depend on the particular circumstances of the banking system and the economy as a whole.

Cyclical Adjustment of Prudential Regulations

Prudential policies should be devoted to creating a framework for sound banks rather than diverted to cyclical demand management. Therefore, prudential requirements should not be viewed as an additional monetary policy tool. While regulations could potentially be adjusted over time to produce procyclical or countercyclical effects on the economy, such an approach to prudential regulation is likely to introduce conflicts of interest within the central bank and weaken the banking system in the long run. For example, expansionary policy could be reinforced by reducing capital requirements.[106] This policy tool, however, could be difficult to reverse, with the result that over time the banking system could tend toward lower levels of capital and greater risk of insolvency.

It has been argued that in some circumstances prudential regulations could weaken the effectiveness of monetary policy instruments. For example, a stimulatory monetary policy may be less effective when capital adequacy regulations constrain bank credit expansion, since the central bank can control access to, or the cost of, borrowed funds, but does not control the supply of bank capital.[107] While that is true, there are many aspects of credit creation that the central bank cannot control, such as the supply of bankable projects and the credit-screening process. Central banks normally do not seek to control these aspects of credit creation, since it is not desirable to expand the supply of questionable credit.

Arguments against maintaining strict prudential standards on monetary management grounds focus excessively on short-term considerations. The central bank should not seek to expand the supply of credit based on an insecure capital foundation. During periods of economic stress, banks should be encouraged not only to maintain the minimum level of capital, but to build up additional capital if possible, for example, by refraining

---

[106] This is suggested by Goodhart (1995).
[107] See Brockelmann (1995).

from paying dividends. In the medium to long term, there is no inconsistency in striving for effective monetary control, strong banks, and sound prudential policies. In fact, an effective system of prudential regulations that fosters a sound banking system will increase the flexibility and effectiveness of monetary policy instruments, which should enhance monetary control in a reasonably stable economy.

Transitional Arrangements in Raising Prudential Standards

Understanding the potential short-run effects of raising prudential standards leads to a policy approach that recognizes that any changes in prudential regulations should be phased to take account of the capacity of the banking system to adjust and of broader macroeconomic trends. An increase or decrease in capital adequacy ratios can leave the banking system starved of or flush with capital. Either could cause problems, depending on current and prospective macroeconomic conditions. For this reason, the Basle Capital Accord was phased in over a period of four years. Similarly, the introduction of new or higher liquidity, interest exposure, loan limits, and other prudential standards needs to be undertaken with due regard for the short-term effects on the banking system and the monetary stance. Prudential policies should be tightened gradually. Any forbearance that may be required must be monitored and phased out under an enforceable compliance timetable.

11

International Governance

The internationalization of banking has created additional concerns in a number of areas. Individual banks operate in multiple jurisdictions and even banks operating from a single jurisdiction may have extensive international risk exposure. Three key concerns arise. First, the complicated corporate structure of international banks and the fact that operations are often based in different jurisdictions make supervision difficult. Second, the portability of many banking transactions may provide opportunities for some institutions to engage in regulatory arbitrage by officially recording transactions in the jurisdiction with the least onerous regulatory regime. This can result in a bank taking on excessive risk, which may be poorly monitored because of the difficulty in supervising international banks. It may also lead to competitive deregulation among jurisdictions eager to see their financial sectors grow. Ill-considered deregulation could result in systemic weakness. Finally, the extent of international linkages between banks and banking systems makes it more and more likely that any significant banking crisis will have international or global dimensions.

As there is no recognized international supervisory authority, responses to these issues have taken the form of bilateral arrangements, multilateral agreements in a few areas, and efforts at coordination on the part of international organizations.

International Cooperation to Reinforce the Operating Environment

Even in an era of global finance, the framework for banking is still country specific and may be enforced by different authorities both within and between countries. For example, foreign branches may be supervised by home-country supervisors using criteria different from those used by host-country supervisors. Just as the domestic operating environment may provide opportunities for regulatory arbitrage between financial institutions subject to different regulatory regimes, international differences in laws, accounting standards, supervisory rules, and exit procedures provide scope for such arbitrage. Regulatory arbitrage can result in competition among banks on an unequal basis and in decreased effectiveness of supervision as financial activities will tend to shift to jurisdictions where oversight is the most lax.

International harmonization of regulatory and supervisory standards can improve the operating environment for banks that are internationally active by simplifying banks' operations in an increasingly integrated international economy. Harmonization can make easier the conduct of consolidated supervision of domestic banks operating abroad, improve the oversight of foreign banks' local operations, and bring additional discipline to local regulatory structures. Harmonization also removes the incentives for competitive deregulation or regulatory arbitrage.

The Basle Committee has played a leading role in international efforts toward supervisory cooperation and regulatory harmonization.[108] The Basle Committee was established at the end of 1974 by the central bank governors of the industrial countries comprising the Group of Ten, in response to the growing awareness of the need to improve international supervisory collaboration, made more acute by the Herstatt and Franklin National Bank crises (Freeland, 1994, and Thompson, 1994). In particular, a lack of internationally coordinated supervision allowed the failure of Bankhaus Herstatt in 1974 to spill over to banks in the United States.

The first significant agreement by the Basle Committee, the 1975 Basle Concordat, was an attempt to clarify the operating environment for banks by establishing a set of principles governing the way in which the supervision of banks' foreign branches, subsidiaries, and joint ventures is carried out. As subsequently revised (see Box 1), the Basle Concordat attempts to ensure that no institution escapes adequate supervision. It should be noted, however, that not all countries participate in or fully implement the Basle Concordat, and that it did not avoid coordination problems when BCCI, Meridien, and Barings failed.

In the context of the EU,[109] a broader effort to harmonize the operating environment of banks across countries has been made. The European Economic Community treaty recognized that the liberalization of capital movements would be necessary to ensure the proper functioning of the common market. Since 1977, the EU has adopted a series of banking directives; these directives oblige EU member states to adapt their nation-

---

[108] Dale (1994) discusses the evolution of international efforts from cooperation to harmonization.

[109] The banking rules of the EU are applied also in the countries of the European Economic Area, comprising all EU member states, plus Iceland, Norway, and Liechtenstein. The rules are therefore applicable in a banking market of 370 million people.

Box 1. The Basle Concordat

The Basle Committee's first priority was to discuss modalities for international cooperation in closing gaps in the supervisory net for international banks and in improving supervisory understanding and the quality of banking supervision worldwide. Its approach was based on two basic principles: that no foreign banking establishment should escape supervision and that supervision should be adequate.

The original Concordat, entitled "Report on the Supervision of Banks' Foreign Establishments," was published in September 1975. It is a set of broad guidelines demarcating responsibilities among national supervisory authorities for banks' foreign branches, subsidiaries, and joint ventures: supervising liquidity should be the primary responsibility of host authorities, while supervising solvency should be the responsibility of home authorities for branches, and of host authorities for subsidiaries.

In May 1983, a revised Concordat on "Principles for the Supervision of Banks' Foreign Establishments" replaced the 1975 text. It incorporates the principle of consolidated supervision and fills some gaps in the supervision of international banks that appeared in some countries, especially offshore banking centers. In April 1990, a "Supplement to the Concordat" was issued to define more clearly how the Concordat was to be implemented in practice, seeking to ensure that adequate information flows between supervisory authorities. In July 1992, following the BCCI incident, the Basle Committee issued more stringent "minimum standards" to reinforce the Concordat.

Note: Prepared by Olivier Frécaut, Monetary and Exchange Affairs Department.

---

al legislation. The First Banking Directive of 1977 establishes the principle of mandatory licensing and sets common basic licensing requirements. The Second Banking Directive (1989) addresses a range of minimum standards, and provides that an institution authorized in one member state can operate in all member states. Along with this "single banking license" principle, other measures to establish harmonized standards of operation, minimum cover for deposit insurance, and the exercise of banking supervision on a consolidated basis have strengthened and unified the operating framework for banking across the EU.

The global framework for financial markets has also been considered in the context of payment system development. International initiatives in this area have been advanced by a number of public and private organizations and groups. Many of the major—and most broadly accepted—initiatives have been led by the Group of Experts on Payment Systems and subsequently by the Committee on Payment and Settlement Systems of the Central Banks of the Group of Ten Countries. Their work has included proposals to minimize foreign exchange settlement risk, as well as risks arising in domestic payments and securities transfer systems. This has included proposing standards for domestic currency and foreign exchange netting systems.[110] In addition, the United Nations Commission on International Trade Law has done considerable work on model laws on credit transfers, while the EU Working Committee on EU Payments Systems has worked on the minimum common features for domestic payment systems within the EU, as well as on the design of both domestic and pan-EU, real-time, gross-settlement systems.[111]

International Cooperation to Reinforce Internal Governance

The most important initiative to reinforce internal governance internationally has been the widespread implementation of minimum capital adequacy standards. While many countries have individually established capital adequacy standards, the most prominent international standard and the primary vehicle for harmonization in this area is the Basle Capital Accord, discussed earlier. While most countries are not bound by the Accord, many have adopted the same standards, and it is doubtless that the attention focused on the issue of capital adequacy by the international agreement has facilitated widespread re-examination of existing standards in many countries other those of the Group of Ten.

Again, in the context of the EU, a broader range of initiatives to reinforce internal governance has been taken. For example, the First Banking Directive requires that "there shall be at least two persons who effectively direct the business of the credit institution." (European Union, 1977, Article 3). Subsequent directives have set concrete conduct of business standards for banks. The minimum level of initial capital has been set at ECU 5 million. A risk-weighted capital adequacy ratio of 8 percent is applied. Banks' holdings of equity in individual nonfinancial institutions are limited to 15 percent of the bank's capital, with the total of such holdings limited to 60 percent of capital. Large exposures to a single borrow-

---

[110] The main initiatives regarding foreign exchange settlement risks were presented in "Report on Netting Schemes" (February 1989), "Report of the Committee on Interbank Netting Schemes" (November 1990), "Central Bank Payment and Settlement Services with Respect to Cross-Border and Multi-Currency Transactions" (September 1993), and "Report of the Steering Group on Settlement Risk in Foreign Exchange Transactions" (March 1996). The main initiatives regarding risks in domestic payments and securities transfer systems were presented in "Delivery Versus Payment in Securities Settlement Systems" (September 1992).

[111] Their main proposals are presented in "Report to the Council of the European Monetary Institute on the TARGET System" (May 1995) and "Minimum Common Features for Domestic Payment Systems" (November 1993).

er or connected group of borrowers are limited to 25 percent of the bank's capital, with an aggregate maximum of 800 percent of capital.

Standards to limit market risk and money laundering have been set on an EU-wide basis. In addition, member states are obliged to exercise supervision over the internal control and accounting systems, although no concrete standards have been set in this area; the actual standards are set by the individual member states. In the context of the bank-licensing process, member states are also obliged to apply fitness and propriety tests to prospective bank managers and to assess the suitability of shareholders. These requirements must be complied with by the banks at all times, not only at the time of licensing.

International Cooperation to Reinforce Market Discipline

Reinforcement of market discipline at the international level has come chiefly in the area of data disclosure. For example, the IMF has recently put forward proposals for the dissemination by countries of economic and financial statistics (International Monetary Fund, forthcoming, mid-1997). These focus on improving the accuracy, consistency, and timeliness of monetary and other macroeconomic statistics. The Basle Committee has also issued recommendations regarding public disclosure of banks' activities. Such improved disclosure standards and additional information on the condition of individual banks would better permit market participants to assess banks' soundness, paving the way for improved market discipline.

Within the EU, standards have been set for bank disclosure, by means of the Directive on the Annual Accounts and Consolidated Accounts of Banks and Other Financial Institutions. This directive specifies the basic layout of the annual financial statements of banks, covering the balance sheet, the profit-and-loss account, and the explanatory notes to the annual statements.

It is notable that there is no international agreement regarding bank closure standards. Thus exit policy as an adjunct to market discipline functions only at the national level, with international cooperation essentially on an ad hoc basis.

International Cooperation to Reinforce Supervision

As in the areas of internal governance and market discipline, there have been efforts to improve international coordination and cooperation in bank supervision. These efforts have been spearheaded by groups of supervisors such as the Basle Committee, working on behalf of their own member supervisory agencies. The IMF has contributed to this effort within the almost universal roster of its membership. The closest cooperation, however, has developed in regional groups, particularly the EU.

Basle Committee and Regional Supervisory Groups

As discussed above, the Basle Committee has promulgated recommendations and standards for consolidated supervision and capital adequacy and has formulated policies in other key areas, such as the regulatory treatment of market risks and operations in derivatives. It serves primarily as a forum for the Group of Ten supervisors. However, Basle Committee recommendations are increasingly seen as the global standard that many countries beyond the Group of Ten seek to adopt. Should the Basle Committee formulate further recommendations, they will in all probability receive serious consideration for adoption by supervisors worldwide.

In principle, international coordination on banking sector issues among a broader range of countries than those participating in the Basle Committee can be accomplished through the regional groups of supervisors that have been organized in east and southern Africa, west and central Africa, for the Arab countries, the Caribbean, central and eastern Europe, the EU, the Gulf Cooperation Council, Latin America and the Caribbean, SEANZA (Southeast Asia, New Zealand and Australia), and for countries with offshore centers. These regional groups seek to share experiences, harmonize practices and, on occasion, develop standards on a regional basis to complement those of the Basle Committee. The Basle Committee supports these groups and has promoted the creation of some of them.[112] Over time, the regional groups may develop into a mechanism for more intensive regional collaboration, which could include regulatory harmonization and supervisory cooperation; thus far they provide a useful forum for contacts between supervisors in neighboring countries.

IMF Surveillance and Policy Advice

The IMF has been concerned with bank soundness for some time; its response to the international debt crisis of the 1980s demonstrated its awareness of the need for soundness of the international banking system and of principal international banks.[113] To the extent that the Fund provides, under adequate safeguards, a financial safety net for member countries, it can affect the performance of markets and the development of financial institutions across countries.[114] IMF surveillance of member

---

[112] See Basle Committee on Banking Supervision (1994).
[113] See Fischer (1995) and Harold James (1995), Chapter 12.
[114] On the role of safety nets in international financial markets, see Dale (1994).

countries' economic policies and the design of Fund-supported macroeconomic programs have in recent years increasingly acknowledged the importance of a sound financial sector. Some of the IMF's surveillance activities in this area are reported in the annual *International Capital Markets* survey and in the *World Economic Outlook* publications. In addition, financial sector reform measures have been included in many Fund-supported adjustment programs.[115]

The IMF's role is not as a banking supervisor, but as an advisor on policy. The IMF conducts regular broad-based consultations with all its members and is often deeply involved in the design and implementation of economic reform programs. In addition, the Fund has acquired knowledge of financial sector issues through its technical assistance and international market surveillance activities. It is particularly well placed in transition countries and some developing countries as a result of its surveillance over the condition of their macroeconomies and its intense involvement in the development of these countries' central banks. IMF consultations help to focus the authorities' attention on the interactions between financial sector policies for banking soundness and macroeconomic and other structural policies, the adequacy of official oversight systems in relation to market developments and the institutional environment, the sufficiency of the bank regulatory framework and its enforcement, and the desirability of adherence to international standards and norms of cooperation on supervisory issues.

The IMF is in a unique position among international institutions to offer such advice because it surveys the economies of virtually all countries and has access to expertise, both in-house and from member central banks, on a broad range of supervisory issues and policies. The Fund is thus well placed to advocate improved regulation, supervision, data disclosure, and resolution strategies, to complement the work of other agencies by setting structural issues in banking in a macroeconomic context, and to contribute to international harmonization of prudential policies.

Bilateral and Multilateral Technical Assistance

Banking supervision and regulation in many developing countries and virtually all economies in transition have benefited from external technical assistance. The World Bank and the various regional development banks have provided technical assistance in addressing banking sector problems in the context of structural adjustment lending and loans to support financial sector development and rehabilitation. Over the last thirty years, the IMF has provided advice and operational support in the

---

[115] See Schadler and others (1995).

strengthening of banking regulation and supervision to a broad range of countries in the context of its technical assistance programs aimed at developing and improving central banking practices in member countries. This work is supported by a network of cooperating central banks, which provide personnel and training support. Banking supervision in many countries has also benefited from assistance provided bilaterally or by regional organizations such as the EU.

Initiatives Within the EU

Globally, the most comprehensive program to improve supervisory cooperation and coordination is taking place within the EU. This cooperation goes beyond the harmonization of rules and regulations. The countries of the EU have also concluded among themselves a series of bilateral Memoranda of Understanding concerning practical cooperation in performing cross-border banking supervision, inspections of bank establishments in other EU countries by the home country supervisory authorities, sharing of information, and the implementation of corrective measures against banks. This is an experiment from which other countries can benefit. The economies in transition in Central and Eastern Europe are watching with particular interest, as most aspire to EU membership and may be expected to tailor their nascent supervisory arrangements to facilitate accession.

International Coordination Failures

In pursuing international coordination of bank supervision, the limits to what can be achieved by regulatory harmonization need to be recognized. Even so, despite the efforts of the past twenty years, much that is feasible remains to be accomplished.

Limits to the Benefits of Regulatory Harmonization

Regulatory harmonization among countries that share similar exposures to factors that threaten bank soundness is both possible and useful; there are practical limits, however, to the ability to achieve international harmonization. Full regulatory harmonization is not always appropriate. For example, the Basle Committee has successfully harmonized capital adequacy standards for the Group of Ten countries, by establishing a minimum standard of 8 percent of risk-weighted assets for banks in these relatively stable and diversified economies. The Committee stressed that higher levels must be adopted in uncertain or volatile conditions. Many countries beyond the Group of Ten have adopted the Basle capital standards even under conditions of high economic volatility and inadequate accounting and asset valuation, where a much stricter standard would be appropriate.[116]

Similarly, appropriate standards of liquidity will depend on local factors such as the characteristics and volatility of the demand for base money and the depth of the money markets. Regulations on loan provisioning should reflect prior experience with recovery of impaired loans, which will depend on local factors such as the legal procedures for loan recovery and for bankruptcy.

In addition, varying institutional frameworks will produce different operating conditions even with harmonized prudential regulations. The official safety net of supervision, lending of last resort, and deposit insurance will differ from country to country; market responses will be conditioned not only by regulations but also by the nature of the financial support that can be expected in the event of a problem[117] The competitive structure of the banking system as well as of the broader financial industry will also determine the degree to which a level playing field across countries can actually be constructed through bank regulations.

Thus the focus on international standards compatible with those of the Group of Ten should not be allowed to detract from the development of a framework for sound banking appropriate to the country concerned. While the value of identifying best practices is clear, the real work must take place in applying those practices to create a sound banking environment in each different economic, political, and institutional context.

Insufficiency of Supervisory Coordination

International coordination is not yet sufficiently developed to offset the differences in operating environment, regulation, and supervisory procedures across jurisdictions. For example, confidentiality provisions make it difficult for supervisors to share information on the condition of banks and their major customers across jurisdictions, even where bilateral arrangements are in place. The only recognized international standards at present are those developed by the Basle Committee. They cover areas of limited relevance to developing and transition countries that do not have the financial infrastructure necessary to facilitate the standards and practices used by the Group of Ten. In addition, while the Basle Committee provides policy recommendations on some specific supervisory issues, it has not involved itself in legislation, accounting, valuation, taxation, or resolution issues.

[116] See Dziobek, Frécaut, and Nieto (1995) and Kane (1995).
[117] See Dale (1994).

Gaps remain in the international oversight framework. Fragmented international supervision allowed the failure of BCCI in 1991 (addressed by subsequent Basle Committee guidelines on consolidated supervision by home country authorities) and of Meridien Bank in 1995 (which occurred despite those guidelines having been issued). International supervisory coordination was also an issue in the Barings and Daiwa cases. Improved information exchanges might have helped supervisors in Singapore, Osaka, and Tokyo perceive that Barings was speculating rather than hedging. Better collaboration between supervisors could have prevented much of the rancor associated with discovery of the Daiwa fraud and the subsequent removal of that bank's license to operate in the United States.

Very little has been done to prevent international spillovers and systemic risk arising from a bank failure. Policies for bank liquidation and restructuring typically are purely domestic. There is little harmonization of exit procedures or standards for early intervention. Crisis resolution is done on an ad hoc basis, despite the clear need for international coordination demonstrated by several significant failures. The spillover effect due to the way in which the 1974 failure of Herstatt Bank was handled is a classic example. In the cases of BCCI and Barings, closure was coordinated across jurisdictions. The failure of Meridien, on the other hand, was marked by a distinct lack of international communication and coordination among supervisors.

The difficulties in improving international cooperation in this area should not be underestimated. Consider the case of a financial services group operating banking, insurance, and securities subsidiaries. Each of these business lines may be regulated by a separate authority, and the banking units may be overseen by the central bank as well as banking supervision and deposit insurance agencies. Operations in different securities markets may be monitored by different regulators as well. Thus in each country multiple agencies may be concerned when the group becomes unsound. Multiply that by the number of countries within which the group may be operating, for example, under the EU's single passport, and one begins to get a sense of the challenge that lies ahead in coming to terms with the international dimensions of unsoundness.

Recently the Basle Committee has been seeking to expand its role by providing training programs through the regional supervisors' groups, and there have been calls for the IMF to assume a more assertive role in monitoring banking systems (Fidler, 1996a and 1996b). It must be recognized, however, that while IMF surveillance can add international and macroeconomic dimensions to banking system oversight, neither the Basle Committee nor the IMF can replace proper banking supervision and improved collaboration between supervisors. The international community is only just beginning to grapple with these issues in a concerted manner.

Part IV

Conclusions: Policy Design and Flexibility

12

Macroeconomic Policy Design

The fact that weaknesses in the banking system can constrain the effectiveness of macroeconomic measures and damage economic performance suggests that promotion of a sound banking system represents a legitimate policy objective—as well as a constraint—in the design of macroeconomic policies. Thus, strategies for dealing with macroeconomic imbalances will need to consider the degree of soundness of the banking system, and in many cases an understanding of banking system problems is a prerequisite for analysis of macroeconomic policies. The need for appropriate structural policies to underpin the soundness of the banking system has been discussed in the preceding chapters. Most structural policy initiatives have their full impact only over an extended period of time. In the meantime, the severity of any banking problems must be assessed in order to adapt the objectives and instruments of macroeconomic policies so as to prevent the system from deteriorating further and facilitate its strengthening. This chapter further explores four key areas in which the linkages between macroeconomic policies and banking system soundness may require adaptation of objectives or instruments: overall macroeconomic policy formulation in the context of stabilization policies, the choice of monetary instruments, the fiscal balance, and dealing with foreign capital flows.

Stabilization Policies

While stabilization generally has a positive impact on the economy as a whole, as well as on the banking system, it can also pose transitional problems. Concern for the soundness of the banking system can bring to the surface trade-offs in the choice of policy objectives and program targets and influence the pace with which such objectives can be pursued. Typically, inflation and balance of payments targets are pursued with monetary, exchange rate, and fiscal policies. In choosing the mix of these policies, their implications for the soundness of the banking system should be considered along with the influence of the banking system on policy flexibility.

It is clear that the effect of banking system soundness on policy flexibility would vary depending upon the specific structure of banks' balance sheets and other initial conditions. Restrictive monetary policy measures that cause high interest rates or large exchange rate adjustments may result in major distress for banks and bank customers exposed to market risks, and this could trigger systemic problems. Thus, the soundness of the banking system could constrain the use of monetary and exchange rate policies to achieve program objectives.

The most extreme case is when a banking system has already deteriorated to the point where a financial crisis is imminent or in process. The experience in most countries is that when this situation is faced, short-term stabilization objectives give way to efforts related to preventing or dealing with the crisis. The prospect of a crisis—which could take the form of a run on banks or a general collapse of financial institutions—tends to subordinate most other policy considerations, including those in the monetary and fiscal domains. Avoiding this undesirable outcome argues for realistic precrisis assessments of weak banking systems, of the trade-offs in each individual situation, and of the probability of crisis. This should lead to an orderly bank-restructuring program that is well integrated with macroeconomic and prudential policies.

The constraint of an unsound banking system must be considered when formulating the targets and phasing of any macroeconomic program; otherwise, early policy gains could be eroded through bank losses or swept away in a banking crisis. There may, therefore, be a need to adjust the objectives or the phasing of a macroeconomic program to support other structural reforms to restore soundness to the banking system and flexibility to policymaking. This may require an allocation of resources, including human resources, to facilitate the structural reforms. Needless to say, concern with banking system unsoundness cannot be seen as an excuse for postponing adjustment, but rather should lead to a sustainable pace of adjustment, and to an appropriately designed adjustment program that combines macroeconomic and structural policies.

For example, a sharp decline in inflation, while beneficial over the medium term, may have negative effects for the banking system in the short term. Banks earning their income from inflation-driven activities need time to refocus their business toward traditional banking in a low-inflation environment. Bank clients could be exposed to large relative price adjustments and rising real interest rates. An inflation target, therefore, may need to be tempered by concerns that a faster reduction in inflation might have an adverse impact on the banking system in the short term, as was the case recently in Mexico. Programs of sharp disinflation would therefore require particular attention to banking soundness issues.

At all times, monetary policy will be constrained by what the banking system can be counted on to accomplish, which is largely dependent on how sensitive banks are to interest rate signals and the extent to which the banking system and the central bank itself are able to control their own balance sheets. For example, attainment of a targeted accumulation of international reserves may be sought through restraint in domestic credit expansion or through a combination of credit policy and an exchange rate adjustment. An unsound banking system saddled with a large share of nonperforming loans may not be able to reduce aggregate credit flows to the extent required by the first course of action. Alternatively, a devaluation can bring a different set of problems, if banks or their customers have significant foreign exchange exposures.

Major changes in the exchange rate can seriously damage a banking system, as can prolonged over- or undervaluation of an exchange rate—although in these situations there are always gainers as well as losers. A shift in the exchange rate will similarly have mixed effects. An exchange appreciation, for example, in response to capital inflows, might hurt some borrowers as well as banks with net external asset positions, but could result in lower interest rates and strengthen banks to the extent that they have net external liabilities (which is often the case after a period of capital inflows). At the same time, the limitations imposed by a weak banking system on the use of interest rate policy will limit the scope for exchange rate management through domestic interest rates—regardless of exchange rate regime. In particular, an unsound banking system may limit the scope for sustaining a currency board arrangement.[118]

While in the long run the scope for substituting fiscal and monetary policies may be limited, insofar as monetary and exchange rate policies are constrained in their short-run effects by weaknesses in the banking sector, an additional fiscal effort may become necessary to reduce resource pressures in the economy. There may be very limited room for such compensatory tightening, however, when public finances are weak and the government already is being called upon to honor various deposit and loan guarantees. This situation would typically call for a well-considered phasing of the necessary fiscal adjustment to support bank restructuring, in parallel with other structural policies.

---

[118] The limitations posed by an unsound financial sector on the classical interest rate defense of an exchange rate and the functioning of a currency board are discussed in Folkerts-Landau, Ito, and others (1995, Chapter VII).

Monetary Instruments

When a banking system is fragile, there is not only a need to carefully evaluate the feasibility and implications of the overall macroeconomic targets and policy mix, but also of the instruments with which these policies will be pursued. This is particularly important in the monetary area.

Use of Indirect Instruments

As explained in Chapter 5, the effectiveness of indirect instruments of monetary control is constrained when weaknesses in banks' loan portfolios or management make banks unresponsive to price signals and lead to interbank market segmentation. If unsound banks' responsiveness to interest rates is in question, safeguards may be required in the operation of central bank credit facilities. For example, participation of weak banks in central bank credit auctions might be limited.[119] Market segmentation is typically reflected in sound banks receiving more deposits than they can lend, and in their quest for safe and liquid assets cutting their interbank exposures and becoming the principal holders of safe instruments like treasury bills, the yields of which tend to decline. At the same time, because unsound banks may not have access to the interbank market, there may be frequent shortfalls in their required reserves, overdrafts in their clearing accounts at the central bank, and distress borrowing. This situation would distort interest rates and complicate the use of market-based instruments.

Under circumstances of extreme market segmentation, indirect instruments may lose their effectiveness altogether and direct instruments of monetary policy may be required for short-term control. This would be true, for example, when interbank markets are not functioning and the central bank has to redistribute bank liquidity. Under such circumstances, bank-by-bank credit ceilings could be useful for credit management on a temporary basis, as could interest rate ceilings to limit distress borrowing. Using such instruments, however, could well weaken banks' profitability and constrain their liquidity management and thus further deepen their financial difficulties. In cases of management intransigence or other extreme circumstances, the only way to establish monetary control over weak banks might be through supervisory intervention, which would imply official administration of problem banks.

Many developing and transition countries are seeking to develop their money markets and shift monetary intervention to market-based instruments. Problems in the banking system may influence the pace of these

[119] See Saal and Zamalloa (1995).

reforms, as was observed in a number of countries in the 1980s; for example, Argentina, Chile, and the Philippines temporarily reintroduced interest rate controls to alleviate the burden of high real interest rates on borrowers and banks.[120] The appropriate instrument mix and the phasing of any new instruments will depend on the general state of development of a country's banking system and broader financial markets, the degree of unsoundness in the system, and the scope for fiscal, prudential, and other structural measures to strengthen bank soundness.

Lender-of-Last-Resort Facilities

Considerations of bank solvency become highly relevant in managing central bank LOLR facilities and related payment system policies. Most central banks provide some form of credit facility, such as a Lombard facility or discount window, which can be used to provide liquidity and facilitate payments settlement for banks in distress. Central bank last-resort lending will generally take the form of liquidity injections directed to a particular bank or set of banks and may need to be sterilized by reducing liquidity elsewhere, for example, through open market operations or other instruments.

The intent of central bank LOLR facilities is not to provide resources to insolvent institutions, but to provide temporary liquidity to sound institutions, typically at a penalty rate. To manage its LOLR facility, the central bank must know (on the basis of information from supervisors) which banks are approaching insolvency or are insolvent. In practice, however, both central banks and supervisors often have difficulty distinguishing illiquid but solvent banks from insolvent ones.[121] This is even more difficult when most banks or the entire system is in distress. Experience shows that banks that have major or protracted liquidity problems invariably also are insolvent.

In exceptional cases, the central bank may be called upon to lend to insolvent banks, for example, to buy time for the design of restructuring strategies when banks are viewed as "too big to fail" or when the lending is part of a systemic restructuring strategy. In all such cases, central bank credit (which essentially provides insolvent banks with equity as well as liquidity) must be fully guaranteed by the government. In the case of central bank lending to insolvent banks, the use of collateral is largely illusory from the public sector's point of view, in the sense that central bank claims crowd out other creditors in the final liquidation of a bank and sad-

---

[120] See Alexander, Balixo, and Enoch (1995), p. 21.

[121] For example, a 1991 study of Federal Reserve LOLR "extended credit" to banks showed that 90 percent of those banks subsequently failed (see U.S. House of Representatives, 1991, p. 94).

dle them with the bank's growing negative net worth, which the government often ends up absorbing in part or in full.[122] These considerations suggest that LOLR facilities must be managed with utmost caution, relying on careful monitoring of banking soundness.

Fiscal Balance

The fact that resolving banking system unsoundness often involves substantial government expenditure means that the fiscal balance becomes a constraint on the type of corrective action that can be taken. Banking system problems are often known but neglected, and supervisors often are prevented from intervening in banks because this would bring the problems out in the open and "cause" government expenditure. Typical justifications for inaction are that there is "no room in the budget" or that the fiscal situation is "too weak" to allow for any consideration of banking problems.

The reasons for a lack of early action are often political, and the opacity of banking problems makes it relatively easy to delay them for a subsequent government to deal with. But from an economic point of view such delays are costly; experience has shown that the longer a solution is delayed, the more difficult the ultimate resolution becomes, as banks may spiral deeper into insolvency. Furthermore, the longer insolvent banks are allowed to continue operations, the more implicated and obligated the authorities become, which makes it more likely that the ultimate resolution will involve fiscal expenditure on a substantial scale. For example, the U.S. General Accounting Office (1987) tracked the condition of U.S. banks whose resolution was delayed and found that in most instances their condition deteriorated further during the delay.

It is essential for efficient resource allocation that banking system problems not be "swept under the rug" in fiscal policy formulation. The government's full costs, including estimated contingency costs, need to be taken into consideration in a transparent way. All government current obligations to banks, including the servicing of any securities for bank capitalization or restructuring, should be brought into the budget. Contingent liabilities (such as loan and deposit guarantees, and any negative net worth of the central bank or state-owned banks) should be estimated as well as possible. The extent and form in which such contingencies should be included in the budget needs to be considered in each case. Excluding such contingencies from the budget does not make the expenditure avoidable; ultimately, the cost of bank unsoundness must be paid.

---

[122] Nevertheless, encouraging adequate collateralization—for example, through short-term repurchase agreements—can help to restore the functioning of the interbank market.

However, if such contingencies were transparent to the public, it would be readily recognized that the fiscal liabilities had already been incurred. This recognition could in turn contribute to pressure for timely action to deal with the problem, ultimately reducing fiscal costs.

On the revenue side, tax policies can also be used to provide transparency and keep banks sound. To prevent tax payments on fictitious profits that would cause gradual decapitalization of banks, it is desirable that loan-loss provisions be fully tax deductible and that interest accrued on nonperforming loans not be recognized as income, until it is actually received.

The impact of a weak banking sector on fiscal balance should be evaluated after projecting the actual and contingency costs of supporting the banking system both for the short and medium term. In addition, current and prospective expenditures resulting from bank-restructuring strategies and loan-recovery arrangements should be considered. Special tax breaks for banks to allow their rehabilitation should be discouraged; it is better to show such transfers openly. Similarly, any support for weak banks through loans or deposits from state-controlled entities should be part of a comprehensive bank-restructuring strategy and not be used merely to keep banks liquid, which would only serve to increase ultimate government resolution costs.

Foreign Capital Flows

Banks facilitate international capital movements and contribute to the integration of international financial markets. Given the central role of the banking system in all countries, the perceived soundness of a banking system will affect capital flows. A sound banking system has greater access to foreign interbank and capital markets and could induce repatriation of capital. If the system is allowed to fall into distress, capital flight can be triggered and bank access to interbank and other foreign capital markets can be constrained; such a loss of access could in turn trigger a systemic crisis.

In recent years, as a result of freer capital movements and increased financial market integration internationally, the management of large capital flows, and especially of swings in such flows, has become a challenge for macroeconomic policymakers and bank supervisors in many countries. The dual relationship between macroeconomic policies and banking system weaknesses has become more transparent with the internationalization of the financial system. In particular, banks now face greater exposure to credit and market risk—including off-balance-sheet risks—on account of their participation in international financial markets. The objective of a sound banking system therefore should be added to the well-known policy dilemma of how to balance monetary, exchange rate, and fiscal policy objectives in the context of an open capital account.[123]

The impact of capital flows and their reversals on a banking system are in some ways similar to the impact of cyclical movements in the domestic economy. A rapid credit expansion and asset-price inflation can be of domestic or external origin. In the case of capital inflows and the resulting rapid growth of liquidity in the banking system—unless the liquidity is appropriately sterilized—there is pressure for bank credit to grow rapidly. Experience has shown that the quality of credit tends to suffer when credit grows too quickly. This becomes particularly worrisome when there are known weaknesses in the banking system, including problems in banks' credit appraisal and internal control procedures, poor compliance with prudential rules, poor loan-valuation practices, or weak capitalization. In the case of capital outflows, banking system liquidity would tighten and—unless expanded by monetary (re)injection of liquidity—banks would be forced to call in credits. This process would expose underlying weaknesses in bank-loan portfolios, which if widespread could also result in a systemic crisis.

The design of prudential as well as macroeconomic policies, therefore, should consider the banking system's capacity to effectively intermediate capital flows. This will be particularly important in the context of capital account liberalization, which may radically change banks' operating environment. Prudential measures should seek to foster a strengthening of credit and other risk-management capabilities in banks, supported by strictly enforced capital adequacy and other prudential regulations. Banks not in compliance with prudential regulations should be barred from entering into new activities, accepting new liabilities, or extending certain credits. A tightening of prudential policies also could have a direct effect on the capital flows, by leading banks to reduce deposit rates insofar as banks become restrained in accepting new liabilities and granting new credits.

If it is known that a banking system is weak and that prudential policies are ineffective or seriously deficient in controlling banks' risk exposures, there is an argument in favor of including in the management of monetary policy the aim of preventing excessive credit expansion or contraction to contain the possible adverse effects on asset quality and banking system soundness of swings in capital flows. These soundness considerations could influence the mix of exchange rate and interest rate adjustments in response to capital flows, and thereby affect the choice of specific operating targets and policy instruments.

---

[123] See Quirk and Evans (1995).

13

The Banking System and Macroeconomic Policy Flexibility

An unsound banking system affects macroeconomic policy formulation across sectors. Monetary and exchange policies are likely to be constrained, as monetary instruments become less effective and their ability to support an exchange rate is diminished. A tightening of monetary policy may be insufficiently effective or cause serious distortions; it could even trigger a crisis and force a reversal of policy stance. Although the reduced effectiveness of monetary policy could be offset to some extent by fiscal tightening, banking sector problems could themselves result in increased budgetary commitments. These consequences of unsoundness, along with the impact on the real sector of prolonged banking system deficiencies, imply that actions to strengthen the soundness of the banking system or to prevent any deterioration should receive high priority in the design of macroeconomic policies.

The degree of unsoundness at which these effects take hold will vary from situation to situation. A banking system can become increasingly unsound and yet continue to function for an extended period of time without a crisis. In cases where confidence is more fragile, such as in many emerging market economies, a small degree of unsoundness could have strong consequences in the form of deposit runs and capital outflows.

Over the long term, structural elements are critical to building a strong banking system. Such a system must be composed of individually sound banks operating in a supportive institutional and economic environment, controlled by a combination of internal governance, market discipline, and official regulation and supervision. These structural policies could themselves affect macroeconomic outcomes, a factor that must be taken into account in the design of prudential regulations. As important as the institutional setting and control mechanisms are, however, over shorter time frames, the soundness of the banking system will be affected most sharply by the economic environment.

In some cases, particularly when bank unsoundness is associated with the business cycle, support of the banking system may not present a conflict with overall macroeconomic objectives. Loose monetary policy was probably appropriate in Thailand in 1986–87, so support of the banking system did not hinder the pursuit of macroeconomic policy goals.[124] The same might be said of Japan in 1994–95 and the United States in 1990–91. Happy coincidence should not be confused, however, with the real ability to freely choose and conduct policy. In most instances, particularly in developing and transition economies, an unsound banking system coincides with macroeconomic imbalances that require stringent financial policies. These may be inconsistent with direct support of the banking system and may in fact exacerbate bank unsoundness.

This presents policymakers with difficult challenges. A sound banking sector is itself a necessary objective of macroeconomic policy. Banking is universally treated as a special economic activity. Given governments' propensity to support banking sectors that become unsound, it would appear shortsighted to implement macroeconomic policies that could weaken the banking sector. The externalities relating to bank soundness, and the interlinkages between a sound banking system and macroeconomic developments and policies, argue for adequately considering the soundness of the banking system in formulating macroeconomic policies and the policy instrument mix. When the authorities are forced, however, to make the stability of an unsound banking system their chief concern, policy flexibility is lost. Therefore, in addition to taking account of the current state of the banking system in macroeconomic policy formulation, microeconomic policies should be designed so that the banking sector is robust enough to withstand macroeconomic adjustments when they become necessary.

[124] Johnston (1991).

Appendices

Appendix I
The Value of a Bank

The value or net worth of a bank is the difference between the values of its assets and its debt liabilities.[125] Most bank liabilities are debt instruments that are fixed in nominal terms,[126] so that their valuation is relatively straightforward in normal times. In addition to securities that a bank holds, the main component of bank assets is loans to businesses, households, and the government, which are also fixed in nominal or indexed terms. As there is a positive probability that these borrowers will default on their loans even in normal times, banks face a challenge in valuing their assets and net worth. As a result, there is always a fair degree of uncertainty in the valuation of bank assets. Lesser problems apply to their liabilities. Valuation uncertainty should be considered to be a normal occurrence—one considered acceptable as long as it results from a fair and consistent application of the accounting norms. While valuation is subject to a number of uncertainties even in normal times, it becomes much more problematic in times of stress.

The economic and accounting concepts of net income require that a bank keep its capital intact so that it can continue to generate income in the future. Thus, net income measures the resources available to the bank after it has covered all of its expenses, including capital replenishment. A nonfinancial firm typically depreciates the value of its buildings and equipment over time and may take funds from its current receipts to build a sinking fund to buy new machinery when the old wears out. Equivalently, a bank should classify its loans and depreciate their value according to the estimated probability and extent of impairment. Similarly, the bank must establish a loan-loss reserve to replenish its financial capital that is depleted by loan defaults.

---

[125] Valuation and accounting issues are addressed in Chapter 5 of the draft *Manual on Monetary and Financial Statistics* (Washington: International Monetary Fund, forthcoming in mid-1997).

[126] Although they may be indexed to keep up with inflation.

Table 17. Methods of Valuation Used in Financial Statements

a. *Historical cost* or *book value* represents the price the company paid for an asset when it acquired it.

b. *Current cost* or *market value* represents the price that the company would have to pay today to acquire an asset.

c. *Realizable value* is the amount that a company would expect to obtain for an asset sold in an orderly disposal.

d. *Present value* is measured as the present discounted value of the net estimated cash flow associated with an asset.

Sources: *American Institute of Certified Public Accountants (AICPA) Professional Standards*, AC Sections 9000A and 9030; and the International Accounting Standards Committee, *International Accounting Standards* (1995).

Valuation Techniques

Banks are dependent on businesses' own valuations of their assets (discussed in the annex to this appendix). While, conceptually, banks and their borrowers have four valuation techniques to choose from (see Table 17), their country's accounting rules will constrain their choice. Moreover, bank supervisors often issue accounting regulations for banks that supplement or even override the conventions that businesses follow.

Loan Valuation in Normal Times

Some businesses with heavy fixed investment that rarely need to redeploy existing resources and are operating in a noninflationary environment rely heavily on depreciated original cost (book values). This approach is satisfactory as long as the business is profitable and readily able to meet its obligations. Most countries require their banks to value their loans and deposits using historical cost.

Other ongoing financial businesses that trade in volatile markets, such as investment banks and money market mutual funds with investments in financial assets, constantly need data on the current value of their investments. Obtaining current values may be problematic in developing and transitional economies where markets are thin, trading is infrequent, and bid-ask spreads are wide. Thus, mutual funds in developed financial markets can more readily mark to market than those with investments in emerging markets.

It has been proposed that the global financial position of some banking institutions be assessed on the basis of current market conditions. This has been tried, but it has proved impracticable. Market values derived from deep and actively traded organized markets are available only for a limited number of assets (marketable securities, a small share of banks' assets), and in a limited number of countries. The largest items on banks' balance sheet are loans and deposits. The economic value of the loan portfolio is affected by each change in the level of the interest rates. But interest rates and market valuations can be volatile. Under market valuations, they would need to be permanently revalued accordingly. For the sake of consistency, the same revaluation process would need to apply to all deposits although this is often not the practice.[127]

In practice, historical costs, although economically inexact, continue to be relied upon for loans (adjusted by provisioning, as described below) and deposits, with the approval of the relevant accounting authorities. Market values are used for specific items only, such as traded securities.

Loan Classification and Provisioning

In an alternative attempt to keep loan valuations contemporary, a bank should employ an approach similar to depreciated historical cost when valuing its loans. A loan's principal value is reduced in a process of loan classification and provisioning that should reflect expected future cash flows as indicated by the likelihood and the expected extent to which the borrower will fail to pay the loan's principal and interest and the bank will be unable to cover its losses by selling any collateral backing the loan.[128] While the details of classification and provisioning vary among countries, the general principles are laid out in Table 18.

Supervisors require banks to make specific provisions against the loans that are impaired. These provisions can be treated in one of two ways. First, as in the German system, the provision directly reduces the value of the loan on the asset side of the balance sheet, so that capital is reduced correspondingly on the liability side.[129] The bank will need to replace that capital if it is to retain its preprovision capital ratio. Second, as in the English and American systems, the loan may be retained at its original value on the balance sheet but is partly written down by an allowance for loan and lease losses that is treated as a contra asset on the balance sheet.

---

[127] This would be a complex, costly, daily task in a large bank. More important, it would lead banks to post a succession of sometimes large, potentially destabilizing, gains and losses on their deposits and loans, despite the fact that, for most of these items, there is a contractually determined amount and payment date.

[128] Thus provisioning is equivalent to reducing a loan's original cost to its estimated present value. Loans that a bank has had to reschedule because the borrower has been unable to meet his obligations should normally remain classified until the borrower has re-established his creditworthiness through a history of timely servicing.

[129] Using this approach makes it clear that losses are being recognized and that they should, therefore, be tax deductible.

Table 18. Rules for Loan Classification and Provisioning

Classification	Criteria[1]	Required Provision
Not classified "unimpaired"	Loan is current and has adequate collateral; original source for repayment is adequate.	Amount based on prior charge-off experience
Classified "substandard"	Inadequately protected by borrower's paying capacity and/or collateral; distinct possibility of loss.	15% to 25%
Classified "doubtful"	As above, but also recovery in full is highly questionable.	50%
Classified "loss"	Extremely high possibility of loss; uncollectible with little value; difficulties in recovery so great that the asset can no longer be considered "bankable."	100% (less the realizable value of collateral)

[1] Some countries base the classification on the period over which the borrower has failed to service the loan. For example, a loan might be classified as nonperforming after interest had not been paid for 90 days. Practices vary enormously, however, over the length of the period required for classification. For example, some supervisors do not classify a loan until interest has been withheld for one or even two years. Best practice appears to be 90 days.

This allowance is not recognized as capital under the Basle capital standards.

Supervisors typically also require banks to make general provisions against their unimpaired loan portfolio. The provision may be set in relation to the historical loss experience relevant to each particular category of loans. The value of the loan portfolio is left unadjusted on the balance sheet and a general reserve is established for possible losses.[130] The Basle standards recognize this item as part of tier 2 capital.

Provisioning will prevent the overstatement of net income and avoid paying taxes on fictitious income. In addition, a bank should not continue to accrue interest on loans that become nonperforming. To do so overstates the bank's income, capital, the tax liability, and ability to pay dividends.

Table 18 sets out a scheme, similar to that which MAE typically recommends in the context of its technical assistance to Fund members, for categorizing loans as "unimpaired" or classifying them into one of three categories of nonperforming loans ("substandard," "doubtful," and "loss") and for making provisions for each category of loans.

[130] This process is similar to that used by a business firm when it builds a sinking fund so that it can ultimately replace a depreciated or obsolete asset.

Ideally, a system of classification and provisioning would replicate the value that a loan would bring on an efficient market. This approximation will only be rough, however, because loan valuation is inexact and subjective, although statistical methods are beginning to be applied to make the process more scientific. Moreover, the loan-loss reserve would keep a bank's financial capital intact.

Valuation of Securities

In principle, both the securities that a bank issues and those that it holds in its asset portfolio can be valued at market prices. However, even when a clear and undisputable market value is available, as in the case of securities traded on a deep and liquid market, supervisors typically believe that this value should not be relied upon to assess the worth of bank assets or liabilities. They take this position because, while the negotiable value of debts may change with market value, neither the legal obligation to repay creditors nor the claim on debtors has altered.

It is reasonable to record debts at original or book values as long as they will be held to their maturity and the obligors are willing and able to meet their commitments. (As described above, the loan-provisioning process can be interpreted as estimating market values for bank loans.) In other situations, market values, estimated present values, or liquidation values are more relevant to decision making.

Securities Issued by a Bank

On the liability side of its balance sheet, a bank may have issued fixed-rate, long-term bonds that are traded on a deep and liquid market. Following a decline in the level of the interest rates, the economic value of these bonds will increase. A market valuation approach would require the bank to post additional liabilities in its balance sheet and the corresponding loss, which could be large for long-term securities, in its income statement. Conversely, a rise in the level of interest rates would reduce the economic value of the bank's liabilities and lead the bank to post a gain in its income statement, part of which could be paid out in the form of additional taxes and dividends. In both cases, however, the amount to be finally repaid to bondholders has remained unchanged.

As long as the bank continues in business, it is obligated to repay the face value of its securities. Therefore, it is preferable to record the obligations in the bank's books at face value, treating them in the same way as deposits, and continuously valuing them on the basis of the contractual repayment price.

The market value or present value of these securities is additional information to the banks' owners and managers at all times and might usefully be recorded in a footnote to the bank's accounts.[131] If the bank were to be sold or liquidated, market, present, or liquidation values would likely become decisive.

Securities Held by a Bank

Countries with well-developed financial systems allow their banks to select between two valuation methods for securities in their asset portfolios. The choice depends on how long a bank intends to keep these securities.[132] Although the details of the rules diverge slightly from one country to the next, the principle is similar: securities in the trading portfolio must be regularly marked to market, with the adjustment in value having a direct impact on the income statement, while securities in the investment portfolio may continue to be valued at historical cost, the difference between this cost and the final redemption price being amortized over the remaining life of the security.

As a result, two identical securities bought at the same date for the same price by the same bank may appear in its balance sheet at different values, if one was bought for trading and the other for investment. As part of the independence of management, the bank determines freely what it intends to do with each line of its securities portfolio. The accounting authorities' role is only to set rules applicable in each case. Again, as with bank liabilities, estimated current values of all of the bank's assets can usefully be incorporated in footnotes to bank accounts.

While book values are appropriate when the bank is expected to continue in business and to hold the asset to maturity, market values are relevant for securities that the bank intends, or is forced, to sell before maturity. Sale could occur not only if the asset is part of a bank's trading portfolio, but also if the bank is illiquid, is to be sold, or is to be liquidated.

Problems in Applying These Techniques

Banks have a recurring problem in that borrowers know more about their own condition and prospects than do their bankers. Therefore, sound banks carefully evaluate their borrowers' condition and prospects before making a loan and monitor borrowers' progress afterward. To prevent competitors from free riding on that information, banks keep information on their borrowers confidential. But some borrowers are intent on deceiving their bankers.

---

[131] The footnote might include an estimate of the option value to the bank of redeeming callable bonds early.
[132] Strict rules govern the conditions under which a bank can change its methods of valuation. It is not allowed to switch back and forth between valuation methods and is penalized if it attempts to do so.

Off-Balance-Sheet Items

Adjusted book values exclude the value of intangible assets, such as goodwill, profit opportunities, and underpriced guarantees, which can produce net income in the future. Banks also earn income or experience losses as a result of their off-balance-sheet activities, which can be very large in relation to their balance sheet items. While the Basle Committee has spent many years in attempting to value off-balance-sheet assets and liabilities in an effort to require banks to keep capital that will buffer them against losses that arise both on and off the balance sheet, it is agreed that they have achieved only a rough approximation of the valuation of off-balance-sheet items.

Valuation During Inflationary Periods

Valuation of business and bank assets and liabilities becomes more complex in an inflationary environment. For example, the depreciated book values of fixed assets tend to understate the market and present values of existing assets and their replacement cost. For example, an industrial firm's sinking fund may be insufficient to keep its physical capital intact. Similarly, a bank's general reserve may fail to keep up with inflation. The purchasing power of financial assets diminishes so that interest rates will be high if the real value of the principal is to be maintained, unless the principal is indexed to the general price level.[133] Similarly, as the valuation of business assets becomes more complex in an inflationary environment, so does the valuation of bank assets and net worth.

Even when a bank requires collateral to protect itself when making a loan, the marketable value of collateral will change with economic conditions. Inflation gives borrowers incentives to service their loans so that they can benefit from the appreciation in the value of their asset. Even if borrowers default, the bank should be able to recoup its loan loss by selling the collateral. Deflation, that occurs, for example, when an asset bubble bursts, exposes banks to defaults and losses on the sale of collateral. An individual bank, conducting credit evaluation according to its usual criteria, may not be able to perceive a problem of, for example, overbuilding in the real estate sector and the sharp reduction in values that could occur when several banks simultaneously attempt to sell their collateral.

---

[133] The International Accounting Standards (IAS) Committee (1995) has set accounting standards for high inflation environments (IAS 29). These standards attempt to value assets and liabilities on the balance sheet at current prices by universally applying an appropriate price index. The income statement then reflects gains and losses that arise from the effects of changes in the price level on the net monetary position of the organization, so as to maintain the general purchasing power of the shareholders' equity.

Valuation in Volatile Economies

Even stable banks and businesses can become volatile when the business environment changes abruptly. Then, established methods of depreciating book values can produce misleading values. Moreover, market values can change suddenly and significantly, or become unavailable (e.g., if there is a halt in trading), and the assumptions underlying realizable and present values need to be sharply revised. As a result, the firm's most recent accounts become less meaningful and there is substantial uncertainty over its values, solvency, and future prospects. In addition, a sharp deterioration in the realized or present value of a firm's assets as compared with their depreciated original cost reduces the firm's ability and incentive to repay its loans.

To the extent that these changes in the valuation of a firm's assets reflect the firm's ability to service its loans, they affect the likelihood of default on, and the value of, the bank's loans. Thus, these changes make it more difficult for the bank to value its portfolio and maintain adequate provisions. Consequently, the value of bank assets may plummet during economic downturns.

Valuation When the Bank's Future Is in Doubt

Depreciated book or market values (where they exist) are usually adequate for ongoing businesses in a stable economic environment; however, when the future of the business is in doubt, especially if it may need to be wound up, traditional financial statements are no longer relevant. If market values are not at hand, depreciated book values may need to be replaced by estimates of realizable or present value. Accountants are poorly equipped to deal with these substitute measures because the estimation processes are less clearly specified and typically involve business forecasts and other forward-looking analysis. Moreover, the necessary adjustments to the balance sheet and income statement may be significant.

Similarly, it becomes more difficult to value the bank when its viability is in doubt. Assets held in the investment portfolio at original cost may have to be sold. Thus, market, realizable, or present values become more relevant than historical cost.

In case of outright bank distress, the approach should be different. The level of uncertainty regarding the bank's (negative) net worth is very high and cannot be substantially reduced. As a consequence, detailed audits are a wasteful diversion of financial resources and, more important, of precious time. Rough estimates are sufficient to prepare adequate policy decisions. The estimates for losses should be prepared preferably in the form of a range, thus also expressing the degree of uncertainty, rather than in the form of a misleading single figure.

A second consequence is that the resolution plan must deal not only with losses, but also with their degree of uncertainty. In the case of plain liquidation, the burden of uncertainty is shouldered by the creditors, because they have to wait until the end of the process to know how much they will recover. In the case of a resolution scheme avoiding liquidation, one party needs to be allocated this additional burden of uncertainty.

Valuation When the Bank Hides Its Condition

The several difficulties in valuing bank assets give bank managers opportunities to disguise their deteriorating condition by continuing to book interest due but not received, rolling over both principal and unpaid interest into new and unclassified loans ("evergreening"). They may be encouraged to do so by tax authorities and owners because overstating their income allows banks to pay taxes and dividends from their exaggerated income.

Difficulties in valuing bank assets increase in volatile economies with very thin markets, where values may change abruptly. Loan classification and provisioning need to take such volatility into account, because it implies a higher probability of large losses. High inflation can also be damaging to bank equity because banks typically hold more monetary assets than liabilities, whose value declines as inflation increases. Under inflation, the real value of capital and reserves of all kinds depreciates, unless inflation hedging and accounting are carefully applied.

Moreover, banks operating in inflationary and volatile environments may seek to avoid disciplinary action and closure by incorrectly classifying bad loans and making even lower provisions than are common in more stable economies.

Necessity of On-Site Inspections

Regular on-site inspections of banks are indispensable. Valuation rules incorporate a material, yet legitimate, degree of flexibility, but this flexibility may be abused by the dishonest. Bank management is expected to prepare "true-and-fair" financial statements, under the oversight of the external auditors. Beyond and above the work of the external auditors, however, is a need for a bank to be inspected by prudential supervisors and for the behavior of its management regarding valuation rules to be assessed. The inspectors should take a qualitative approach to the assessment of the valuation methods and assess the adequacy of the provisions.

Inspectors need to focus on the degree of genuineness of the financial statements and to check if and to what extent management has taken advantage of the flexibility of the valuation rules. Bank managers might wish to minimize apparent losses, relying on varied techniques that might not raise formal objections from the external auditors. For instance, they may have renewed the evergreened fragile loans and capitalized accrued interest. In some other cases, banks might also want to exaggerate losses, for instance to reduce tax liabilities or following a management shake-up.

Summary

In short, valuing bank assets and liabilities will always demand experience and honesty; nevertheless, there is room to apply modern statistical techniques (developed initially to facilitate credit scoring) to portfolio valuation.

Annex: Business Accounting

Even in normal times, bank borrowers themselves confront problems in valuing their assets. In addition, valuation becomes far more difficult under high inflation or when the economic environment deteriorates abruptly. Moreover, valuation is always an estimate, sometimes a range of estimates, and can change over time.

Business managers need information about what resources they command, which uses have proved the most profitable and secure, and who owns them. To meet its informational needs, a business constructs a balance sheet and statements of net income and material changes in the company's condition and performance.[134] These financial statements are made on the assumptions that flows are measured when they accrue, not when cash changes hands, and that the business is a "going concern," that is, it is not expected to be liquidated. In these statements, accountants currently use four different approaches to valuing assets, summarized in Table 19.

Financial statements have several desirable properties that are also listed in Table 19, but two are particularly important for valuing bank assets. In general, honest accountants and their clients prefer an objectively verifiable measure (a market or book value) to a subjective value (realizable or present value), which is only as valid as the assumptions on which it is based. (Others, bent on deception, tend to prefer a manipulable measure,

---

[134] Financial statements should present a true-and-fair representation of the position of the company, so that they meet the informational needs of external users (investors, employees, lenders, suppliers, trade creditors, customers, governments and their agencies, and the public), to enable them to make informed decisions. Financial statements are the prime source of information for these groups on the company's ability to generate cash and meet its obligations.

Table 19. Reporting and Presentation of Financial Statements

Components of financial statements

Statements should report:

(1) The company's position in a *balance sheet* that values *assets* from which benefits are expected to flow; *liabilities* that are expected to necessitate, either by law or self-imposed obligation, an outflow of resources; and *equity*, which represents the owners' residual interest in the assets after all liabilities are met;

(2) The company's performance in a statement of *net income* that reports the difference between income and expenses, where *income* represents both ordinary and extraordinary increases in the value of assets (the latter from both realized and unrealized gains in the value of assets) or reductions in liabilities, while *expenses* are reductions in benefits either from ordinary or extraordinary transactions (the latter include both realized and unrealized losses in the value of assets); and

(3) Material changes in the company's position and performance.

Desirable properties of financial statements

Financial statements should be:

(1) Understandable to the informed reader, especially when conveying complex material;

(2) Relevant so that they confirm or contradict impressions derived from other sources, to enable the reader to evaluate past and present events and future obligations;

(3) Material because important omissions or misstatements could lead to mistaken decisions;

(4) Reliable so that they can be depended upon to be free from material error or bias;

(5) Faithful in representing transactions; consequently, items subject to undue uncertainty such as goodwill are omitted;

(6) More representative of substance than form, so that fictitious transactions that appear to, but do not, convey ownership are represented accurately;

(7) Neutral and free from bias;

(8) Prudent; exhibiting a degree of caution when making estimates that avoids both overoptimism and the omission of hidden reserves;

(9) Complete, so that no material information is omitted;

(10) Comparable over time and across different companies;

(11) Timely, so that the information is still useful when it is made available; and

(12) Cost-effective, so that the benefits of the information to users exceed the costs of obtaining and preparing it.

Sources: *AICPA Professional Standards*, AC Sections 9000A and 9030; and the International Accounting Standards Committee, *International Accounting Standards* (1995).

often to overstate income and net worth.) In addition, a current value is more useful than an original cost. The four valuation methods emphasize the two desirable characteristics of objectivity and current relevance to different degrees.

Market values derived from deep and actively traded markets are current, objective, and verifiable. Employing such values tends to make financial statements volatile, but such volatility may merely reflect a reality that needs to be recognized. For less frequently traded assets held by firms that are expected to continue in business, accountants favor historical cost for the balance sheet, which is objective and readily verifiable. They attempt to make their valuation current by adopting one of several professionally recognized methods for depreciating the value of an asset over its productive life.

Appendix II
Supervisory Instruments

The work of bank supervisors consists of (1) promulgating prudential regulations; (2) licensing new banks; (3) monitoring the activities, performance, and condition of operating banks; (4) acquiring and using (and, in some instances, also disclosing) relevant information to banks and their customers; (5) enforcing bank laws and regulations and correcting banks' deficiencies; and (6) intervening, for example, by revoking bank licenses where necessary.[135] Their objective is to protect the banking system rather than individual banks, but it also encompasses protecting the interest of small depositors who are not able to monitor banks directly.

Regulatory Action

Banks intermediate between savers and borrowers by risk, denomination, maturity, and currency. They typically convert small deposits, the claims of risk-averse depositors, into larger riskier loans and take on credit and market risks; turn short-term liabilities into longer-term assets and so incur interest rate and liquidity risks; and borrow in one currency to invest in another, exposing themselves to foreign exchange risk. It is management's responsibility to actively manage banks' risk activities and price them appropriately, but discipline and incentives from the markets and supervisors can help banks to manage these and other risks.

First, supervisors may establish regulations that limit the bank's risk exposure and set minimum standards for capital to enable the bank to survive setbacks. This role is particularly important in economies where corporate governance and market discipline are weak. Second, some activities, such as significant investments in nonfinancial subsidiaries, are subject to limitations. Alternatively, rather than limiting or forbidding certain other activities, regulators may require banks to hold higher levels of capital when they engage in these activities. Third, some regulators

---

[135] Because supervisors impose sanctions of various kinds in the exercise of their duties, provision should be made for their actions to be subject to administrative or judicial review to discourage them from acting in an arbitrary manner. At the same time, a balance must be struck to avoid unwarranted interference that inappropriately impedes justifiable supervisory actions.

price banks' risk taking, for example, by charging higher fees to riskier banks for on-site inspections and deposit insurance.

A summary of key prudential practices, including those recommended by the Basle Committee on Bank Supervision, those adopted in the EU and the United States, and those recommended by MAE, in its technical assistance to Fund members, are contained in Table 20. It does not describe the practices that these entities have adopted with respect to disciplining and closing deficient banks. No international consensus appears to have been reached on these issues. The Basle Committee has not issued any guidelines, and practices differ within the EU.

Capital Adequacy

Until 1988, capital requirements traditionally were set as "leverage" or "gearing" ratios, which measured equity (plus loan-loss reserves and subordinated debt) in relation to total, on-balance-sheet assets. The Basle capital standards, established in 1988 for banks in the Group of Ten countries, acknowledged that bank assets have different degrees of exposure to credit risk and that off-balance-sheet items also expose a bank to risk. Nevertheless, the Basle risk-based standards allow banks a substantial degree of choice in their portfolio composition by requiring capital ratios that roughly reflect the risks banks take, both on and off their balance sheets.

As illustrated in Table 21, the Basle Committee has placed bank assets into different risk categories and applied different weights that roughly correspond to banks' perceived credit-risk exposure. The Committee wanted to keep the risk-weighting system simple and was, therefore, prepared to adopt a "broad-brush" approach. The risk weights, chosen after negotiation, although not statistically derived, intend to reflect default probabilities observed over a period of time in the Group of Ten countries. The Basle standards have been criticized, however, for having a small number of risk categories that fail to account for measurable differences in risk, for not adequately distinguishing between differences in risks within risk categories, and for aggregating risk-weighted assets without considering the covariances among assets that may reduce, or in some cases increase, risk exposure.[136]

The Committee focused on total capital, which it divided into two tranches (tier 1 and tier 2). It recommended that banks maintain total capital equal to at least 8 percent of their risk-weighted assets and that at least 4 percent should be tier 1 (principally equity) capital (see Table 22).

---

[136] See Folkerts-Landau, Ito, and others (1995), p. 138 and Kane (1995).

Table 20. Key Prudential Practices

Practice	Basle Committee	European Union	United States	MAE Advice[1]
Minimum capital for new banks	No guidance.	Minimum capital set at ECU 5 million ($6 million).	In practice minimum $2 million.	Minimum $1 million.
Minimum capital adequacy ratio	Total capital to risk-weighted assets of at least 8%.	Compulsory, at least 8% total capital to risk-weighted assets.	Similar to Basle standards; additionally, a leverage ratio of 4% at a minimum.	At least 8%; more in a high-risk environment.
Loans to one borrower	Guide to best practice; not more than 25% of total capital.	Not more than 25% of total capital to one borrower, and not more than 8 times capital to all large borrowers[2] in total, applied on a consolidated basis.	Federal limits 15% of total capital; state rules from 10% to 25%.	25% of total capital applied to a single borrower or group of related parties.
Lending to related parties	No guidance, but special attention needed.	Less than 20% to related enterprises.	At arm's length, less than 15% of total capital to each and 100% to all related borrowers.	At arm's length, between 15% and 25% of total capital applied to related parties and in total not more than 100%.
Liquidity ratios	Guidelines on measuring and managing liquidity risk.	Country specific.	Guidelines; case-by-case assessment.	Guidelines are necessary and ratios are useful.
Foreign exchange exposure	New capital charges adopted, position limits recommended.	Country specific; normally 10% to 15% for individual currencies and 20% to 40% in total; capital charges required.	Guidelines; case-by-case assessment.	Limits necessary either as a ratio or in absolute amounts.

[1] MAE = Monetary Affairs Department of the IMF
[2] Defined as exposures of 10 percent or more of capital.

Table 21. Essential of the Basle Risk-Based Capital Standards

Assets Included	Risk Category	Risk Weight (In percent)
Balance sheet items		
Cash and loans to governments and central banks	1	0
Claims on public sector entities	2	10
Claims on OECD banks	3	20
Loans secured by mortgages on residential property	4	50
All other assets, including commercial loans	5	100
Off-balance-sheet items		
Each off-balance-sheet item is scaled by a		Applicable
conversion factor	6	weight

The Committee has recently enlarged its capital standards to cover market risks, which are defined as the risk of loss arising from position-taking in debt and equities in the trading portfolio and in foreign exchange (Basle Committee, 1996). The scheme is to be implemented not later than year-end 1997. The Committee offers banks two alternatives for estimating their capital needs. First, a bank may use the traditional "add-on" measurement approach, which requires it to hold an additional amount of capital to cover its exposure to market risk. Alternatively, in some cases, a bank may use its own internal risk-management systems to assess its exposure instead of the traditional measure and thus avoid a possible conflict between the two approaches and the added burden of meeting two capital standards: one internal and one external. Perhaps the best-known internal system for measuring bank exposure to market risks is the "value-at-risk" (VAR) system.[137]

Given the likelihood that it will become increasingly difficult to set meaningful capital standards in the modern, fast-moving world of global finance, supervisors may wish to rely increasingly on banks' own assessment of their capital needs. One way to do this would be to adopt the "pre-commitment approach" to bank supervision. Under this method, each bank would be required at the beginning of each reporting period to

---

[137] VAR estimates attempt to calculate the maximum loss that a bank might incur from market risk over a given, short time period. The VAR system of estimates has been criticized because it is dependent on a large number of assumptions and historical relationships, which may be invalidated by market events. It also demands sophisticated modeling, extensive computer capacity, and a large amount of data, which may become irrelevant when the environment changes (as it often does when banks become unsound). Thus, VAR is currently usable only by the largest banks—these, however, are the principal dealers in derivatives. Small banks will need to use the add-on approach. Moreover, VAR says nothing about the size of the losses that might be incurred in the tail of the distribution beyond the usual 1 percent cut-off level. These omissions may be important if the distribution is not normally distributed.

Table 22. Tier 1 and Tier 2 Capital

Capital Measure	Components	Recommended Ratio
Tier 1	Paid-up capital (common stock) and disclosed reserves.	At least 4%.
Tier 2	Undisclosed, revaluation, and general loan-loss reserves, subordinated debt, and hybrid debt instruments.	Limited to 100% of tier 1 capital.
Total	Tier 1 plus tier 2 (where tier 1 can range between 50% and 100% of the total).	At least 8%, of which at least 4% is tier 1 capital.

evaluate its need for capital (over and above the regulatory minimum) in the ensuing period in relationship to its desired level of risk exposure. It would manage its portfolio to limit its cumulative trading losses during this interval to an amount less than its capital allocation, so that it does not fall below the established capital requirements. While the bank would choose its capital commitment, both the commitment and the adequacy of the risk-management system that generated it would be subject to supervisory evaluation and approval. To provide incentives to maintain adequate capital, penalties would be imposed if a bank's losses exceed its capital allocation.[138]

Many supervisors in countries with more volatile economies have adopted the Basle standards even when conditions do not warrant their use. There are several reasons why they may be inappropriate. First, the default probabilities of Group of Ten countries do not apply, so that supervisors need to require their banks, whose values are volatile because of economic conditions, to hold higher levels of capital in relation to their risk-weighted assets to achieve the same probability of insolvency as faced by banks in the Group of Ten countries.[139] Second, supervisory techniques in general and loan classification and provisioning practices in particular in many countries may be so weak that assets are overvalued and reported measures of capital are, therefore, grossly overstated and infor-

---

[138] See Kupiec and O'Brien (1995), who suggest a capital surcharge in future periods or fines as incentive-compatible penalties. The Basle Committee adopted elements of the precommitment approach in its scheme for incorporating market risks into the capital accord. A bank is required to hold additional capital in the next period if "backtesting" demonstrates that its capital allotment was insufficient in the previous period. A bank that can demonstrate by backtesting that its capital allotment was adequate escapes the addition.

[139] See Dziobek, Frécaut, and Nieto (1995), Kane (1995), and Hausmann and Gavin (1995).

mation in general is unreliable. Third, the legal infrastructure makes it less likely that banks will succeed in getting their loans serviced. Hence, many observers argue that good practice requires that banks in volatile economies with undeveloped financial and legal infrastructures maintain (possibly much) higher levels of capital.

Liquidity Standards

There are two supervisory approaches to liquidity risk. The first is to issue guidelines to banks for the measurement and management of this risk. The approach is adequate in industrial countries, where a deep interbank market can assist banks in maintaining liquidity.

In many other countries, supervisors adopt a second approach and require banks to meet certain prudential ratios of liquid assets (cash, claims on the central and correspondent banks, and short-term, negotiable, government securities) to deposits or total assets to enable them to satisfy requests to withdraw deposits. The ratios may be of several different types, some of which weight assets and liabilities according to their liquidity. Supervisors may require banks to strike a more complex balance between the maturities of their assets and liabilities.

Because of the difficulty of measuring liquidity (a time- and place-specific concept) the Basle Committee, the EU, and the United States have not established formal liquidity ratios. While many countries still use liquidity ratios, because of the diversity in approaches currently in use, it has not been possible to reach an international consensus on this issue. However, in September 1992, the Basle Committee issued a set of nonbinding guidelines in "A Framework for Measuring and Managing Liquidity." The guidelines set out the main elements of a model system for measuring and managing liquidity. They rely on a maturity ladder and the calculation of a cumulative net excess or deficit of funds.

Limits on Lending to Single Borrowers and Insider Transactions

Supervisors in most countries impose limits on loans to single borrowers to limit risk concentration and on loans to related parties and insiders to reduce conflicts of interest and possible concentration in the portfolio. As shown in Table 20, banks may not be permitted to lend more than 15 to 25 percent of their capital base to a single borrower or group of related interests—concepts that need to be clearly defined in the regulation. Loans to insiders typically are quantitatively restricted as a percentage of capital and are accompanied by a requirement that they be made "at arm's length" (i.e., not on preferential terms).

Foreign Exchange Exposure

There are two main supervisory approaches to foreign exchange risk. The first is to issue guidelines to banks for the measurement and management of this risk. The guidelines would typically encompass standards for internal controls; recording, accounting, and reporting of data; establishing risk-management responsibilities and a separation between front- and back-office functions; and allocating other responsibilities. Supervisors would request that these guidelines be followed and incorporated into a written statement of policies and procedures, approved by the bank's board and made available to the supervisors.

The second approach, which can be combined with the guidelines, consists of specifying prudential limits on open positions, expressed as a percentage of the capital base. There are generally limits for open positions in each currency (typically 15 percent of capital) and for aggregate exposure (frequently set at 25 percent of capital). The definition of the aggregate open position used to vary widely from country to country, but recently an international consensus definition, "the shorthand aggregate position," has been adopted by the EU and the Basle Committee.[140] In addition, the Basle and EU capital standards have been extended to require that additional capital be held in relation to foreign exchange positions, which are viewed as a type of market risk.

Regulations Relating to Internal Controls

Supervisors will encourage banks to introduce good management and strong internal controls through on-site supervision to ensure that management adequately controls risk taking, continues to meet the "fit-and-proper" standards set when they were licensed, follows a "four-eyes" principle of management review, separates trading from back-office operations, and requires an internal audit function that reports directly to the board.[141] Some supervisors issue guidance on the roles and responsibilities of directors.[142]

Consolidated Supervision

It is important that supervisors oversee the consolidated position of both domestic and foreign subsidiaries, participations, and groups. Failure to do so has led to serious banking problems in many countries.

---

[140] The shorthand aggregate position is the sum of either the short or long positions in individual currencies, whichever is greater.

[141] Because Barings Bank in Singapore and Daiwa Bank in New York failed to separate these activities, "rogue" traders were able to expose these banks to very large losses.

[142] The U.S. Office of the Comptroller of the Currency (1987) issued a book of guidelines. See also Perú (1995) and De Nederlandsche Bank (1987).

Oversight needs to be consolidated internationally. Particularly in recent years, banks have increased their international activities through the development of regional operations abroad and offshore branch networks or closely related foreign subsidiaries. In such cases, supervisory authorities must insist on consolidated supervision, which includes offshore affiliates, in banks' reporting and analysis. The 1975 Basle Concordat demarcated responsibilities among home and host country supervisory authorities. These guidelines have been strengthened since then, most recently in 1992 (after the BCCI incident), to establish minimum standards for supervision of international banks and banking groups and a principle of consolidated supervision by the home country. All supervisory authorities that have international banks operating in their jurisdictions are expected to implement these guidelines.

Licensing Banks

New banks are needed to provide actual and potential competition to enable the banking system to serve the public interest efficiently. Nevertheless, the licensing process needs to offer some assurance to depositors that the new bank is sound and stable in order to protect small depositors and the banking system from destructive competition from undercapitalized, ill-conceived banks or those operated by unqualified or less reputable owners and managers. Consequently, new banks are required to meet certain standards to enable them to operate successfully.

These requirements, summarized in Table 23, set a corporate framework to ensure good internal governance by "suitable" owners, fit-and-proper boards of directors and managers with strong policies, procedures, and internal controls; a sound business plan to attain profitability as soon as possible; and enough capital of good composition to enable the bank to undertake initial lending activities, cover operating expenses, and provide a sufficient buffer against potential losses that might be experienced in the initial start-up years. During periods of banking distress, licensing laws may allow for a temporary moratorium on new banks; this would permit the formulation and implementation of a strategy for resolving banking problems in an orderly fashion and provide for procedures to relicense banks, or to otherwise facilitate exit of weak and insolvent banks and the enforcement of requirements aimed at strengthening remaining banks.

With the exception of the EU, there are no international agreements on licensing standards (although countries have trade-related bilateral agreements regarding the application of reciprocity in granting licenses to branches and subsidiaries of each other's banks). Nevertheless, a host country should not license a foreign bank branch, subsidiary, or represen-

Table 23. Basic Elements of a Licensing Process for Banks

(1) The licensing process should be made transparent by publishing and uniformly applying the laws, regulations, and requirements for a license, the process for applying for one, the decisions made on license applications, and the register of licensed banks. The law should give the supervisory authorities the right to demand pertinent information, a strong responsibility to maintain its confidentiality, and specify penalties for violating confidentiality.

(2) The requirements for a license should specify the nature of a joint-stock banking company and the provision of limited liability. They should set the ground rules for corporate governance, "suitability" standards for owners, and fit-and-proper specifications for boards of directors and managers to insure the honesty, trustworthiness, skill, and experience of bank owners, officers, and managers. They should determine whether commercial and industrial firms can own banks and set bounds for the organizational structure and administration of the bank, including its internal controls, internal and external audit functions, and any provisions necessary to prevent conflicts of interest.

(3) The laws or regulations should set minimum levels for initial capital and the composition of that capital.

(4) The license application should include a feasibility study and a business plan. An application should not be considered complete until all demanded information has been provided.

(5) The scope of the license, specifying activities that the bank can undertake—whether and to what extent it can take equity positions in nonbanks, engage in securities and insurance brokering and underwriting, leasing, factoring—should be clearly specified in the applicable laws and regulations.

(6) The corporate structure should be transparent.

(7) The bank should be licensed by the country in which it will conduct the major part of its business.[1]

---

[1] Sometimes a bank will obtain a license in a country that does not conduct consolidated oversight and then operate mainly through branches and subsidiaries in other countries. BCCI and Meridien were able to escape oversight in this way.

tative office without the approval of the home country's supervisory authorities.

Monitoring Banks

Banking supervisors monitor the condition of banks, so that corrective actions can be taken when banks deteriorate. Prudential supervision is best carried out through a combination of off-site monitoring and on-site inspections, although these techniques receive varying degrees of emphasis by different countries. There is, however, a recent tendency toward recognizing the importance of on-site inspection as the only way to assess the quality of internal controls and management.

Off-Site Supervision

The purpose of off-site supervision is to monitor compliance with regulations, provide early identification of problems that require prompt correction, set the priorities among banks for on-site inspections, and assess general information, press reports, and market data. Off-site monitoring is typically based on submitted reports containing, inter alia, balance sheet data, profit-and-loss statements, cash flows, and supplementary information, especially that on asset quality. The usefulness of the analysis is only as good as the quality of the data, however.

Less-sophisticated supervisory authorities limit themselves to relatively straightforward calculations of prudential ratios, including capital adequacy, liquidity, loan performance, and provisions for loan losses. In other countries, the performance of a bank is compared both over time and against that of similar banks in peer group analysis.[143]

Some supervisory authorities construct computer models to forecast banks' financial condition and analyze sectoral trends. The accuracy of such forecasts can be improved by the inclusion of data from the most recent on-site inspection.

On-Site Supervision

On-site inspections verify the accuracy and reliability of data included in a bank's financial reports and assess the quality of management and internal controls, and so on. Many countries make a full-scope evaluation of the condition of a bank by constructing a CAMEL rating[144] assessing capital adequacy, the quality of its assets, the adequacy of its management and system of internal controls, earnings, and liquidity. These assessments cannot be made satisfactorily off-site; in particular, the assessment of management capability has to be made on-site. More limited, targeted on-site inspections can focus on compliance with prudential regulations or on specific problems a bank is experiencing.

The frequency of on-site inspection is important, particularly where a bank's condition can change rapidly. A worthy goal is to conduct on-site examinations when they are needed, which is typically at least annually; but problem banks may need more frequent attention; while too-big-to-fail troubled banks that carry systemic risks may need to have inspectors continually in attendance so that they do not use their guarantee to increase their risk exposure (see Chapter 3).

---

[143] Experience has shown, however, that peer group analysis that identifies outlier banks in need of correction will fail when banks as a group make the same mistakes (Cole, Cornyn, and Gunther, 1995).

[144] A CAMEL rating is a measure of the relative soundness of a bank and is calculated on a 1–5 scale, with 1 being a strong performance. The term stands for capital, asset, management, earnings, and liquidity.

Early Warning Indicators

Bank supervisors can use experience and statistical modeling to detect threats to solvency and liquidity at an individual bank. They can assess the strength of the banking system as a whole from a distribution of banking assets by probability of insolvency.

Role of External Auditors

Some countries use external auditors as either substitutes for, or complements to, oversight by a supervisory agency, but some aspects of their use are controversial in some countries.[145] There is an increasing tendency for countries to require external auditors to report the deficiencies they identify not only to the bank's management but also to the supervisory agency. This development is thwarted, however, when a country's commercial law (as in the United Kingdom and the United States) confines external auditors' responsibility to shareholders,[146] so external audits are not a source of information for supervisors.[147]

In this situation, the supervisory agency (as in the United Kingdom) that does not wish to expand its on-site inspection function, may subcontract its supervisory role to external auditing firms, which conduct on-site examinations on its behalf. An audit is not the same as an on-site inspection, however. An audit is, in large part, backward looking, whereas a loan evaluation conducted by supervisors is anticipatory. While external auditors can verify accounting data that banks report, they normally do not have the skills needed to conduct on-site inspections that evaluate the quality of the loan portfolio and adequacy of provisions for losses.[148]

Other countries, such as Australia, Chile, and those in the EU, view external audits as complements to the on-site supervisory process and are increasingly moving to share supervisory responsibilities with external auditors.[149] For example, the EU has recently placed responsibilities on a bank's auditors to notify the supervisors of deficiencies that it identifies.[150] Sharing responsibilities means that letters to the bank from the supervi-

---

[145] See American Institute of Certified Public Accountants (AICPA, 1989, Section 10,040).

[146] There are a number of instances, however, where auditors have been sued by shareholders for failing to detect damaging deficiencies.

[147] Baring's external auditors notified management of deficiencies in internal controls relating to derivatives activities in writing during the 1992 audit (United Kingdom, House of Commons, 1995, paragraph 10.33). That information might have alerted the Bank of England to the bank's problems if it had been shared with the supervisory agency. The United Kingdom will need to amend its commercial law to reflect the new EU requirement discussed below.

[148] In the United States, responsible external auditors have been sued and found guilty in a number of instances for issuing "clean bills of health" to banks and thrifts that failed soon afterwards.

[149] See AICPA Professional Standards, Section 10,040.

[150] See European Union (1995).

sors are shown to the auditors and conversely. Moreover, auditors are present at supervisory meetings with management and supervisors attend auditors' final conferences with management and directors.

Role of Banks' Internal Controls

Supervisors' and auditors' traditional reliance on periodic on- and off-site evaluation based on time-specific accounting data is based on a premise that a bank's condition will not change markedly between reporting and inspection periods. (It is not reasonable to expect a bank to report on a continuous basis.) That assumption is less valid today when a bank can change the composition of its portfolio overnight and its risk exposure momentarily through, for example, the use of derivatives. While most banks fail as a result of credit losses, new approaches to their supervision need to be developed.[151] Supervisors in very few countries are trained to evaluate the creditworthiness of derivative portfolios. Consequently, risk restraint is becoming increasingly dependent on the bank's own risk-management systems to ensure the bank's safety, while the supervisor's task is to assess the adequacy of these systems.[152]

One suggestion is to place increasing reliance on banks' own systems of internal control. This reliance is feasible when information about banks and their borrowers is inexpensive, plentiful, frequently updated, and reliable. Then, the supervisors' role is to ensure the adequacy of these controls. The precommitment approach to capital adequacy, discussed earlier, falls in this category.

Enforcement and Corrective Actions

Supervision intends to monitor compliance with prudential standards and safe and sound banking operations of the bank. In case of noncompliance or unsafe and unsound banking practices, supervisors can first seek improvement through moral suasion, then through "informal" followed by "formal" actions. The relative emphasis placed on these tools varies from country to country. When moral suasion fails, the supervisor may choose to take an informal action (e.g., by issuing a letter of reprimand or obtaining a memorandum of understanding) that is not legally enforceable, but which notifies the institution that its noncompliance has been noted and should be remedied and that it has been recorded to establish a track record. Continued noncompliance would normally be met by legal-

---

[151] See Folkerts-Landau, Ito, and others (1995).
[152] If the assessment of a bank's risk-management system is that it is inadequate, supervisors can conduct an in-depth analysis of its risk exposures.

ly enforceable formal actions that include cease-and-desist orders, removal of major officers or prohibition orders, and fines.

Alternative Approaches

Some countries favor a system of prompt corrective actions (PCA) established by law or regulation that specifies actions that the regulators should or must take as the condition of a bank deteriorates. Each step in the graduated process will be triggered by clearly defined deficiencies; most notably when the bank reaches a certain capital level. Such a legal obligation to take action will be particularly necessary where supervisors are prone to forbear or are subject to political interference.

The PCA system in Table 24 describes the system used in the United States. It defines a critical minimum capital ratio below which closure is required; categories of banks according to their capital ratios; and corrective actions that either must or may be applied to banks with capital deficiencies.

Other countries prefer to grant full discretion to their supervisors to take remedial measures as needed. This system can be assisted by an incentive system that rewards supervisors (perhaps financially) for maintaining a sound system and holds them accountable when they fail to do so. To operate a discretionary system successfully requires that supervisors be free from political interference.

Closing Nonviable Banks

If the institution continues to deteriorate, the supervisor should have the right to take the institution from its owners, place it in conservatorship to be sold, merged, or restructured, or call for its liquidation. Grounds for conservatorship and liquidation are listed in Table 25.

Data Creation and Disclosure

Bank supervisors can play a role in obtaining and verifying for their own use and supplying accurate data on bank condition to the public and on borrower condition to banks. Very few publish their information at present, however, although banks usually have a legal obligation to publish audited annual financial statements. Where supervisors do not collect and supply the data themselves, they can encourage private suppliers to provide data services. Data from private sources or from supervisors can cover the condition of individual banks, the system as a whole, and bank borrowers, and report market conditions as they affect banks and their customers. Regulations can assist in improving the availability of information

Table 24. Prompt Corrective Actions in the United States

1. The critical minimum capital ratio is typically defined as either zero or 2 percent for either the unadjusted ratio of equity to assets or the total risk-adjusted capital ratio.

2. Categories of banks

Level 1. Banks that maintain capital ratios that are significantly in excess of the minimums established are called "well capitalized."

Level 2. Banks that meet or exceed the minimum ratios established but do not belong to level 1 are referred to as "adequately capitalized."

Level 3. Banks that are not in compliance with minimum capital standards but are not in level 4 or 5 are "undercapitalized."

Level 4. Banks that maintain capital ratios that are above the critical minimum, but significantly below the prescribed ratios are called "significantly undercapitalized."

Level 5. Banks that have one or more capital ratios below the critical minimum are "critically undercapitalized."

3. Corrective actions for undercapitalized banks

• All undercapitalized banks shall submit, within a specified time, a capital restoration plan to their supervisor. The plan will specify how the bank will meet applicable capital standards without increasing risk (including credit and interest rate risk, and other types of risk) and the activities in which it will engage. The plan will also provide any other information that the regulators will require. The plan must be approved or disapproved in a timely manner by the supervisory agency, which has the right to demand that appropriate changes be made to the plan.

• The supervisory agency shall prohibit any undercapitalized bank from increasing its liabilities. Limited exceptions may be granted.

• For banks in levels 4 and 5, the regulators may (1) require banks to sell shares, (2) prevent them from paying dividends, (3) restrict the interest rates they pay, (4) prohibit the payment of bonuses or excessive compensation to executive officers, (5) require approval for the opening of new branches, (6) prohibit the receipt of deposits from correspondent banks, (7) require the election of new directors, and (8) restrict other activities.

• In addition, banks in level 5 will be prevented from (1) paying interest on subordinated debt, (2) undertaking any material transaction, and (3) changing accounting methods.

• Banks that do not improve and so remain in level 5 will be placed in conservatorship or receivership/liquidation after 120 days.

Source: The U.S. FDIC Improvement Act of 1991, Section 131.

by establishing requirements regarding what data should be reported and the timing and format of the reports. Nevertheless, supervisors provide a service only when the data they obtain and disseminate are valid—there is a danger of obfuscation to achieve political ends. "Disinformation," which has been a problem in some countries, deters market discipline and weakens the system in the long run.

Table 25. Grounds for Conservatorship and Liquidation

Conservatorship	Liquidation
• Serious deterioration with regard to capital adequacy; for example, capital falls below 25% of the required minimum	• The bank defaults on its obligations
	• Negative capital (insolvency)
• Serious breaches of laws or regulations	• Other reasons for assuming that the bank is not viable
• Seriously unsafe and unsound banking practices	
• Willful violation of a cease-and-desist order	
• Willful and unlawful concealment of data or noncooperation with the supervisor	
• Criminal activities	

Data on Borrowers

Good credit assessment is a decisive factor in banking. When he applies for a loan, a borrower typically knows the condition and prospects of his business better than his bank. Moreover, an existing loan can be impaired if economic conditions worsen or a borrower takes on an excessive amount of debt from another source. Consequently, bank supervisors can help to redress this asymmetry of information by collecting data on bank borrowers and supplying nonconfidential parts of the data to banks.

In France and some other EU countries, for example, each bank is required to report large corporate loans to the central bank.[153] In return, banks are told every month the total indebtedness of all large borrowers to the banking system. To retain confidentiality among banks, the names of other lenders are not revealed. As an alternative, a country can take a decentralized approach by permitting the development of private rating services for borrowers.[154]

Credit evaluation by a bank's loan officers is a complex, data-intensive process that requires good judgment that may take years of training and experience to acquire. Credit bureaus that monitor borrowers' credit history can assist banks in making credit decisions. Supervisors can encourage the provision of such bureaus in countries where they do not exist,

---

[153] A BIS (Bank for International Settlements) working group is trying to improve the comparability of credit registers in several countries, although neither that working group nor the Basle Committee is directly involved in the international exchange of credit register information.

[154] Agencies, such as TRW and Equifax in the United States, sell information about small business and consumer borrowers and several companies (such as Moody's and Standard & Poor's) rate larger borrowers.

especially as recent advances in credit-evaluation techniques are making the process more systematic. Credit-scoring techniques, derived from estimation of borrowers' default probabilities, applied first to judging applications for consumer credit in the United States, are now being used to evaluate mortgage applicants. Such techniques could assist banks in making initial credit decisions and monitoring the continuing condition of borrowers in other countries. Credit-scoring methods would also assist supervisors in classifying individual loans and setting the appropriate provisions against them, but there is no evidence that the technique has been adopted by any country to date.

Data on Bank Condition

Public disclosure of information can facilitate reduced reliance on supervision and orient the system toward market discipline and so strengthen banking system soundness. Releasing data is feasible if most banks are sound. Then, the provision of accurate data can enable the public to migrate from unsound banks to stronger ones without precipitating a run to cash or abroad. Such discipline will serve to keep the system strong by rewarding sound actions and penalizing unduly risky activities.

The public has a right to good data on the condition of banks and there is evidence from many countries that the public (which includes the bank's principal creditors) tries to distinguish sound banks from unsound banks to protect its interests by relocating funds to a safe place. Credible, well-publicized information that a bank is sound is likely to prevent a run on it and other sound banks in the system, even when some banks in the same region or in the same location are unsound. In fact, an uninformed public is more likely to run from a sound bank that it considers similar in some way to a failed bank than an informed one. Thus, good information can avert a generalized run. While transfers from weak to strong banks in a flight to quality can be disruptive, they are easier for the authorities to handle than a general flight to cash or abroad, because a flight to quality within the banking system does not reduce bank reserves in the aggregate or cause a decline in the money supply.

Publishing information when there are few if any strong banks and no credible guarantee of deposit repayment is more problematic. While the supervisory agency has an obligation to keep the public well informed about the condition of the banking system, it does not want to initiate a panic, but if it does not inform the public and the public incurs losses, it may be held responsible for these losses. In an unsound system, perhaps the best that can be achieved is to include provisions for the future full disclosure of accounting data and even supervisory ratings after the banking system, including the legal, regulatory, and supervisory infrastructure in which banks operate, has been successfully restructured. Then, the public could exert constructive, discriminating discipline on banks, and regulators would no longer be allowed to hide behind a cloak of secrecy.

Data on Market Conditions

The damage to several countries' banking sectors caused by recent bubbles in the real estate and stock markets suggest that countries that do not already do so may want to keep close track and take account of the behavior of asset prices and the condition of real estate and other asset markets. This information is important so that supervisors can anticipate when they will need to pay special attention to banks with portfolio concentrations in these industries.[155] Supervisors can obtain the information themselves, or use private sector data when they exist. For example, as a result of the collapse of the real estate market in the United States, the Federal Deposit Insurance Corporation (FDIC) now publishes a regular survey of the real estate markets in major regions. Supervisory agencies in other countries might find the provision of similar information cost effective in discouraging asset concentration or, at least, encourage private agencies to provide these data services.

Conclusion

Effective bank supervisors help to keep the banking system sound and protect small depositors. Supervision should, however, complement and not replace good corporate governance and the constructive force of market discipline. As is well known, overregulation can detract from economic efficiency, innovation, and growth. Finding the right balance is an important challenge.

---

[155] Carse (1995) points out that banks in Hong Kong failed to appreciate the industry risk inherent on property lending in an inflated market. The lending decisions of individual banks that may have appeared prudent in isolation were collectively rash. Consequently, the Hong Kong Monetary Authority required banks with high exposure in real estate to supply a policy statement detailing lending procedures and exposure limits.

References

References

Akhtar, M.A., "Causes and Consequences of the 1989–92 Credit Slowdown: Overview and Perspective," *Quarterly Review*, Federal Reserve Bank of New York, Vol. 18 (Winter 1993–94), pp. 1–23.

Alexander, William E., Tomás José T. Baliño, and Charles Enoch, eds., *The Adoption of Indirect Instruments of Monetary Policy*, IMF Occasional Paper, No. 126 (Washington: International Monetary Fund, 1995).

Alexander, William E., and Francesco Caramazza, "Money Versus Credit: The Role of Banks in the Monetary Transmission Process," in *Frameworks for Monetary Stability*, ed. by Tomás J. T. Baliño and Carlo Cottarelli (Washington: International Monetary Fund, 1994), pp. 397–422.

Allen, Linda, and Anthony Saunders, "Forbearance and Valuation of Deposit Insurance as a Callable Put," *Journal of Banking and Finance*, Vol. 17 (June 1993), pp. 629–43.

American Institute of Certified Public Accountants, *The Relationship Between Bank Supervisors and External Auditors* (New York, July 1989).

Aoki, Masahiko, and Hugh Patrick, eds., *The Japanese Main Bank System: Its Relevance for Developing and Transforming Economies* (Oxford, New York: Oxford University Press, 1994).

Baer, Herbert, and Daniela Klingebiel, "Systemic Risk When Depositors Bear Losses: Five Case Studies," in *Banking, Financial Markets, and Systemic Risk*, Vol. 7 of *Research in Financial Services Private and Public Policy*, ed. by George G. Kaufman (Greenwich, Connecticut: JAI Press, 1995), pp. 195–302.

Bank for International Settlements, *Report of the Committee on Interbank Netting Schemes of the Central Banks of the Group of Ten Countries* (Basle, November 1990).

_____, *Delivery Versus Payment in Securities Settlement Systems* (Basle, September 1992).

_____, *Central Bank Payment and Settlement Services with Respect to Cross-Border and Multi-Currency Transactions* (Basle, September 1993).

_____, *Report of the Steering Group on Settlement Risk in Foreign Exchange Transactions* (Basle, December 1996).

Bank of England, "Is There a Credit Crunch?" *Quarterly Bulletin*, Bank of England, Vol. 31 (May 1991), pp. 256–59.

Bank of Japan, "Characteristics of Interest Rate Indicators," *Quarterly Bulletin*, Bank of Japan, Vol. 2 (November 1994), pp. 35–62.

Barker, David, and David Holdsworth, "The Causes of Bank Failures in the 1980s," Federal Reserve Bank of New York, Research Paper No. 93–25, August 1993.

Basle Committee on Banking Supervision, *Report on the Supervision of Banks' Foreign Establishments* (Basle: Bank for International Settlements, September 1975).

———, "Principles for the Supervision of Banks' Foreign Establishments" (Basle: Bank for International Settlements, May 1983).

———, *Report on International Developments in Banking Supervision*, No. 9 (Basle: Bank for International Settlements, September 1994).

———, "Communiqué" (Basle: Bank for International Settlements, December 1995).

———, "Amendment to the Capital Accord to Incorporate Market Risks" (Basle: Bank for International Settlements, January 1996).

Beatty, Anne, Sandra L. Chamberlain, and Joseph Magliola, "Managing Financial Reports of Commercial Banks: The Influence of Taxes, Regulatory Capital and Earnings," The Wharton Financial Institutions Center, Paper No. 94–02, August 1993.

Benston, George J., "Federal Regulation of Banking: Historical Overview," in *Deregulating Financial Services: Public Policy in Flux*, ed. by George G. Kaufman and Roger C. Kormendi (Cambridge, Massachusetts: Ballinger Publishing Company, 1986), pp. 1–48.

Berg, Jesper, "The Nordic Bank Crisis—Lessons to Be Learned" (unpublished, Washington: International Monetary Fund, July 1995).

Berglöf, Erik, "Corporate Governance in Transition Economies: The Theory and Its Policy Implications," in *Corporate Governance in Transitional Economies: Insider Control and the Role of Banks*, ed. by Masahiko Aoki and Hyung-Ki Kim (Washington: The World Bank, 1995), pp. 59–95.

Blum, Jürg, and Martin Hellwig, "The Macroeconomic Implications of Capital Adequacy Requirements for Banks," *European Economic Review*, Vol. 39 (1995), pp. 739–49.

Bockelmann, Horst, "Comments [on Goodhart]," in *Financial Stability in a Changing Environment*, ed. by Kuniho Sawamoto, Zenta Nakajima, and Hiroo Taguchi (New York: St. Martin's Press, 1995), pp. 498–505.

Bonin, John P., *Banking in the Transition: Privatizing Banks in Hungary, Poland, and Czech Republic*, issue paper for Institute for East West Studies, Comparative Privatization Project, State Withdrawal: Creating Market-Oriented Banking Sectors for the Economies in Transition (London, European Bank for Reconstruction and Development, December 4–5, 1995).

Borish, Michael S., Millard Long, and Michel Noël, *Restructuring Banks and Enterprises*, World Bank Discussion Paper, No. 279 (Washington: The World Bank, 1995).

Bosworth, Barry, "Institutional Change and the Efficacy of Monetary Policy," *Brookings Papers on Economic Activity: 1* (1989), pp. 77–110.

Brinkmann, Emile J., and Paul M. Horvitz, "Risk-Based Capital Standards and the Credit Crunch," *Journal of Money, Credit, and Banking*, Vol. 27 (August 1995), pp. 848–63.

Brock, Philip L., ed., *If Texas Were Chile: A Primer on Banking Reform* (San Francisco: ICS Press, 1992).

Brunner, Karl, and Allan M. Meltzer, "Money and Credit in the Monetary Transmission Process," *American Economic Review*, Vol. 28 (May 1988), pp. 446–51.

Calvo, Guillermo A., and Fabrizio Coricelli, "Credit Market Imperfections and Output Response in Previously Centrally Planned Economies," in *Building Sound Finance in Emerging Market Economies*, ed. by Gerard Caprio, David Folkerts-Landau, and Timothy D. Lane (Washington: International Monetary Fund and World Bank, 1994), pp. 257–94.

Calvo, Guillermo A., and Morris Goldstein, "Crisis Prevention and Crisis Management after Mexico: What Role for the Official Sector?" paper presented at the Institute for International Economics Conference on Private Capital Flows to Emerging Markets after the Mexican Crisis, held in Vienna, Austria, September 1995.

Calvo, Guillermo A., and Manmohan S. Kumar, "Money Demand, Bank Credit, and Economic Performance in Former Socialist Economies," *Staff Papers*, International Monetary Fund, Vol. 41 (June 1994), pp. 314–49.

Cantor, Richard, and John Wenninger, "Perspective on the Credit Slowdown, *Quarterly Review*," Federal Reserve Bank of New York, Vol. 18 (Spring 1993), pp. 3–36.

Caprio, Gerard Jr., and Daniela Klingebiel, "Bank Insolvency: Bad Luck, Bad Policy, or Bad Banking?" paper presented at the World Bank Annual Bank Conference on Development Economics, Washington, April 25–26, 1996.

Carse, David, "Market Entry and Asset Quality," *Quarterly Bulletin*, Hong Kong Monetary Authority (February 1995), pp. 42–49.

Chari, V. V., Larry E. Jones, and Rodolfo E. Manuelli, "The Growth Effects of Monetary Policy," *Quarterly Review*, Federal Reserve Bank of Minneapolis, Vol. 19 (Fall 1995), pp. 18–32.

Clair, Robert T., Joanna O. Kolson, and Kenneth J. Robinson, "The Texas Banking Crisis and the Payments System," *Economic Review*, Federal Reserve Bank of Dallas (First Quarter 1995), pp. 13–21.

Clare, Andrew D., "Using the Arbitrage Pricing Theory to Calculate the Probability of Financial Institution Failure," *Journal of Money, Credit, and Banking*, Vol. 27 (May 1995), pp. 920–26.

Cole, Rebel A., and Jeffrey W. Gunther, "Separating the Likelihood and Timing of Bank Failure," *Journal of Banking and Finance*, Vol. 19 (September 1995), pp. 1073–89.

Cole, Rebel A., Barbara G. Cornyn, and Jeffrey W. Gunther, "FIMS: A New Monitoring System for Banking Institutions," *Federal Reserve Bulletin* (January 1995), pp. 1–15.

Cottarelli, Carlo, and Angeliki Kourelis, "Financial Structure, Bank Lending Rates, and the Transmission Mechanism of Monetary Policy," *Staff Papers*, International Monetary Fund, Vol. 41 (December 1994), pp. 587–623.

Dale, Richard, "International Banking Regulation," in *International Financial Market Regulation*, ed. by Benn Steil (Chichester; New York: John Wiley and Sons, 1994), pp. 1–15.

De Gregorio, José, and Pablo E. Guidotti, "Financial Development and Economic Growth," IMF Working Paper 92/101 (Washington: International Monetary Fund, December 1992).

de Juan, Aristóbulo, "Does Bank Insolvency Matter? And What to Do About It?" Economic Development Institute of the World Bank Working Paper

(Washington: Economic Development Institute of the World Bank, 1991).

De Nederlandsche Bank, "Memorandum on the Role of the Supervisory Board of a Bank," December 31, 1986, *Quarterly Bulletin* (Amsterdam: De Nederlandsche Bank, December 1987).

Demirgüc-Kunt, Asli, "Deposit-Institution Failures: A Review of Empirical Literature," *Economic Review*, Federal Reserve Bank of Cleveland, Vol. 25 (Fourth Quarter 1989), pp. 2–18.

Diamond, Douglas W., and Phillip H. Dybvig, "Bank Runs, Deposit Insurance, and Liquidity," *Journal of Political Economy*, Vol. 91 (June 1983), pp. 401–19.

Dimsdale, Nicholas, "Banks, Capital Markets, and the Monetary Transmission Mechanism," *Oxford Review of Economic Policy*, Vol. 10 (Winter 1994), pp. 34–48.

Dittus, Peter, *Corporate Governance in Central Europe: The Role of Banks*, BIS Economic Paper, No. 42 (Basle: Bank for International Settlements, August 1994).

Dooley, Michael P., and Peter Isard, "The Role of Incentives and Planning in Market-Oriented Transition," in *Finance and the International Economy 6*, ed. by Richard O'Brien (Oxford: Oxford University Press, 1992), pp. 19–31.

Dornbusch, Rudiger, and Stanley Fischer, *Macroeconomics* (New York: McGraw-Hill Book Company, 6th ed. 1994).

Drees, Burkhard, and Ceyla Pazarbaşioğlu, "The Nordic Banking Crises: Pitfalls in Financial Liberalization," IMF Working Paper 95/61 (Washington: International Monetary Fund, June 1995).

Dziobek, Claudia, "Regulatory and Tax Treatment of Loan Loss Provisions," IMF Papers on Policy Analysis and Assessment 96/6 (Washington: International Monetary Fund 1996).

_____, Olivier Frécaut, and María Nieto, "Non-G-10 Countries and the Basle Capital Rules: How Tough a Challenge Is It to Join the Basle Club?" IMF Paper on Policy Analysis and Assessment 95/5 (Washington: International Monetary Fund, March 1995).

European Union, Directive 95/26/EC of the European Parliament and Council Directive, *Official Journal of the European Communities*, No. L 168/7 (June 29, 1995).

_____, Directive 77/780CEE of the European Parliament and Council Directive, *Official Journal of the European Communities*, No. L322/30 (December 12, 1977).

Faig-Aumalle, Miquel, "Implications of Banking Market Structure for Monetary Policy: A Survey," IMF Working Paper 87/25 (Washington: International Monetary Fund, April 1987).

Fairlamb, David, "Beyond Capital," *Institutional Investor*, Vol. 19 (August 1994), pp. 16–26.

Fama, Eugene F., "What's Different About Banks?" *Journal of Monetary Economics*, Vol. 15 (January 1985), pp. 29–39.

Fidler, Stephen (1996a), "IMF urged to do more in monitoring banking," *Financial Times*, March 26, 1996, p. 4.

_____ (1996b), "IMF urged to be bolder in fight to stem bank crises," *Financial Times*, March 27, 1996, p. 6.

Fischer, Klaus P., and Jean-Pierre Gueyie, "Financial Liberalization and Bank Solvency," paper presented at the symposium on Business Finance in Emerging Markets, held at the University of Laval, Québec, August 31–September 1, 1995.

Fischer, Stanley, "International Capital Flows, the International Agencies and Financial Stability," in *Financial Stability in a Changing Environment*, ed. by Kuniho Sawamoto, Zenta Nakajima, and Hiroo Taguchi (New York: St. Martin's Press, 1995), pp. 26–37.

Folkerts-Landau, David, Takatoshi Ito, and others, *International Capital Markets: Developments, Prospects, and Policy Issues*, World Economic and Financial Surveys (Washington: International Monetary Fund, 1995).

Freeland, Charles, "The Work of the Basle Committee," in *Current Legal Issues Affecting Central Banks*, Vol. 2, ed. by Robert C. Effros (Washington: International Monetary Fund, 1994), pp. 231–40.

Fries, Steven M., and Timothy D. Lane, "Financial and Enterprise Restructuring in Emerging Market Economies," in *Building Sound Finance in Emerging Market Economies*, ed. by Gerard Caprio, David Folkerts-Landau, and Timothy D. Lane (Washington: International Monetary Fund and World Bank, 1994), pp. 21–46.

Galbis, Vicente, "Financial Sector Reforms in Eight Countries: Issues and Results," IMF Working Paper 95/141 (Washington: International Monetary Fund, December 1995).

———, "High Real Interest Rates Under Financial Liberalization: Is There a Problem?" IMF Working Paper 93/7 (Washington: International Monetary Fund, January 1993).

Garcia, Gillian, "Comparing and Confronting the Recent Banking Problems in Indonesia, Turkey, and Venezuela" (unpublished, Washington: International Monetary Fund, December 1994).

———, "Lessons from Bank Failures Worldwide," paper presented at the conference on Regulating Depository Institutions, held at Koç University, Istanbul, November 3, 1995.

———, "Deposit Insurance: Obtaining the Benefits and Avoiding the Pitfalls," IMF Working Paper 96/83 (Washington: International Monetary Fund, August 1996).

———, and Matthew I. Saal, "Internal Governance, Market Discipline, and Regulatory Restraint, "in *Rethinking Bank Regulation*, proceedings of the 32nd Annual Conference on Bank Structure and Competition, May 1996 (Chicago: Federal Reserve Bank of Chicago, forthcoming).

Gertler, Mark, "Financial Structure and Aggregate Economic Activity: An Overview," *Journal of Money, Credit, and Banking*, Vol. 20 (August 1988, Part 2), pp. 559–88.

Gilbert, R. Alton, and Sangkyun Park, "Value of Early Warning Models in Bank Supervision," draft working paper, Federal Reserve Bank of St. Louis and Federal Reserve Bank of New York, 1994.

Goldstein, Morris, and others (1993a), *International Capital Markets: Part I: Exchange Rate Management and International Capital Flows*, World Economic and Financial Surveys (Washington: International Monetary Fund, 1993).

——— (1993b), *International Capital Markets: Development, Prospects, and Policy Issues*, World Economic and Financial Surveys (Washington: International Monetary Fund, 1992).

Goodfriend, Marvin, "Money, Credit, Banking, and Payments System Policy," *Economic Review*, Federal Reserve Bank of Richmond (January/February 1991), pp. 7–23.

Goodhart, Charles, "Price Stability and Financial Fragility," in *Financial Stability in a Changing Environment*, ed. by Kuniho Sawamoto, Zenta Nakajima, and Hiroo Taguchi (New York: St. Martin's Press, 1995).

Gorton, Gary, "Banking Panics and Business Cycles," *Oxford Economic Papers*, No. 40 (December 1988), pp. 221–55.

Griffith-Jones, Stephany, "Introductory Framework," in *Financial Reform in Central and Eastern Europe*, ed. by Stephany Griffith-Jones and Zdeněk Drábek (New York: St. Martin's Press, 1995), pp. 3–15.

Guitián, Manuel, "A Neglected Dimension of Monetary Policy" (unpublished, Washington: International Monetary Fund, January 25, 1993).

Gulde, Ann-Marie, "Liquid Asset Ratios—An Effective Policy Tool?" IMF Monetary and Exchange Affairs Department Operational Paper 95/04 (unpublished, Washington: International Monetary Fund, May 1995).

Hall, Stephen, and David Miles, "Monitoring Bank Risk: A Market Based Approach," Birkbeck College Department of Economics Discussion Paper in Financial Economics FE–3/90 (April 1990), pp. 1–19.

Hargraves, Monica, and Garry J. Schinasi, "Monetary Policy, Financial Liberalization, and Asset Price Inflation," Annex I in *World Economic Outlook* (Washington: International Monetary Fund, May 1993), pp. 81–95.

Hausmann, Ricardo, and Michael Gavin, "The Roots of Banking Crises: The Macroeconomic Context," paper presented at the Inter-American Development Bank Conference on Banking Crises in Latin America, held in Washington, October 6–7, 1995.

Hinds, Manuel, "Economic Effects of Financial Crises," Policy, Planning, and Research Working Paper, No. 104 (Washington: World Bank, October 1988).

Hong Kong Monetary Authority, *Annual Report* (Hong Kong, 1994).

International Accounting Standards Committee, *International Accounting Standards* (Rochester, England: The Stanhope Press, 1995).

International Monetary Fund, *Theoretical Aspects of the Design of Fund-Supported Adjustment Programs*, IMF Occasional Paper, No. 55 (Washington: International Monetary Fund, September 1987).

———, "The Special Data Dissemination Standard: Standards for the Dissemination by Countries of Economic and Financial Statistics" (Washington: International Monetary Fund, April 1995).

———, *Manual on Monetary and Financial Statistics* (Washington: International Monetary Fund, forthcoming in mid-1997).

Jaffee, Dwight, and Mark Levonian, "Russian Banking," in *Weekly Letter*, Federal Reserve Bank of San Francisco, No. 95–35 (October 20, 1995), pp. 1–3.

James, Christopher, "Some Evidence on the Uniqueness of Bank Loans," *Journal of Financial Economics*, Vol. 19 (December 1987), pp. 217–35.

James, Harold, *International Monetary Cooperation Since Bretton Woods* (New York: Oxford University Press, 1995).

"Japan Lifts Another Veil," *The Banker*, November 1995, p. 8.

Johnston, R. Barry, "Distressed Financial Institutions in Thailand: Structural Weaknesses, Support Operations, and Economic Consequences," in *Banking Crises: Cases and Issues*, ed. by V. Sundararajan and Tomás J.T. Baliño (Washington: International Monetary Fund, 1991), pp. 234–75.

———, and Ceyla Pazarbaşioğlu, "Linkages Between Financial Variables, Financial Sector Reform, and Economic Growth and Efficiency," IMF Working Paper, WP/95/103 (Washington: International Monetary Fund, October 1995).

Kaminsky, Graciela L., and Carmen M. Reinhart, "The Twin Crises: The Causes of Banking and Balance-of-Payments Problems," International Finance Discussion Paper No. 544 (Washington: Board of Governors of the Federal Reserve System, March 1996).

Kane, Edward J., "Difficulties of Transferring Risk-Based Capital Requirements to Developing Countries," *Pacific-Basin Finance Journal*, Vol. 3 (July 1995), pp. 193–216.

Kapur, Ishan, and others, *Ghana: Adjustment and Growth, 1983–91*, IMF Occasional Paper, No. 86 (Washington: International Monetary Fund, September 1991).

Kaufman, George G., "Are Some Banks Too Large to Fail? Myth and Reality," *Contemporary Policy Issues*, Vol. 8 (October 1990), pp. 1–14.

———, "Bank Contagion: A Review of the Theory and Evidence," *Journal of Financial Services Research*, Vol. 8 (1994), pp. 123–50.

Kim, Myung-Sun, and William Kross, "The Impact of the 1989 Change in Bank Capital Standards on Loan Loss Provisions" (unpublished, New Brunswick, New Jersey: Rutgers University, August 1995).

Kneeshaw, J. T., "Survey of Non-Financial Sector Balance Sheets in Industrialized Countries: Implications for the Monetary Policy Transmission Mechanism," BIS Working Paper No. 25 (Basle: Bank for International Settlements, April 1995).

Kupiec, Paul H., and James M. O'Brien, "A Precommitment Approach to Capital Requirements for Market Risk," in *The New Tool Set*, proceedings of the 31st Annual Conference on Bank Structure and Competition, May 1995 (Chicago: Federal Reserve Bank of Chicago, 1995), pp. 552–62.

Kyei, Alexander, "Deposit Protection Arrangements: A Survey," IMF Working Paper 95/134 (Washington: International Monetary Fund, December 1995).

Lane, Timothy D., "Market Discipline," *Staff Papers*, International Monetary Fund, Vol. 40 (March 1993), pp. 53–88.

Leone, Alfredo M., "Institutional and Operational Aspects of Central Bank Losses," IMF Paper on Policy Analysis and Assessment 93/14 (Washington: International Monetary Fund, September 1993).

Louis, Jean-Victor, "Banking in the European Community After 1992," in Vol. 2 of *Current Legal Issues Affecting Central Banks*, ed. by Robert C. Effros (Washington: International Monetary Fund, 1994), pp. 69–81.

Luckett, Dudley G., "Credit Standards and Tight Money," *Journal of Money, Credit, and Banking*, Vol. 2 (November 1970), pp. 420–33.

Ludwig, Eugene A., letter to the Chief Executive Officers of National Banks, including a Survey of Underwriting Policies and Practices, November 7, 1995.

Maciejewski, Edouard, and Ahsan Mansur, eds., *Jordan—Strategy for Adjustment and Growth*, IMF Occasional Paper, No. 136 (Washington: International Monetary Fund, May 1996).

Marston, David, "The Use of Reserve Requirements in Monetary Control," IMF Monetary and Exchange Affairs Department Operational Paper (unpublished, Washington: International Monetary Fund, 1996).

Mathieson, Donald J., and Richard D. Haas, "Establishing Monetary Control in Financial Systems with Insolvent Institutions," *Staff Papers*, International Monetary Fund, Vol. 42 (March 1995), pp. 184–201.

Mishkin, Frederic S., "Asymmetric Information and Financial Crises: A Historical Perspective," in *Financial Markets and Financial Crises*, ed. by R. Glenn Hubbard (Chicago: University of Chicago Press, 1991), pp. 69–108.

———, "Preventing Financial Crises: An International Perspective," NBER Working Paper No. 4636 (Cambridge, Massachusetts: National Bureau of Economic Research, February 1994).

Montes-Negret, Fernando, and Luca Papi, "Are Bank Interest Rate Spreads Too High?" *Viewpoint* (Washington: The World Bank, Financial Sector Development Department, February 1996).

Nascimento, Jean-Claude, "Crisis in the Financial Sector and the Authorities' Reaction: The Philippines," in *Banking Crises: Cases and Issues*, ed. by V. Sundararajan and Tomás J. T. Baliño (Washington: International Monetary Fund, 1991), pp. 175–233.

National Bank of Commerce, Tanzania, "Press Statement" *Guardian* (Dar es Salaam: July 24, 1995).

Otani, Ichiro, and Chi Do Pham, eds., *The Lao People's Democratic Republic— Systemic Transformation and Adjustments*, IMF Occasional Paper, No. 137 (Washington: International Monetary Fund, May 1996).

Padoa-Schioppa, Tommaso "Cooperation Between Banking and Market Regulators," paper presented at the XX Annual Conference of the International Organization of Securities Commissions (IOSCO) held in Paris, July 12, 1995.

Pérez-Campanero, Juan, and Alfredo M. Leone, "Liberalization and Financial Crisis in Uruguay, 1974–87," in *Banking Crises: Cases and Issues*, ed. by V. Sundararajan and Tomás J.T. Baliño (Washington: International Monetary Fund, 1991), pp. 276–375.

Perotti, Enrico C., "Bank Lending in Transition Economies," *Journal of Banking and Finance*, Vol. 17 (September 1993), pp. 1021–32.

Perú, Superintendencia de Banca y Seguros, *Guía del Director de Empresas Bancarias, Financieras y de Crédito de Consumo* (Lima, 1995).

Pozdena, Randall J., "Is Banking Really Prone to Panics?" *Weekly Letter*, Federal Reserve Bank of San Francisco, No. 91–35 (October 11, 1991).

Premchand, A., *Effective Government Accounting* (Washington: International Monetary Fund, 1995).

Prowse, Stephen, *Corporate Governance in an International Perspective*, BIS Economic Paper, No. 41 (Basle: Bank for International Settlements, July 1994).

———, "Alternative Methods of Corporate Control in Commercial Banks," *Economic Review*, Federal Reserve Bank of Dallas (Third Quarter 1995), pp. 24–36.

Quirk, Peter J., and Owen Evans, *Capital Account Convertibility: Review of Experience and Implications for IMF Policies*, IMF Occasional Paper, No. 131 (Washington: International Monetary Fund, October 1995).

Reserve Bank of New Zealand, "Review of Banking Supervision: Reserve Bank's Policy Conclusions," *Reserve Bank Bulletin*, Vol. 58 (June 1995), pp. 73–78.

Rojas-Suárez, Liliana, and Steven R. Weisbrod (1995a), "Banking Crises in Latin America: Experience and Issues," paper presented at the Inter-American Development Bank Conference/Group of Thirty Conference on Banking Crises in Latin America, October 6–7, 1995.

_____ (1995b), *Financial Fragilities in Latin America: The 1980s and 1990s*, IMF Occasional Paper, No. 132 (Washington: International Monetary Fund, October 1995).

Romer, Christina D., and David H. Romer, "Credit Channel or Credit Actions? An Interpretation of the Postwar Transmission Mechanism," in *Changing Capital Markets: Implications for Monetary Policy*, a symposium sponsored by the Federal Reserve Bank of Kansas City, August 19–21, 1993 (Kansas City: Federal Reserve Bank of Kansas City), pp. 71–116.

Rosett, Claudia, "Banking Crisis Erupts in Russia Amid Rumors of Unsoundness," *Wall Street Journal*, August 25, 1995, p. A4.

Rostowski, Jacek, "Systemic Requirements for Monetary Stability in Eastern Europe and the Former Soviet Union," IMF Working Paper 94/24 (Washington: International Monetary Fund, February 1994).

Saal, Matthew I., and Lorena M. Zamalloa, "Use of Central Bank Credit Auctions in Economies in Transition," *Staff Papers*, International Monetary Fund, Vol. 42 (March 1995), pp. 202–24.

Sandmo, Agnar, "Public Goods," *The New Palgrave Dictionary of Economics*, Vol. 3 (London and Basingstoke: MacMillan, 1987), pp. 1061–66.

Saunders, Anthony (1994a), *Financial Institutions Management: A Modern Perspective* (Burn Ridge, Illinois: Richard D. Irwin Inc., 1994).

_____ (1994b), "Banking and Commerce: An Overview of the Public Policy Issues," *Journal of Banking and Finance*, Vol. 18 (March 1994), pp. 231–54.

Schadler, Susan, and others, *IMF Conditionality: Experience Under Stand-By and Extended Arrangements, Part I: Key Issues and Findings*, IMF Occasional Paper, No. 128 (Washington: International Monetary Fund, September 1995).

Sheng, Andrew, "Bank Restructuring in Malaysia, 1985–88" in *Financial Regulation: Changing the Rules of the Game*, ed. by Dimitri Vittas (Washington: The World Bank, 1992), pp. 195–236.

_____, ed., *Bank Restructuring—Lessons from the 1980s* (Washington: The World Bank, 1996).

_____, and Tannor, Archibald A., "Ghana's Financial Restructuring, 1983–91," in *Bank Restructuring—Lessons from the 1980s*, ed. by Andrew Sheng (Washington: The World Bank, 1996), pp. 123–32.

Shinagawa, Ryoichi, "Impact of Capital Requirements on the Behavior of Banks and Its Macroeconomic Implications: Japan's Experience," in *FDICIA: An Appraisal*, Proceedings of the 29th Annual Conference on Bank Structure and

Competition, May 1993 (Chicago: Federal Reserve Bank of Chicago, 1993), pp. 156–70.

Siegel, Mark M., "Sterilization of Capital Inflows Through the Banking Sector: Evidence from Asia," *Economic Review*, Federal Reserve Bank of San Francisco, No. 3 (1995), pp. 17–34.

Siems, Thomas F., "Quantifying Management's Role in Bank Survival," *Economic Review*, Federal Reserve Bank of Dallas (First Quarter 1992), pp. 29–41.

Simons, Katerina, and Stephen Cross, "Do Capital Markets Predict Problems in Large Commercial Banks?" *New England Economic Review*, Federal Reserve Bank of Boston (May/June 1991), pp. 51–56.

Sundararajan, V., "The Role of Prudential Supervision and Financial Restructuring of Banks During Transition to Indirect Instruments of Monetary Control," paper presented at the symposium on Business Finance in Emerging Markets, held at the University of Laval, Québec, August 31–September 1, 1995.

_____, and Tomás J.T. Baliño, "Issues in Recent Banking Crises," in *Banking Crises: Cases and Issues*, ed. by V. Sundararajan and Tomás J.T. Baliño (Washington: International Monetary Fund, 1991), pp. 1–57.

Swiderski, Karen A., ed., *Financial Programming and Policy: The Case of Hungary* (Washington: International Monetary Fund, 1992).

Thompson, C.J., "The Basle Concordat: International Cooperation in Banking Supervision, in Vol. 1 of *Current Legal Issues Affecting Central Banks*, ed. by Robert C. Effros (Washington: International Monetary Fund, 1994), pp. 331–448.

Thomson, James B., "Modeling the Bank Regulator's Closure Option: A Two-Step Logit Regression Approach," *Journal of Financial Services Research*, Vol. 6 (1992), pp. 5–23.

Thorne, Alfredo, "Eastern Europe's Experience with Banking Reform," Policy Research Working Paper 1235 (Washington: World Bank, December 1993).

Timewell, Stephen, "Latvia: The Brutal Truth," *The Banker* (August 1995), pp. 35–37.

Tuya, José, and Lorena Zamalloa, "Issues on Placing Banking Supervision in the Central Bank," in *Frameworks for Monetary Stability*, ed. by Tomás J.T. Baliño and Carlo Cottarelli (Washington: International Monetary Fund, 1994), pp. 663–90.

United Kingdom, House of Commons, *Report of the Board of Banking Supervision Inquiry into the Circumstances of the Collapse of Barings* (London: HMSO, July 18, 1995).

United States, General Accounting Office, *The Net Worth Certificate Program and the Condition of the Thrift Industry* (Washington: General Accounting Office, 1985).

_____, *Thrift Industry: Forbearance for Troubled Institutions, 1982–1986*, Briefing Report to the Chairman, Committee on Banking, Housing, and Urban Affairs, United States Senate, GAO/GGD–87–78BR (Washington, May 1987).

United States, House of Representatives, *Federal Deposit Insurance Corporation Improvement Act of 1991: Report to Accompany H.R. 3768* (Washington, 1991).

United States, Office of the Comptroller of the Currency, *The Director's Book* (Washington, August 1987).

_____, *Bank Failure: An Evaluation of the Factors Contributing to the Failure of National Banks* (Washington, June 1988).

_____, *A Director's Guide to Board Reports* (Washington, 1989).

VanHoose, David D., "Deregulation and Oligopolistic Rivalry in Bank Deposit Markets," *Journal of Banking and Finance*, Vol.12 (September 1988), pp. 379–88.

Velasco, Andrés, "Liberalization, Crisis, Intervention: The Chilean Financial System, 1975–85," in *Banking Crises: Cases and Issues*, ed. by V. Sundararajan and Tomás J.T. Baliño (Washington: International Monetary Fund, 1991), pp. 113–174.

Vittas, Dimitri, "The Impact of Regulation on Financial Intermediation," in *Financial Regulation: Changing the Rules of the Game*, ed. by Dimitri Vittas (Washington: The World Bank, 1992), pp. 59–84.

Vos, Rob, "Financial Liberalization, Growth, and Adjustment: Some Lessons from Developing Countries," in *Financial Reform in Central and Eastern Europe*, ed. by Stephany Griffith-Jones and Zdenek Drábek (New York: St. Martin's Press, 1995), pp. 179–220.

Whalen, Gary, "A Proportional Hazards Model of Bank Failure: An Examination of Its Usefulness as an Early Warning Tool," *Economic Review*, Federal Reserve Bank of Cleveland, Vol. 27 (First Quarter 1991), pp. 21–31.

Williams, Michael, "Many Japanese Banks Ran Amok While Led by Former Regulators," *Wall Street Journal*, January 19, 1996, pp. A1 and A6.

"The World's 100 Largest Banks," *Institutional Investor*, Vol. 29 (August 1995), pp. 51–61.